Developing a Dream Destination

DEVELOPING A

DREAM DESTINATION

Tourism and Tourism Policy
Planning in Hawai'i

JAMES MAK

University of Hawai'i Press | Honolulu

Library of Congress Cataloging-in-Publication Data
Mak, James.
Developing a dream destination : tourism and tourism
policy planning in Hawai'i / James Mak.
p.   cm.
Includes bibliographical references and index.
ISBN 978-0-8248-3243-8 (pbk. : alk. paper)
1. Tourism — Hawaii.   2. Tourism — Government
policy — Hawaii.   I. Title.
G155.U6M325   2008
338.4'791969 — dc22   2007043303

Designed by April Leidig-Higgins

Printed by Versa Press

Contents

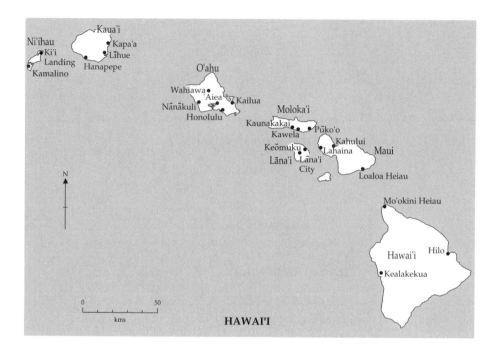

Ni'ihau

Ki'i
Landing
Kamalino

Kaua'i

Kapa'a
Līhue
Hanapepe

O'ahu

Wahiawā
'Aiea   Kailua
Nānākuli
Honolulu

Kaunakakai
Kawela

Moloka'i

Pūko'o

Kahului
Keōmuku   Lahaina   Maui
Lāna'i   Lāna'i
City
Loaloa Heiau

Mo'okini Heiau

Hawai'i   Hilo

Kealakekua

N

0   50

kms

HAWAI'I

Preface

This book began almost thirty years ago as a collaborative project between Tom Hamilton and myself. Thomas Hale Hamilton had served as the seventh president of the University of Hawaii from 1963 to 1968. After that he was briefly the managing director of the Hawaii Visitors Bureau. I did not know Tom in either of those capacities. When I first worked with him in the mid-1970s, I was a relatively junior faculty member in the Economics Department at the University of Hawaii and he was special advisor to the trustees of the powerful Bishop Estate, a multibillion-dollar charitable trust and the largest private landowner in Hawaii. But for those who knew him, he was the most astute observer and student of tourism in Hawaii. He was *the* guru of Hawaii tourism during the '70s.

In the 1970s, tourism was booming in Hawaii. From less than a quarter of a million tourists that came in 1959—Hawaii's statehood year—the number had exploded to nearly 1.8 million by 1970. Boeing 747 jumbo jets were bringing in hundreds of tourists at a time at the Honolulu International Airport. It was the beginning of mass tourism in Hawaii. Nothing—not even the Arab oil embargo in 1973—seemed to interrupt this tidal wave of humanity.

For many locals, the changes brought by this avalanche were more than just a bit unsettling. Some very serious questions were being raised about Hawaii's tourism. Some of them were apt, relevant, and justified. Others were simply part of the larger picture of the antibusiness and antiestablishment tenor of the times. It was, after all, the Vietnam War era. Even those who supported the growth of tourism had doubts about the flood of in-migrants moving to the state and what that might do to the quality of life in Hawaii.

Some of these questions had to do with what tourism might or might not be doing to the environment and the delicate ecological balance of the islands. Questions also were raised as to how valuable tourism really was economically as far as the people of Hawaii were concerned. There were complaints that tourists were monopolizing the beaches, and that local citizens no longer had free and easy access. Crowding in Waikiki, transportation, sewage problems, and a diminution of the Aloha Spirit all came in for criticism. There were debates, some very bitter, about how many visitors (and residents) the small landmass of Hawaii could accommodate. In the 1960s, a number of studies were done on tourism. But until the 1970s most studies were filed and forgotten. At most, another study was authorized. Thus Hawaii approached America's bicentennial year with a number of social and economic uncertainties.

In January of 1970, the late governor John A. Burns convened the first Governor's Travel Industry Congress. There were two important features of this congress: One was that excellent staff work was done before it convened, and the other was that it was representative of all sectors of Hawaii society. Eight hundred invitations were issued, and four hundred individuals actually participated in the two-day discussion. Media coverage before, during, and after the congress was excellent.

This was the largest group of representative citizens in any political jurisdiction ever to meet to discuss the visitor industry as it related to their lives. It sensitized the state to tourism in a new and constructive way. And this sensitivity has remained. More important than the recommendations that came out of this congress was the focusing of statewide community attention on the visitor industry.

From this beginning, a number of studies, task forces, and groups were formed to continue the examination of tourism. Tom Hamilton was at the center of this process. He was more often than not the chair of a citizen task force, a study group, or a committee on tourism, and the one responsible for holding everyone together to complete each assignment, no matter how little money was available to accomplish the work. His absolute integrity and diplomacy made him an ideal person to chair such citizen committees. It did not hurt that he was enormously well liked and already highly respected in the community. Bryan Farrell described Tom Hamilton as a person who "never shirked from confronting the industry or the community with critical situations as he saw them."[1]

In 1975, I worked with Tom when I was an economic consultant to yet another unpaid citizen committee on tourism that he chaired. Partly as a result of the reports that were drafted, the 1976 Legislature passed Act 133, which was signed by the governor.

Act 133 was unique in the history of tourism policy planning in Hawaii, as it was the first statute that called for continuing and comprehensive planning for Hawaii's visitor industry. The law called for the development of an interim tourism policy that would be replaced by the policies of a State plan—a broader and more inclusive scheme—when and if such a plan was approved by the Legislature. The law also called for the development of "a ten-year master plan for the growth of tourism for presentation to the 1978 session of the Legislature." This time, money—and quite a lot of it—was made available to pay for technical studies.

After the technical studies were completed and submitted to the Department of Planning and Economic Development—which had the responsibility for crafting the tourism master plan—Tom and I met privately at the Willows Restaurant (at his "usual" table next to the bar) to discuss the possibility of writing a book on the planning process and the plan itself after it was accepted. To the best of our knowledge, no other tourist destination had done anything this comprehensive for an exotic business that was spreading globally.

It was finally decided that there would be two volumes. The first volume would be designed for the general reader and tourism's practitioners. It would contain some historical material and a general description of the plan for Hawaii's tourism. The second volume would be for the scholar, the technician, and the government planner. Tom would be largely responsible for the first volume, and I would be assigned the second. Tom presented the idea to the director of the University Press of Hawaii (Bob Sparks) and received his blessing. With this encouragement, Tom charged ahead, and within a year or so he completed the first four chapters of volume one. Unfortunately, the project was never completed as Tom passed away.

Tom's four chapters were filed away in my office for nearly thirty years. In 2004, when I was cleaning out my research files after having finished my book, *Tourism and the Economy* (University of Hawaii Press, 2004), I came across the file containing Tom's chapters. They were so enjoyable to read again that my interest in finishing the project was rekindled. Of course, nearly thirty years of tourism history had slipped by since Act 133 was enacted, and the original plan is no longer appealing. Too much else has happened since then.

In the 1970s, people were concerned about an industry that was perceived to be growing too fast. Act 133 was intended to address the concerns of that time. But in the 1990s, tourism was in the doldrums, which raised quite a different set of issues. Then there is the matter of sheer numbers. In the early '70s, there were fewer than 3 million visitors a year to Hawaii, versus over 7 million visitors a year (and rising) in 2005. Questions about tourism proliferated with the increasing scale of tourism. In the '70s, the phrase "sustainable tourism" had not yet been invented. The book, if it is going to be complete, has to tell the story of how public policies toward tourism changed over this whole period. This is that story.

Some of the materials in Tom's four chapters have been incorporated in chapters 2 and 3 of this book. Everything else is new. Readers should be warned that this book is not a history of tourism in Hawaii. That book has yet to be written. This book is about the development of public policy toward tourism in Hawaii, roughly between statehood (1959) and 2005. The year 2005 is an appropriate soft ending date, partly for data reasons, but—more importantly—by then the tourist industry in Hawaii had fully recovered from the effects of the September 11, 2001, terrorist attacks and other terrible global shocks. Also, in 2005 the State revealed its new ten-year (2005–2015) strategic tourism plan, and in 2006 the counties revealed their parallel strategic plans (2006–2015); thus, 2006 begins a new chapter in Hawaii's tourism saga.

As an economist, I have tended to focus on policy issues that have an economic slant. However, anyone who has reviewed the news events of this period will agree that the tourism policies that I have chosen to write about are also those that have been at the center of people's concerns in Hawaii.

Developing a Dream Destination should appeal to students studying tourism policy planning and development as well as to tourism professionals and policy makers. Although this book is about the development of tourism in Hawaii, the lessons from Hawaii's lengthy experience in developing a modern "dream destination" should be of interest to readers both in and outside of Hawaii.

There are various models of tourism development, ranging from the *command-and-control* model (e.g., Bermuda, Vietnam, and China), where the government plays the central role in directing tourism development, to the *market-driven* laissez-faire model, where tourism is largely left to the private sector. It is widely believed that to maintain a destination's competitiveness and sustainability, tourism development needs to be tightly controlled. Hawaii's model of tourism development—which I characterize as "market-friendly interventionism"—relegates the government to an important but secondary role. The book also points out that government can be a part of the problem as well as a solution. Destinations interested in adopting a form of tourism development with less government intrusion should find Hawaii's experience enlightening.

I thank Shelley Mark (director of the Department of Planning and Economic Development under the late governor John Burns), Seiji Naya (director of the Department of Business, Economic Development and Tourism under former governor Ben Cayetano), Pearl Imada Iboshi (State economist), Sumner LaCroix (University of Hawaii–Manoa), Kelly Yamanouchi *(Honolulu Advertiser),* Jan TenBruggencate *(Honolulu Advertiser),* Paul Brewbaker (Bank of Hawaii), Leroy Laney (Hawaii Pacific University), John Knox (John M. Knox & Associates), Greg Schmidt (Hui Nalu Canoe Club), and Richard P. Perdue (Virginia Polytechnic Institute and State University) for helpful comments and suggestions. Reuel Reyel (student assistant) did an excellent job of organizing the manuscript and putting it together. Cy Feng (Department of Business, Economic Development and Tourism) made data from DBEDT files readily available whenever I made a request. Bill Hamilton, director of the University of Hawaii Press, was both helpful and supportive of this project. Lee Motteler did a wonderful job in catching mistakes in the manuscript and making it readable; he also prepared the index. Any remaining errors, of course, are mine.

This book is appropriately dedicated to the memory of Tom Hamilton.

Note

1. Farrell (1982).

Reference

Farrell, Bryan H. 1982. *Hawaii: The Legend That Sells.* Honolulu: University Press of Hawaii.

Chapter One

Introduction

Americans love rankings! There are "best" rankings for appliances, new and used cars, restaurants, hotels, colleges and universities, places to live and places to retire, the "best" (and "worst") dressed woman (man), books, music and movies, and, to quote the King of Siam, "Etcetera, etcetera, etcetera." Cable television's Travel Channel even has a top-ten ranking for the best restaurant bathrooms in the world.[1] Advocates of such rankings argue that they quantify the unquantifiable. They provide information to consumers on products and services that are difficult to compare before they are purchased. This would be particularly true of services—and tourism.

Hawaii: A Dream Destination

When it comes to tourist destinations, Hawaii consistently ranks among the very best. That's no small feat, considering the number of potential competitors. Just counting the number of countries alone, the membership of the World Tourism Organization currently lists over 150 countries and territories all vying for the tourist dollar. Within each country there are regions, provinces, states, cities, towns, villages, and so on. Hawaii also has to compete against the growing popularity of ocean cruises.

Mark Twain once described the Hawaiian Islands as "the loveliest fleet of Islands anchored in any ocean."[2] For millions of people around the world, Hawaii is a dream destination—the vacation of a lifetime. The *National Geographic Traveler* magazine recently included Hawaii in its list of "50 Places of a Lifetime: The World's Greatest Destinations."[3] A survey of over nine thousand U.S. households by NFO Plog Research revealed that Hawaii was the most "satisfying" domestic vacation destination in 2002. Remarkably, Hawaii topped the NFO Plog's "Delightful Dozen" list for six consecutive years.[4] A telephone poll of 1,028 American adults conducted in May

2005 for the Associated Press found that Hawaii was the top destination choice for vacations if money was no object.[5] In 2004, the "LuxeReport"— an annual poll of six thousand luxury travel agencies—ranked Hawaii as the third most popular destination to view marine life (after the Galapagos Islands and the Sea of Cortez) and the fourth most popular group tour destination (after Italy, Alaska, and Russia).[6] For the eleventh consecutive year, Maui was voted the "best island in the world" in 2004 by the *Conde Nast Traveler* Readers' Choice Awards Poll. Among Pacific Rim Islands, Kauai came in second; the Big Island fourth; Lanai sixth; and Oahu seventh.[7] Maui also captured the "Best of the Best Crown" in the same poll.[8] A poll of over half a million travelers by *Travel + Leisure Magazine* and America Online's Travel Channel in 2004 rated Honolulu their favorite American city.[9] *Travel Weekly*, the industry publication, named Hawaii the "Best Overall Destination" in the United States and Maui the "Best Destination in Hawaii" in its 2006 Readers Choice Awards.[10] And where did cartoonist Dean Young send Dagwood and Blondie on their seventy-fifth anniversary in 2005? Hawaii. You get the picture. The top rankings keep rolling in for Hawaii—and so do the tourists.

From less than 250,000 visitors at the time of statehood in 1959, Hawaii now receives over 7 million visitors per year (see chapter 2). On a typical day in 2005 there were roughly 185,000 visitors in Hawaii versus roughly 1.2 million residents.[11] On average, nearly one out of every eight people you run into in Hawaii is likely to be a tourist. After more than forty-five years, Hawaii's tourism product still receives high marks from visitors—and from residents. For example, over 97 percent of the U.S., Japanese, Canadian, and European visitors surveyed in 2005 rated their Hawaii vacations as either "excellent" or "above average."[12] About the same percentage indicated that their trips "met" or "exceeded" their expectations. Likewise, a statewide survey of residents found that three out of four people in 2006 agreed that "tourism has brought more benefits than problems to their island."[13] The positive responses have remained relatively unchanged since systematic surveys of residents began in 1988.[14]

Hawaii's success in developing tourism is much envied by other tourist destinations. Pan American Airlines' Paul Kendall once observed that tourism flourished in Hawaii because it enjoyed "an accidental head start in climate and environment."[15] But there are other tropical resort destinations that have wonderful weather and beautiful scenery as well. Yet Hawaii has remained at the top of travelers' popularity list for over half a century.

Certainly the odds of staying at the top are stacked against Hawaii. For one thing, there are many more destinations competing for tourists today than there were a few decades ago.[16] In contrast to Hawaii's lengthy history in tourism, the beach resorts of Australia, Indonesia, Thailand, and elsewhere in Asia and the Pacific are relative newcomers.

Second, popularity can also be ruinous to a destination. "See it before they spoil it" is a well-known cliché in tourism. Esteemed travel writer and author Paul Theroux observed that "when a place gets a reputation as a paradise, it very quickly turns into a purgatory, and then goes to hell."[17] It has been well established that tourist destinations tend to follow a predictable life cycle from birth to maturity, old age, and finally decline.[18] A now classic theory, put forth by Stanley Plog, is that once a destination becomes popular, it begins to attract less desirable tourists (which he labels the "Dependables" and "Near Dependables") who will drive away the desirable tourists (the "Venturers" and "Near-Venturers"). Eventually, fewer tourists will come to visit. Plog then ranks tourist destinations by the "psychographics" of their visitors. He surmises that Honolulu is already in the Near-Dependable area and the Neighbor Islands are approaching it.[19]

But decline is not inevitable. Plog concludes that "Destinations can be preserved and still enjoy continued, growing prosperity. Tourism planners need to look no further than the mirror to know who must fix the problems."[20] The key, he argues, is planning and tight control of tourism development. One needs to look no further than Bermuda to find a gem of an island destination whose success has been attributed to careful planning and tight government control.[21]

Growing Importance of Tourism

Interest in how best to develop tourism has risen in tandem with tourism's growing global importance. Indeed, what we have here is the phenomenon of one of the world's major economic and social forces of the second half of the twentieth century, little understood by those who formulate public policy on the one hand and unattended—even avoided until recently—by scholars on the other.

For travel destinations, winning the hearts and choices of tourists can be hugely lucrative. Since World War II, tourism has become an enterprise of enormous global significance. The statistics are startling. Global international tourist arrivals totaled 809 million in 2005, and these visitors spent nearly $680 billion in their host countries.[22] And that doesn't include the cost of getting them there and back or the money tourists spend on travel clothes, luggage, passport fees, and other accessories before their trips. By comparison, in 1950 there were only 25 million international visitor arrivals and $2 billion in spending. Ever since mass tourism became a megabusiness beginning in the 1970s, international tourist arrivals have been growing 1.4 times as fast as the world's economy. And there is no end in sight. The World Bank recently predicted a 3 percent annual growth rate of the world's economy for the next fifty years.[23] This means there will be lots more money available around the world to be spent on travel. And the pool of potential tourists is huge; as of 1996, only 3.5 percent of the world's population had ever traveled abroad.[24] The World Tourism Organization's *Tourism 2020 Vision* predicts international tourist arrivals will grow to about 1 billion by 2010 and over 1.56 billion by 2020, despite the ongoing global war on terrorism.[25]

Figures for domestic tourism are much harder to find. The conventional wisdom is that there are ten times as many domestic visitors as there are international visitors.[26] In the United States, domestic residents took 63.5 million trips abroad in 2005,[27] compared to over 1.992 billion domestic person trips of 50 miles (one way) or more away from home, of which 75 percent were leisure trips.[28] And the money they spent on travel generated income, jobs, and tax revenues for the destinations fortunate enough to have them.

The economic benefits of tourism have not escaped public notice. The World Travel and Tourism Council (WTTC) estimates that tourism accounts for more than 10 percent of the world's gross domestic product, about 8 percent of total worldwide employment, and 12 percent of total world exports.[29] The World Tourism Organization (UNWTO) notes that tourism is the largest item in world exports, and—among the world's developing countries and especially the least developed ones—tourism is "almost universally the leading source of economic growth, foreign exchange, investment, and job creation."[30] Not surprisingly, just about every country, region, state, and city wants a piece of the growing tourism pie. In 2005, tourism-related output in the United States—which includes all goods and services sold directly to visitors and the supporting output—topped $1 trillion.[31] Total tourism employment grew to 8.2 million jobs.[32]

But tourism development is not a free lunch. It requires a lot of infrastructure to service tourists: airports, harbors, roads, sewers, water, solid waste disposal, not to mention private facilities such as hotels and tourist attractions. Then you have to promote the destination, train the workers, pay the policemen, firemen, lifeguards, and so on.

The social and cultural impacts of tourism are much harder to measure, but surely they are not trivial. Tourism is often promoted as a "clean" industry, but Oliver Hillel of the United Nations Environment Programme observes that "Tourism is not a smokestack-free industry. It is exactly as polluting as any other major industry."[33] The *Economist* magazine observes that as large as tourism has become, "Its potential for making a mess of it is equally large."[34] Frances Brown writes convincingly that tourism can be a blight and a blessing for the host community.[35]

Some destinations are finding that there is such a thing as having too many tourists or that tourism can grow too rapidly. In Majorca (Spain), the local government requires that before a developer is permitted to build a new hotel, another hotel with more beds must first be demolished.[36] Bermuda limits the number of cruise ship passengers it accepts each year at 225,000. It also limits the number of cruise ships permitted.[37] Since the 1990s, Maui residents have successfully fought the extension of the island's airport runway because they feared that existing public infrastructure and services were unable to accommodate massive increases in tourists; the State Department of Transportation had wanted to extend the runway to accommodate jumbo jets in order to facilitate direct flights from the U.S. mainland and Asia to Maui.[38]

The idea that a destination has a limit, or "carrying capacity," for tourism gained increasing acceptance with the spread of mass tourism. The UNWTO defines carrying capacity as "the level of visitor use an area can accommodate with high levels of satisfaction for visitors and few impacts on resources."[39] The concept of carrying capacity is often taken to mean that an area can host only so many tourists—some predeterminable number etched in stone. That notion is no longer widely accepted. Clearly, a destination that can properly manage its resources and educate its visitors to behave responsibly can host more tourists "with high levels of satisfaction for visitors and few impacts on resources." The term "carrying capacity" has become outmoded,[40] and it was replaced in the 1990s by the more fashionable concept of "sustainable tourism."[41]

The World Tourism Organization defines sustainable tourism as development that "meets the needs of present tourists and host regions while protecting and enhancing opportunities for the future."[42] It is based on the very sensible notion that decisions regarding tourism development today must not jeopardize the well-being of tourists and residents in the future.

Sustainable tourism "is envisaged as leading to management of all resources in such a way that economic, social, and aesthetic needs can be fulfilled while maintaining cultural integrity, essential ecological processes, biological diversity, and life support systems."[43] It has become the buzz phrase in tourism. Governments, the industry, and nongovernmental organizations (NGOs) around the world have endorsed it as the guiding principle in planning for future tourism development. But putting it into practice is another matter. Two highly respected tourism scholars, M. Thea Sinclair and Mike Stabler, who have studied this matter quite thoroughly, believe that a lot of the professed commitment to sustainable tourism is merely lip service.[44] However, a recent *National Geographic Traveler* magazine survey finds that there are more than a few destinations around the world that score quite highly on the magazine's "stewardship index."[45]

Why Study Hawaii?

In this book, I examine the development of tourism in Hawaii, focusing specifically on the development of public policies toward tourism in the Aloha State.[46] But why study Hawaii? The most obvious reason is to see if there are lessons in tourism development and tourism policy planning that can be learned from an acknowledged successful destination. To be sure, Hawaii is not perfect. Hawaii Tourism Authority's (HTA) *Draft Strategic Tourism Plan 2005–2015* acknowledges that Hawaii suffers from inadequate public and private infrastructure, insufficient visitor-resident interaction, geographic isolation, lack of "new" experiences, lack of postarrival information, and other problems.[47] In 2003, the *National Geographic Traveler* magazine asked two hundred specialists in sustainable tourism to rate 115 destinations worldwide. The following is what they said about Hawaii:[48]

- Significant improvements to save the culture are currently underway.
- Danger of overuse of some areas still exists.
- Too much emphasis on increasing number of visitors without adequate management planning or impact assessment.
- The tourism products and experience have changed and some are degraded, but as a whole the islands of Hawaii still offer such a broad range of opportunities.
- Hawaii is still a paradise when visitors plan properly.

Second, developing a successful and sustainable tourism destination over time is believed to require comprehensive planning and tight government oversight and control. However, unlike Bermuda, Vietnam, or China, Hawaii has not imposed rigid government control over tourism development. Indeed, comprehensive tourism planning came rather late to the state—in the late 1970s (see chapter 3). Even then, Hawaii's State government saw itself not as the architect of tourism but as a coordinator, facilitator, and regulator (when needed). Perhaps the most appropriate characterization of Hawaii's model of tourism development is "market-friendly intervention-ism." Tourism planners might find Hawaii's comparative lack of government intrusion intriguing.

Third, one of the factors that hampered tourism research was the lack of reliable data. For many years, there was not even agreement as to how one defined "tourist." Although the UNWTO has proffered its own definition and subsequently advised how to collect the data, there is still some controversy over this.[49] Even when there came to be some agreement as to terms and data began to be collected, historical or trend studies were made difficult or impossible by the absence of comparable facts for past years. Hawaii, for a number of reasons (see chapter 5), has been more fortunate than most destination areas in having excellent data on tourism. Its remote insular geography certainly simplified keeping track of those who arrived.

Organization of the Book

This book is an interpretive history of tourism and tourism policy development in Hawaii between statehood (1959) and around 2005—roughly a forty-six-year period. It is certainly long enough for us to draw lessons and inferences from its development experience. The book is informally divided into three parts. Part one recounts the history of tourism in Hawaii and how and why it has changed over the years. It also examines tourism's imprints on Hawaii. Part two reviews the development of public policy toward tourism, beginning with the story of the planning process that started around 1970, fully a decade before the first comprehensive State Tourism Plan was crafted and implemented. Part two also examines State government policies and actions taken relative to the taxation of tourism, tourism promotion, convention center development and financing, the environment, Honolulu County's efforts to improve Waikiki, and how the Neighbor Islands have coped with explosive tourism growth. Along the way, I offer interpretations

Table 1-1. Population and land areas for Hawaii: 2000

	Land area (sq. mi.)	Resident population (thousands)	Defacto population (thousands)
State	6,422.6	1,211.5	1,338.0
Honolulu County			
Oahu	596.7	876.2	927.2
Hawaii County (Big Island)	4,028.0	148.7	167.0
Maui County			
Maui	727.2	118.0	156.2
Molokai	260.0	7.4	8.1
Lanai	140.5	3.2	4.2
Kauai County			
Kauai	522.3	58.3	75.0
Niihau	69.5	0.2	0.2

Source: State of Hawaii DBEDT, *2005 State of Hawaii Data Book,* sections 1 and 5.

of what has worked and what has not—and why. Part three concludes with a final chapter on lessons learned from Hawaii's experience in developing a dream destination over the past forty-six years.

Hawaii's Geographic and Political Divisions

For the benefit of readers who are unfamiliar with Hawaii, it is the only island state in the United States. The closest state to Hawaii—California—is about 2,400 miles or five hours of flying time away. Hawaii is actually a chain of 130 islands spread over 1,500 miles in the Pacific Ocean. The total area of the islands is about 6,400 square miles (Table 1-1). Only seven of the islands are inhabited. These islands extend from Kauai lying to the northwest to the island of Hawaii in the southeast. The island of Hawaii, at over 4,000 square miles, is geographically larger than all the other islands combined; not surprisingly, it is more commonly referred to in Hawaii as the Big Island. However, Oahu, the third largest of the islands after Maui, is the most populous. Table 1-1 also presents statistics on the "defacto population," which includes the average daily census of tourists present in Hawaii minus residents who are temporarily away.

The islands are divided politically into four counties. The City and County of Honolulu comprises the entire island of Oahu and the Northwestern

Hawaiian Islands. Hawaii County covers the entire island of Hawaii. Maui County includes the populated islands of Maui, Molokai, and Lanai, as well as unpopulated Kahoolawe. The County of Kauai includes the islands of Kauai and tiny Niihau. Hawaii, Maui, and Kauai Counties are collectively referred to as the Neighbor Islands.

Notes

1. The top ranking goes to the posh Expedition Restaurant in Moscow, where patrons are required to spend two hours in a spa before dining.

2. Lind (1969), p. viii.

3. *National Geographic Traveler* (1999).

4. Mak (2004), p. 205, fn. no. 7. Hawaii topped the Delightful Dozen List in 2003 as well, the last year accessible on the Internet.

5. *Honolulu Advertiser* (May 28, 2005), p. A1.

6. HVCB (April 19, 2004).

7. *Honolulu Advertiser* (October 12, 2004), p. C1. In *Travel + Leisure* magazine's World's Best Islands Poll in 2004, Kauai was ranked second, Maui was third, and Hawaii came in fifth. See http://www.travelandleisure.com/worldbest.

8. *Honolulu Advertiser* (October 12, 2004), p. C1.

9. "America's Favorite Cities," (April 2004).

10. *Travel Weekly Daily Bulletin* (December 15, 2006), Article # 54195.

11. State of Hawaii Department of Business, Economic Development and Tourism (DBEDT), *2005 Annual Visitor Research Report,* Honolulu (2006), p. 11.

12. DBEDT, *2005 Visitor Satisfaction and Activity Report* (2006), Table 4-2.

13. Market Trends Pacific Inc. and John M. Knox & Associates (November 2006), p. 13.

14. Ibid., p. 48.

15. Kendall (June 24, 1975).

16. At its peak, the International Union of Official Travel Organizations—the predecessor of the World Tourism Organization, which was founded in 1975—had a membership of 109 national tourism organizations. Today the UNWTO has over 150 member countries and territories.

17. Tsai (January 4, 2005), p. E3.

18. Plog (June 2001), p. 18. Also see his 1974 classic paper. The concept of tourist area life cycle is described more fully in Butler (1980) and Goncalves and Aguas (1997).

19. Ibid., p. 21. Plog includes Las Vegas, Florida, Caribbean cruises, and theme parks in the Near-Dependable group.

20. Ibid., p. 24.

21. Chaplin, "Hawaii delegation's observations on Bermuda" (June 23, 1975).

22. World Tourism Organization (2006).

23. World Bank (2003), p. 4.

24. *UNESCO Courier* (1999), p. 27.

25. See www.world-tourism.org/market_research/facts/menu.html.

26. Tisdell (2001), p. 19.

27. U.S. Department of Commerce, ITA, Office of Travel and Tourism Industries at http://tinet.ita.doc.gov/.

28. See http://www.tia.org.

29. See www.wttc.org/tsal.htm. Using a broader definition of tourism, which includes not only economic activities generated by tourist spending alone but also all tourism-related expenditures, such as government spending for tourism promotion as well as exports of commercial passenger airplanes, which are subsequently used in tourism, and so on.

30. See www.world-tourism.org/sustainable/wssd/brochure-eng.htm (last accessed on December 6, 2002).

31. Kuhbach and Herauf (2006).

32. Ibid.

33. *Newsweek International* (2002), p. 44.

34. Roberts (January 10, 1998), p. 3.

35. Brown (2000).

36. *Newsweek International* (2002), p. 46.

37. See www.twcrossroads.com/, hereafter referred to as *Travel Weekly Daily Bulletin,* Article # 43051. The number of cruise ship passengers permitted in Bermuda will likely rise somewhat as older, smaller ships are replaced by newer and larger ships.

38. Blackford (2001).

39. Lindberg et al. (2000), p. 557.

40. Some argue that it should not be used at all. Ibid., p. 559.

41. See Mak (2004), chapter 14.

42. World Tourism Organization (2002); Mak (2004), p. 182.

43. World Tourism Organization (2002); Mak (2004), p. 182.

44. Sinclair and Stabler (1997), p. 14.

45. Tourtellot (March 2004).

46. Ritchie and Crouch (2000, p. 2) define tourism policy as "a set of regulations, rules, guidelines, directives, and development/promotion objectives and strategies within which the collective and individual decisions directly affecting tourism development and the daily activities within a destination are taken."

47. Hawaii Tourism Authority (July 2004), p. 5.

48. See Nationalgeographic.com/traveler/scorecard/. The story is found in the March 2004 issue of *National Geographic Traveler.*

49. Mak (2004), chapter 1; see also World Tourism Organization (1993). While most of us associate tourism with pleasure travel, the World Tourism Organization includes in its definition of tourism all forms of travel (other than commuting

to work) not exceeding one year. About 62 percent of international travel is pleasure travel, 18 percent business travel, and the remaining 20 percent is for other purposes, such as religious pilgrimage, medical treatment, education, and so on. In the United States, the Travel Industry Association of America reports that in 2005 there were 1.992 billion domestic trips taken that were at least 50 miles one way from home, and pleasure trips accounted for 75 percent of the total.

References

"America's Favorite Cities." 2004. *Travel + Leisure* (April): 159–168.

Blackford, Mansel G. 2001. *Fragile Paradise: The Impact of Tourism on Maui, 1959–2000.* Lawrence, KS: University Press of Kansas.

Brown, Frances. 2000. *Tourism Reassessed: Blight or Blessing?* Boston: Butterworth Heinemann.

Butler, Richard W. 1980. "The Concept of the Tourist Area Cycle of Evolution: Implications for the Management of Resources." *Canadian Geographer* 24: 5–12.

Chaplin, George. 1975. "Bermuda: Planned Growth Keeps It a Gem." *Honolulu Advertiser,* June 23.

Goncalves, Vitor Fernando Da Conceicao, and Paulo Manuel Roque Aguas. 1997. "The Concept of Life Cycle: An Application to the Tourist Product." *Journal of Travel Research* 36(2) (fall): 12–22.

Goolsbee, Austan. 2004. "Rankings Can Be Misleading." *Honolulu Advertiser,* April 13: A6.

"Hawaii Delegation's Observations on Bermuda." 1975. *Honolulu Advertiser,* June 23.

"Hawaii Named the Best Destination." 2004. *Honolulu Advertiser,* December 16: C1.

Hawaii Tourism Authority (HTA). 2004. *Draft State of Hawaii Tourism Strategic Plan 2005–2015.* Honolulu: HTA.

Hawaii Visitors and Convention Bureau (HVCB). 2004. *HVCB Tourism Industry Update.* April 19 and June 7. Honolulu: HVCB.

Kendall, Paul. "Trip Improves Communication on Tourism." 1975. *Honolulu Advertiser,* June 24.

Kuhbach, Peter, and Bradlee A. Herauf. 2006. "U.S. Travel and Tourism Satellite Accounts for 2002–2005." *Survey of Current Business* (June): 14–30.

Lind, Andrew W. 1969. *Hawaii, the Last of the Magic Isles.* London: Oxford University Press.

Lindberg, Kreg, Stephen McCool, and George Stankey. 2000. "Rethinking Carrying Capacity." In Clem Tisdell, ed., *The Economics of Tourism,* vol. 2 (Northampton, MA: Edward Elgar Publishing): 556–560.

Mak, James. 2004. *Tourism and the Economy: Understanding the Economics of Tourism*. Honolulu: University of Hawaii Press.

Market Trends Pacific Inc. and John M. Knox & Associates. 2006. *2006 Survey of Resident Sentiments on Tourism in Hawaii: Analysis and Report*. Honolulu.

National Georgraphic Traveler. 1999. *50 Places of a Lifetime: The World's Greatest Destinations*. Special Collector's Issue.

Newsweek International. 2002. "The Future of Travel." July 22/July 29: 34–65.

Plog, Stanley C. 1974. "Why Destination Areas Rise and Fall in Popularity." *Cornell Hotel and Restaurant Administration Quarterly* 14(4) (February): 55–58.

———. 2001. "Why Destination Areas Rise and Fall in Popularity: An Update of a Cornell Quarterly Classic." *Cornell Hotel and Restaurant Administration Quarterly* (June): 13–24.

Ritchie, J. R., and Geoffrey Crouch. 2000. "The Competitive Destination: A Sustainable Perspective." *Tourism Management* 21(1): 1–7.

Roberts, Mark. 1998. "Home and Away." *The Economist* (January 10): 3–16.

Sinclair, M. Thea, and Mike Stabler. 1997. *The Economics of Tourism*. New York: Routledge.

State of Hawaii Department of Business, Economic Development and Tourism (DBEDT). 2006. *2005 State of Hawaii Data Book*. Honolulu: DBEDT.

———. 2006. *2005 Visitor Satisfaction and Activity Report*. Honolulu: DBEDT.

State of Hawaii Department of Planning and Economic Development (DPED). 1976. *What Hawaii's People Think of the Visitor Industry: Results of a Public-Opinion Poll Taken October 5–15, 1975*. Honolulu: DPED.

Tisdell, Clem. 2001. *Tourism Economics, the Environment and Development*. Northampton, MA: Edward Elgar Publishing.

Tourtellot, Jonathan B. 2004. "Destination Scorecard, 115 Places Rated." *National Geographic Traveler* (March): 60–67.

Travel Weekly Daily Bulletin (various issues). At http://www.travelweekly.com.

Tsai, Michael. 2005. "Hawaii Essay a Labor of Love." *Honolulu Advertiser,* January 4: E1 and E3.

UNESCO. 1999. "The Globalization of Tourism." *UNESCO Courier* (July/August).

World Bank. 2003. *Sustainable Development in a Dynamic World*. World Development Report. New York: Oxford University Press.

"World's Best Island." 2003. *Honolulu Advertiser,* November 30: E1.

"World's Top Love Spot." 2004. *Honolulu Advertiser,* June 6: E1.

World Tourism Organization (UNWTO). 1993. *Recommendations on Tourism Statistics*. Madrid: UNWTO.

———. 2001. *Tourism after 11 September 2001: Analysis, Remedial Actions and Prospects*. Madrid: UNWTO.

———. 2006. *Tourism Highlights, 2006 Edition*. Madrid: UNWTO. At http://www.world-tourism.org/facts/menu.html.

Chapter Two

Tourism in Hawaii: An Overview

Tourism, as it now exists in Hawaii, is essentially a post–World War II phenomenon. The great growth in numbers actually occurred after 1959. There was a visitor industry in Hawaii before 1959, of course, but the difference in degree is sufficiently great as to constitute a difference in kind.

As early as 1830, there were several rooming houses and hotels in Honolulu, primarily serving sailors and a few visitors. By no stretch of the imagination could they have been classified as luxury resort establishments.[1] It was not until 1867 that one can say Hawaii really had a tourist trade. In that year, more or less regular steamship travel started between Hawaii and the U.S. mainland. In those days, cargo and passengers were handled on the same ship.

In the late 1860s, there were suggestions of the need for a first-class hotel. Private capital was not interested, so the government of the monarchy built the original resort hotel, the Hawaiian. For a number of years there was wrangling over how the financing of this hotel had been handled by the government, and the details were never made clear. In any event, this first hotel was completed in 1872—not in Waikiki but in downtown Honolulu— on the site of what later became the Armed Forces YMCA.[2] A few years later a small annex was built in Waikiki and expanded in 1894 as the Seaside Annex. This was the first major beach hotel in the Islands. In the late 1880s, some two thousand visitors came to Hawaii each year. Small growth continued until the end of the century.

As the twentieth century progressed, steamship service between the U.S. West Coast and Hawaii became more frequent, comfortable, and faster. This certainly played a role in the early stimulation of the industry. In 1922, there were 9,676 visitors who came to Hawaii, spending some $4 million in the territory.[3] In 1927, the first ship that carried only passengers made its maiden voyage. This was the 650-passenger *Malolo*.

In the same year, the John Rogers Airport—predecessor of the Honolulu International Airport—was dedicated.[4] In 1929, Inter-Island Airways, the forerunner of Hawaiian Airlines, began somewhat irregular airline service between the islands. On October 21, 1936, Pan American inaugurated its famous passenger Clipper service from the West Coast to Hawaii.[5] The "luxury flying boats" had sleeping berths, and cabin crews served "hotel-style" meals.[6] The first flight brought to Hawaii seven passengers at a one-way fare of $356.[7] Those were in Depression-era dollars. Today that sum would convert to roughly $5,000. For the next few years, Pan Am flew a once-a-week schedule from San Francisco to Manila via Honolulu. Although it was touted glamorously as passenger air travel, Pan Am made its money primarily by carrying U.S. government mail. Until well after World War II, most visitors still arrived by ship. "Boat Day" was a joyous and colorful affair. But the era of air travel was just beyond the horizon.

The increase in transportation facilities during the first three decades of the twentieth century was matched by an expansion of hotel facilities. The Haleiwa Hotel opened in 1899. Others followed: the Manoa (1901), the Halekulani (1917), the Royal Hawaiian (1927), and the Alexander Young (1930). Volcano House was enlarged in 1922 and the Kona Inn built in 1928, both on the Big Island of Hawaii.

Until the Pearl Harbor attack on December 7, 1941, Hawaii on the eve of World War II had a total of about 32,000 visitors. All but a handful arrived by ship, for Clipper capacity was limited. Only about 5 percent of the total came from countries other than the United States. The West Coast, particularly California, was the residence of most visitors—perhaps as much as 70 percent of the total. According to Anson Chong, there were 2,502 hotel rooms in the state in 1940–1941.[8] Some 2,035 of these were on Oahu and 467 were on the Neighbor Islands of Hawaii, Maui, and Kauai. These totals included many "family hotels" and semiresidential hotels that were found in Hawaii until the 1950s.

Certainly tourism in 1941 was far more leisurely as, indeed, the entire society was. The average length of stay for westbound (mostly U.S. mainland) visitors was more than two and a half times the present nine to ten days.[9] And this was understandable. One did not pay the relatively high ship fare and spend almost ten days sailing to and returning from Hawaii for a long weekend or even a week. It would appear that the 1941 tourist spent considerably more per day than does the contemporary visitor when the dollar is corrected for its loss in purchasing power.

More expensive and slower transportation, longer stays, larger daily expenditures—all these tend to buttress the opinions of those who lived and worked in the period that pre–World War II was a time in which Hawaii was largely a tourist destination for the wealthy. Some, however, hold that this may be overstated. The summers brought a significant number of less-than-affluent schoolteachers.

World War II, quite simply, put Hawaii's tourism out of business from 1941 to 1946. Transportation and hotel facilities were used by the military. Even the Hawaii Visitors Bureau (then known as the Hawaii Tourist Bureau) went out of business from 1942 to 1945 and returned the money it had collected from its members. Following World War II, it took Hawaii's visitor industry over a year to get back into gear on anything like the prewar scale. Hotels and transportation had to be demilitarized. The marketing function had to be revived.

World War II had demonstrated the importance of aviation to Hawaii. In 1947, United Airlines began flying to the Islands from San Francisco.[10] In the same year, Pan Am introduced its first land plane service to Hawaii using DC-4s. The new planes were faster and cheaper to operate than the flying boats. As a result, flying time was cut by five and a half hours to twelve hours and the one-way fare was reduced to around $225.[11] The following year, Northwest Orient Airlines inaugurated service to Hawaii from Portland and Seattle.[12] By 1948, the visitor count exceeded the earlier banner year of 1941 by 4,500.[13] And the growth of the 1950s began.

The popular impression is that the number of tourists increased slowly in the 1950s and precipitously in the 1960s. Actually, the annual percentage increases of the '50s equaled those of the '60s, and over each of the two decades, tourism grew roughly the same: over four times. The difference rested in the base to which these annual increases were applied. The fourfold increase of the '50s resulted at the end of the decade in fewer than a quarter of a million visitors. The Hawaii Visitors Bureau reported that 242,994 visitors came to Hawaii in 1959 and stayed at least one night.[14] A slightly lower overall growth rate of the '60s by 1969 had brought the total to a million and a half.[15] And to a citizen of Hawaii viewing the industry, it was the total number, not the annual rate of increase, that mattered more.

The 1950s saw a renewal of interest in the building of hotels in Hawaii. The inventory of rooms had not increased markedly since the 1930s. As occupancy rates increased, so did the demand for rooms and the potential for profit. A number of hotel interests built new or enlarged old facilities. In

Waikiki these included Kelley, Matson (later Sheraton), and Kaiser-Burns (later Hilton). Upscale national and international hotel chains like Sheraton and Hilton, with their efficient global marketing and reservations systems, did not make a presence in Hawaii until much later. On the Neighbor Islands, comprehensive destination resorts came into being at Kailua-Kona (Hawaii), Kaanapali (Maui), and elsewhere. In 1949 the total number of rooms in Hawaii stood at 1,980, including the disappearing family type and semiresidential hotels. By 1959 the number had increased about three and a half times to 6,800.

Statehood and the Coming of Mass Tourism

One can certainly make a strong case that 1959 was a watershed year for Hawaii tourism. First, Hawaii became the fiftieth and latest member of the United States. Statehood brought a huge surge in tourist travel to Hawaii from the U.S. mainland. Statehood came at just the time when other factors were favorable to a great growth in the number of tourists. For Hawaii, the cost in money and time of air travel has been a critically important determinant of tourism development. It is also one factor the control over which is largely out of the hands of State officials. The airlines and the federal government pulled nearly all the strings when it came to travel between overseas cities and Hawaii. In late 1959, Pan Am began its Jet Clipper service from the West Coast, and soon other airlines adopted jet aircraft.[16] By the middle of the 1960s, almost all the slow propeller-driven planes were replaced by jets. Then in 1969, after years of vacillation, the Civil Aeronautics Board (CAB) made a momentous decision to allow five additional domestic passenger airlines—Western, Continental, Braniff, TWA, and American—to fly from the U.S. mainland to Hawaii.[17] Numerous cities on the mainland became more accessible to Hawaii—either directly or via more convenient connecting flights—in addition to the traditional West Coast gateway cities of Los Angeles, San Francisco, Seattle, and Portland.

Airfares from the U.S. mainland to Hawaii were still set by the CAB and did not necessarily reflect market conditions.[18] But between 1960 and 1970, the price of a one-way coach ticket between San Francisco and Honolulu—adjusted for inflation—fell by almost one-half (46 percent). Most of the decline occurred during the first half of the decade, shortly after the introduction of jet service to Hawaii.[19] At the same time, real income per person in America rose by 38 percent.[20] Americans took advantage of dramatically lower airfares and travel times and rising incomes to take their dream vacations in Hawaii.

Another important event occurred in 1970. In March of that year, Pan Am brought the Boeing 747 jumbo jet into Hawaii service. The new plane (and later other jumbo jets, such as the DC-10) did not cut the travel time from the West Coast by much—it still took about five hours to fly the distance one way—but it nearly doubled the passenger capacity over the earlier generation jets and thus lowered operating costs. The Boeing 747 helped to launch the era of "mass tourism" in Hawaii.

Dr. Richard R. Kelley, board chairman of his family-owned Hawaii hotel chain, Outrigger Enterprises Inc., recalled the dramatic transformation of Hawaii tourism from the '50s to the '70s this way:[21]

> I remember back in '51, I don't think we even had 10,000 visitors at that point. . . . Back in the '40s and '50s, everybody came in by boat. HVB [Hawaii Visitors Bureau] had a tug rented and we'd go offshore and greet people. It was all individual treatment. Reservations were made and confirmed by mail with a three-cent stamp. But by 1970 larger numbers of tourists started to come. Jet planes were soon followed by the jumbo jet. All of a sudden we were dealing with an entirely different level. These weren't individuals; this was the day of mass tourism. The only way to get a cheap airfare was to book a packaged tour. Everybody was doing that. Suddenly we had 200 people in our lobby all at once, then you have nothing for a couple of days, then another 200 show up. We had to get into sales and marketing, working with wholesale travel companies.
>
> It was just a rapid evolution of the business.

Even a cursory examination of Figures 2-1 to 2-4 reveals the very large growth in the volume of tourists, visitor spending, and hotel rooms that occurred since 1960. The increases were staggering! Just looking at the numbers of annual visitor arrivals, they rose from 296,000 in 1960 to 1.7 million in 1970, 3.9 million in 1980, 6.7 million in 1990, and 6.9 million in 2000.[22] Visitor counts in the late 1960s and early 1970s were also bolstered by huge numbers of U.S. military personnel on rest and recreation (R & R) from the Vietnam War.[23]

Perhaps more impressively, over a span of thirty-one years between 1959 and 1990, there was only one year (1980) in which the visitor count fell below that of the previous year. And that decline was a small one: less than

1 percent. Indeed, until 1990 tourism in Hawaii grew year after year despite national recessions, global oil crises in 1973 and 1979, and a disruptive twenty-nine-day United Airlines strike in May and June 1985 that discouraged people from traveling.[24] Hawaii was seemingly immune from negative national and international shocks.

One other factor stimulated growth in Hawaii tourism beginning in the late '70s, and that was the economic deregulation of the U.S. airline industry in 1978. After forty years of tight federal government control over airfares and market entry, the regulatory apparatus was dismantled.[25] No one, however, has yet figured out how large the impact of deregulation was on Hawaii. Nonetheless, it had such a large nationwide impact on air travel that it deserves to be mentioned. Alfred Kahn, the acknowledged father of airline deregulation in the United States, once summarized the effects of U.S. airline deregulation by observing that "It has meant—you may put it in a favorable way—the democratization of travel."[26] In other words, deregulation made it possible for millions of middle-class Americans to fly. For the country as a whole, average airfares, adjusted for inflation, declined by around 40 percent and passenger miles flown tripled in the years following deregulation, especially on long-haul routes. Airfares fell substantially more for recreational travel than for business or first-class travel.[27] Thus, deregulation spurred the growth of mass tourism in the United States. No doubt, Hawaii shared in the subsequent boom in tourist travel.[28]

Hawaii has also benefited from airlines' frequent flyer programs, another popular product of airline deregulation. Over the years, so many frequent flyer program members have opted to redeem their reward miles for "free" travel to Hawaii that airlines serving Hawaii often complain about flying too many nonpaying passengers on their U.S. mainland–Hawaii routes. With credit card companies, hotels, car rental companies, and other businesses also offering reward miles today, getting free airline tickets to Hawaii has become increasingly difficult as airlines ration seats on their Hawaii-bound planes.

Open competition under a deregulated environment produces winners and losers. Only the fittest competitors survive. Among the airlines that succumbed to the wide-open competition on the Hawaii–U.S. mainland routes were Pan Am, Braniff, TWA, and Western Airlines. On the other hand, deregulation made it a lot easier for Hawaii's two major interisland carriers—Aloha and Hawaiian Airlines—to extend their services to the U.S. mainland.[29]

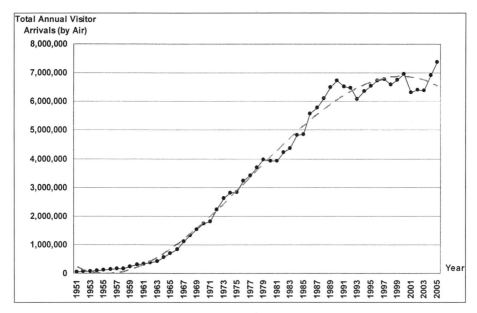

Fig. 2-1. Visitor arrivals: 1951–2005.
Source: Charts kindly supplied by John M. Knox of John M. Knox & Associates, Inc.
Original source of data provided by State Statistician Eugene Tian, April 21, 2006.

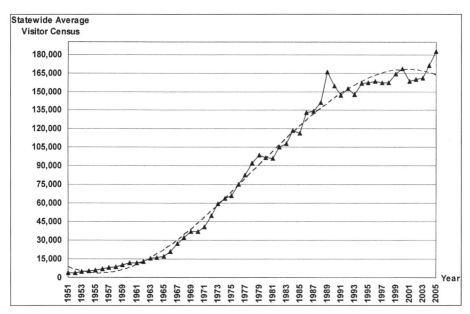

Fig. 2-2. Statewide average daily visitor census: 1951–2005.
Source: Charts kindly supplied by John M. Knox of John M. Knox & Associates, Inc.
Original source of data provided by State Statistician Eugene Tian, April 21, 2006.
Note: Visitors arriving by air.

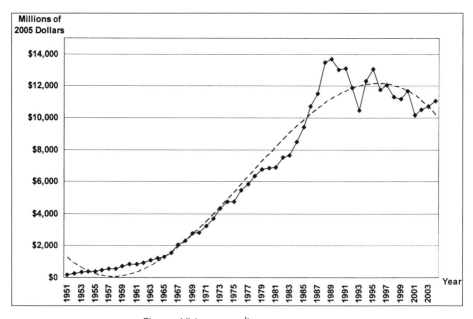

Fig. 2-3. Visitor expenditures: 1951–2005.
Source: Charts kindly supplied by John M. Knox of John M. Knox & Associates, Inc.
Original source of data from 2005 *State of Hawaii Data Book.*

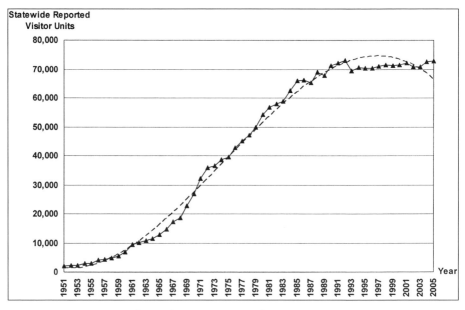

Fig. 2-4. Statewide visitor accommodation units: 1951–2005.
Source: Charts kindly supplied by John M. Knox of John M. Knox & Associates, Inc. Original
source of data from Hawaii Visitor & Convention Bureau, *Annual Visitor Plant Inventory*
(for data from 1951–1964) and DBEDT (data from 1965 on); 1995 data interpolated.

Figures 2-1 to 2-4 indicate that even as the tourist numbers kept rising, the annual *rate* of increase slowed down in each successive decade. The average annual rate of increase in visitor arrivals in the '60s was 20 percent, 8.8 percent in the '70s, 5.6 percent in the '80s, and 0.4 percent in the '90s. The S-curved figures provide a nearly perfect example of Richard Butler's characterization of the typical life cycle of a tourist destination: very rapid growth at the beginning (the "exploration stage") followed by development, consolidation, stagnation, and finally (possibly) decline.[30]

Changing Patterns in the Visitor Industry

Figures 2-1 through 2-4 do not disclose the full story of an industry that was undergoing rapid internal changes. Two of the most important changes in tourism after statehood were the explosion of Japanese travel to Hawaii beginning in the 1970s and the expansion of tourism to the Neighbor Islands.

THE RISE OF JAPANESE TOURISM

Japanese travel to Hawaii peaked in 1997 at 2.152 million arrivals. In that year, an average of eight of every ten foreign visitors to Hawaii and nearly three of ten among all visitors (U.S. and foreign) were Japanese. At Japan's airports, one of eight among Japanese overseas travelers was going to Hawaii.

Thirty years earlier, only a trickle of Japanese visitors came to Hawaii. Lonny Carlile reports 69,000 Japanese visitor arrivals in Hawaii for 1969.[31] Indeed, until 1964 the Japanese government did not even allow its own citizens to take vacation trips abroad. Japanese could go abroad for business but not for pleasure. The prohibition was put in place primarily because the Japanese government did not want its citizens to fritter away hard-to-come-by U.S. dollars on luxuries like foreign vacations when those dollars were needed to pay for essential imports like modern machinery to spur economic growth. After the Tokyo Olympics in 1964, the Japanese government lifted the ban but still kept in place restrictions on the amount of dollars Japanese could exchange to spend on overseas vacations. For example, the permissible amount between 1964 and 1968 was $500 per person. In 1969 it was raised to $700; a year later it was raised again to $1,000. After 1976, all currency restrictions were eliminated.[32] The introduction of the jumbo jet in 1970, which enabled the movement of large groups of travelers at a time, made it possible to put together economical and convenient prepaid group package tours to foreign destinations. Prepaid package tours became enormously popular with the increasingly affluent and time-constrained, hard-working Japanese.[33] Faced with embarrassingly large yearly trade surpluses and foreign political pressure, the Japanese government did an about-face in the '80s and began to urge its citizens to travel abroad. All of these factors, accompanied by the rapid appreciation of the yen (relative to the dollar), produced an explosion of Japanese travel abroad.[34] In 1964, the Japan Ministry of Transport reported 127,749 overseas departures from Japan. A decade later, the number of Japanese departures had increased by a factor of eighteen to 2.3 million. The number more than doubled to 4.7 million departures by 1984, and five years later it more than doubled again to 9.7 million.[35] Japanese tourists were eagerly sought by tourist destinations around the world because they tended (though becoming less so) to be relatively big spenders. By 1989, Japan became the world's biggest spender on international tourism, surpassing the United States and Germany.[36] In 1992, Japanese visitors accounted for one-fourth of all visitor arrivals in Hawaii but over one-third of total visitor spending.[37] Until around 2000, Hawaii was the most popular international destination among Japanese tourists.[38]

Why did the Japanese like Hawaii so much? Kazuhiko Shiraya, president of the Japan-Hawaii Tourist Association, offered the following reasons:[39]

- Perfect tropical weather year-round.
- The natural beauty of white sand beaches, ocean, and blue skies.
- The time and distance factor—Hawaii is not too far from Japan.
- The range of accommodations available, from deluxe to economy.
- A lack of crime and violence.
- The fact that Japanese is spoken at many hotels, restaurants, and other businesses and attractions.
- Hawaii's famous hospitality, the "Aloha Spirit."

Shiraya observed that by the 1990s, Hawaii's early advantage over other destinations had diminished.[40] Weather was no longer as important as before because the Japanese now had more flexibility to choose when they travel. Other destinations such as the Gold Coast of Australia and the Caribbean also offered natural beauty. The quality of tourist accommodations was getting higher elsewhere. Crime and violence in Hawaii were rising.[41] Other destinations were training their tourism employees to speak Japanese. And while the Aloha Spirit was still alive and well in the outer islands, that was not always so in Honolulu. He suggested that Hawaii needed to develop new attractions to keep the Japanese coming. Efforts to entice the Japanese to visit the Neighbor Islands have achieved only limited success.[42] They included the introduction of direct flights by Japan Airlines from Japan to Kona (Big Island) in June 1996.

Japanese travel to Hawaii declined every year between 1997 and 2003, bottoming out at 1.340 million arrivals, a decline of nearly 38 percent from the peak of 1997. The total number of Japanese overseas departures also fell between 1997 and 2003, but the decline was not nearly as much percentage-wise and not in every year. The reasons for the sharp decline of Japanese travel to Hawaii remain somewhat of a mystery. In 2005, the number of Japanese visitor arrivals in Hawaii grew again to reach 1.517 million.[43]

The growth of Japanese tourism in Hawaii was accompanied by at least two waves of tourism-dominated Japanese investment, one in the late '60s and early '70s and another in the late '80s.[44] In 1962, Japanese tycoon Kenji Osano made headlines locally when he purchased the Moana and the Princess Kaiulani Hotels for $19.4 million. He was also the owner of the Kyo-ya Restaurant in Waikiki.[45] By 1991, all but two of Hawaii's major hotels were purchased or financed, at least in part, by Japanese investors.[46] Unlike the generally welcome reception waiting for Japanese tourists, Japanese takeover of existing Hawaii tourism businesses and, in particular, undeveloped land, golf courses, and residential housing, stirred up much controversy and public resentment, despite the fact that the State government had worked vigorously to attract Japanese capital to Hawaii. Rumors spread quickly that the Japanese would be bringing in their own workers and local workers would not be able to find employment. There was also speculation that profits from Japanese businesses in Hawaii would be taken back to Japan and that Hawaii would not gain much from the investment other than revenue from the 4 percent excise tax.

Careful research showed that in 1972, Japanese owned ninety-four businesses in Hawaii, which represented only 0.6 percent of all businesses in the state and less than 5 percent of all "outside" businesses in Hawaii. Japanese business interests controlled less than 3.8 percent of all corporate assets in Hawaii.

Despite their marginal role in the overall economy, the 1972 study revealed that residents tended to view Japanese investment more negatively than investment from the other forty-nine states.[47] Opposition to Japanese investment was strongest among Native Hawaiians and Pacific Islanders.[48]

Some 90 percent of those who viewed Japanese investment negatively also believed that Japanese firms tended to discriminate against non-Japanese in their hiring. Indeed, the study found that Japanese firms (tourism and nontourism combined) tended to hire workers of Japanese ancestry in disproportionate numbers. For example, while the Japanese-Americans represented 26.8 percent of Hawaii's population, they comprised 70.3 percent of the employees of Japanese-owned firms. By contrast, Hawaiians comprised 17.2 percent of the state's population but only 1.7 percent of the employees of Japanese firms in Hawaii.[49]

But a 1975 study of employment patterns by ethnicity found much higher representation of Hawaiians and part-Hawaiians in Hawaii's tourist industries. On Oahu, 15 percent of hotel employees were Hawaiians (and part-Hawaiians); on the Neighbor Islands, it was 24 percent. About the same percentages apply in "other" visitor industries.[50] Hawaiians made up 16 percent of the food service workers, 25 percent of nonfood service/housekeeping workers, 19 percent of clerical employees, and 12 percent of the managerial and professional employees.[51] Advancement of Native Hawaiians in management ranks appears not to have improved since the 1970s study.[52] The president of the Hawaii Hotel Association noted in October 2005 that Native Hawaiians comprised only a scant 10 percent or so of all decision makers in tourism.[53]

Public criticisms of Japanese investment receded after each investment boom was over. Fortunately, there was neither time nor the will for lawmakers to enact laws to curb the inflow of foreign direct investment to Hawaii.[54] Numerous real estate antispeculation tax bills were introduced in the State Legislature during the late 1980s and early 1990s, but none passed.[55] The State's approach was to try to mitigate the problems that arose from foreign direct investment but not to curb the inflow of capital into what is widely regarded as a capital-short state. Following the burst of the Japanese economic bubble in 1991, Japanese investors began to liquidate their tourism-related investments in Hawaii, often at distress prices. Between 2001 and 2004, the dollar volume of Japanese-owned hotels sold totaled more than $1.3 billion.[56] The liquidation is still in progress. While the Japanese are a much smaller player in the Hawaii hotel business today, the remaining owners still control some of the most prized hotels, such as the Halekulani in Waikiki.

TOURISM IN THE NEIGHBOR ISLANDS

Until the mid-1970s, tourist travel to the islands of Maui, Kauai, Hawaii (the Big Island), Molokai, and Lanai—collectively referred to as the Neighbor Islands—was typically side trips from a primary destination base in Waikiki.[57] (This is largely still true of Japanese visitors.) By the early 1970s, nearly 95 percent of the westbound visitors to the state visited Oahu and over 60 percent of them visited at least one of the Neighbor Islands. The percentage of westbound tourists visiting only the Neighbor Islands and not visiting Oahu was tiny: less than 4 percent. With an increasing volume of repeat visitors to the state looking for new experiences, improvements to the tourism infrastructure on the Neighbor Islands, more aggressive marketing, and the initiation of direct flights from the U.S. West Coast to the Big Island in 1967 and the other major Neighbor Islands in 1983 and 1984, tourism on the Neighbor Islands grew much faster than on Oahu.[58] Maui saw the fastest pace of tourism growth, followed by the Big Island and Kauai (see chapter 8). Tourists who used to visit both Oahu and the Neighbor Islands were now bypassing Oahu and visiting the Neighbor Islands only.

The shift in the pattern of travel within Hawaii is reflected in the faster growth of hotel rooms on the Neighbor Islands than on Oahu. In 1965, Oahu had 78 percent of the 12,903 hotel rooms in Hawaii (10,031 units), while the Neighbor Islands had 22 percent (2,872 units). By 1991, the 72,275 hotel rooms in the state were about equally distributed between Oahu and the Neighbor Islands. In 2004, the Neighbor Islands had inched slightly ahead of Oahu, with 50.4 percent of the 72,614 hotel rooms in the state located in the three Neighbor Island counties. The figures for hotel rooms cited here do not include thousands of illegal vacation rentals and bed-and-breakfast units.[59]

In addition to the rising trend in Neighbor Island travel, there has also been a growing preference for single-island travel. Instead of dividing up their vacations into brief stays on several islands, more and more visitors have opted to spend their entire vacations on a single island. By the early 1990s, about 70 percent of tourists visited only one of the Hawaiian Islands. One-quarter of them visited only one of the Neighbor Islands.[60] As a result, the average number of days spent on each one of the Neighbor Islands more than doubled after 1983 (when direct flights to Maui and Kona from the West Coast began), even though the average total number of days spent in Hawaii decreased slightly.[61] In 2005, 5.7 million of the state's 7.4 million tourists visited only one of the Hawaiian Islands.[62]

The implications of these changes on the visitor industry in Hawaii are quite significant. While visitor industry officials do not discuss this publicly, Hawaii, which has long been promoted as a single destination, now has fragmented into several competing destinations, with each island trying to develop its own distinctive market brand.[63] This will require tourism officials to rethink how they market Hawaii. It also means less demand for interisland air travel.

The Struggling '90s

Hawaii's visitor industry struggled during the 1990s. From the beginning of the decade, the industry appeared to have become more susceptible to negative external events. Visitor arrivals fell for three straight years between 1990 and 1993 and again in 1998. For the entire 1990s decade, tourism growth was virtually at a standstill. The performance of the industry became more volatile and less predictable.

There were a number of plausible reasons why tourism declined in those years: A prolonged economic recession in California, the first Gulf War in 1991, the collapse of Japan's economic bubble in the same year, the devastation of Kauai by Hurricane Iniki in September 1992, and an airfare war among the major airlines on the U.S. mainland during the summer of 1992, which unfortunately excluded Hawaii, all combined to create the Perfect Storm that slammed Hawaii's tourist industry at the beginning of the decade.[64] The Asian Financial Crisis of 1997–1998 discouraged foreign travel to Hawaii (reductions of −2.0 percent in 1997 and −10.1 percent in 1998), accounting for the overall decline in visitor arrivals for 1998. The decline in 2001 can easily be blamed on the terrorist attacks on September 11, which shut down air travel in the United States for several days, and the subsequent coalition invasion of Afghanistan.[65] The decline in 2003 can be attributed to the Iraq War and the outbreak of the severe acute respiratory syndrome (SARS) in Asia.[66]

There was much discussion among local tourism observers about whether the downturns of the 1990s were merely transitory or the beginning of a long slide. Some held the view that it was the latter. Just about everyone agreed that Hawaii had become a mature destination.[67] The most

obvious evidence of that was that most—indeed, nearly 60 percent—of Hawaii's tourists were repeat visitors. Among U.S. mainland visitors, roughly
two-thirds had been to Hawaii before, and many had visited the Islands four
or five times or more.[68] By comparison, in the 1950s roughly 75 percent of
all visitors were first-timers.[69] Waikiki, still the flagship of Hawaii's tourist
industry in the '90s, looked somewhat shabby and in need of major physical
renovation (see chapter 7). Hawaii was losing market share in all of its major
foreign markets—including Japan, Australia, New Zealand, and Canada—
to other tourist destinations.[70] Likewise, Americans were showing more
interest in travel to overseas foreign destinations than to Hawaii.[71]

On the other side of the ledger, there was also evidence that Hawaii had
not yet reached the top of the Butler destination life cycle and was about to
begin a long descent. Visitor surveys showed no decline in satisfaction with
their travel experiences in Hawaii. The Hawaiian Islands had not suddenly
lost their tourism appeal.

Whether transitory or long term, tourism's malaise in the '90s was a
worrisome matter that could not easily be ignored. The stakes were much
higher than just the tourist industry. As tourism went, so did the economy.
So when the industry was ailing during the 1990s, so was the state economy
as a whole.[72] Some placed part of the blame on the airlines, suggesting that
they were not assigning enough seats to their Hawaii routes. The airlines
countered that they reduced seat capacity because of declining demand.
Little came out of this debate, except now the Department of Business, Economic Development and Tourism produces quarterly forecasts of available
seats to Hawaii. Well-respected tourism experts did come forward with
ideas on how to fix the ailing industry.[73] Hawaii's State and local governments also took action to rejuvenate the industry. For example, the State
spent $350 million to build a convention center in Honolulu to attract con-
vention/business travel to Hawaii, doubled the amount of money available
for destination tourism marketing, and established the Hawaii Tourism
Authority to oversee the marketing and development of tourism in Hawaii
(see chapter 5). It also passed controversial legislation to provide tax incentives to encourage hoteliers to renovate their properties and a one-time $75
million tax credit to Ko Olina resort developer Jeff Stone to build a world-
class aquarium in Honolulu (see chapter 4). After years of neglect, the City
and County of Honolulu finally spent a meaningful amount of money to
improve Waikiki (see chapter 7).

9/11, the Iraq War, and Other Terrible Global Events

The terrorist attacks on September 11, 2001, which shut down the nation's air transportation system for several days, struck Hawaii's tourist industry a particularly hard blow, as the state is totally dependent on air travel.[74] It occurred just as tourism was making a strong recovery; the first eight months of 2001 set new records for visitor arrivals. The coalition invasion of Afghanistan later in the year and the Iraq War and SARS epidemic in 2003 also dampened people's desire to travel. Visitor arrivals in Hawaii fell sharply in 2001 (–9.3 percent) and in 2003 (–0.1 percent).[75]

One of the immediate casualties of 9/11 was American Classic Voyages, a Miami-based cruise company that had been offering cruises among the Hawaiian Islands using the last of the old oceangoing passenger vessels built in the United States. On October 12, 2001, the company declared bankruptcy, citing financial losses due to 9/11. It was not the only reason but, for public consumption, a convenient one.[76] The collapse of the company eliminated 2,150 jobs, including 1,100 jobs based in Hawaii.[77]

In December 2001, the Norwegian Cruise Line (NCL) began offering weekly interisland cruises, but as required by the 1886 Passenger Vessel Services Act (PVSA), its foreign-built ship—the *Norwegian Star*—had to make a stop at a foreign port if it wanted to cruise the Hawaiian waters. To comply with the PVSA, the *Norwegian Star*'s weekly voyage included a 1,200-mile round-trip to Fanning Island in the Republic of Kiribati, which took more than three days of the seven-day cruise. The ship stayed at Fanning Island for six hours before heading back to Hawaii. The weeklong interisland cruise allowed seven hours in Hilo, nine hours on Maui, and eight hours on Kauai.

The PVSA is protectionist legislation patterned after the famous seventeenth-century British Navigation Acts.[78] Its purpose was to protect domestic shipbuilding and maritime shipping from foreign competition, ostensibly to advance national security. In a nutshell, the PVSA reserves domestic ocean passenger commerce exclusively for companies using U.S.–built and flagged ships and American labor. The companies must also abide by all applicable U.S. laws that govern labor (e.g., wages and benefits), taxation, and the environment.[79] Hawaii's senior U.S. senator, Democrat Daniel Inouye, helped to establish a Hawaii-based cruise tourism industry by deftly shepherding a controversial piece of legislation through a Republican-controlled Congress (February 2003), which granted the Norwegian Cruise Line the exclusive right to offer interisland-only cruises among the Hawaiian Islands using three foreign-built cruise ships operating under U.S. registry.[80] To

gain the support of Alaska and Florida lawmakers, the legislation granting NCL the exemption from the PVSA further stipulated that the three
ships "shall not transport passengers in revenue service to ports in Alaska,
the Gulf of Mexico or the Caribbean Sea."[81] The 2003 federal government
appropriations bill that contained the exemption passed overwhelmingly
by a vote of 228-83 in the House and 76-20 in the Senate.[82] With the legal
hurdle overcome, the first of the three NCL cruise ships went into service in
2004. It was far from being a smooth launch, as there were many passenger
complaints about glitches and the poor quality of the onboard service. NCL
had great difficulty—and continues to experience difficulty—in recruiting
U.S. workers to comply with the requirement of the PVSA. The company
worked hard on these problems. By mid-2006, the last of the three modern
cruise ships toured the Hawaiian waters without apparent major incidents.
However, the rapid increase in capacity could not be profitably absorbed in
such a short period of time.[83] In 2007, NCL announced that it would move
the largest of the three ships to Europe in 2008.

In 2005, about 239,000 visitors flew to Hawaii to board cruise ships,
and another 78,000 visitors arrived in Hawaii on cruise ships. In just three
years, between 2004 and 2006, the number of cruise ship passengers in Hawaii increased from 240,000 to about 398,000.[84] A noteworthy fact about
cruise tourism in Hawaii is that its peak months of cruising (as of 2005) are
September, October, and December, during what are normally the slack
months for Hawaii tourism.[85]

Everything considered, Hawaii's experience after 9/11—at least compared
with the rest of the country—was fortunate in a couple of respects. First,
around the country business travel declined more sharply than pleasure
travel,[86] and Hawaii's tourist industry caters mostly to pleasure travelers.
Second, the widely unpopular U.S.–led invasion of Iraq not only has made
the United States a less attractive tourist destination to many potential foreign visitors, tougher U.S. entry requirements after 9/11 have also made
America a much more difficult country to visit.[87] Likewise, many Americans have also lost interest in overseas travel abroad. As a result, foreign
travel to the United States fell sharply after 9/11, but some of the lost business was offset by the increase in domestic travel.[88] While Hawaii tourism
officials are generally reluctant to talk about it publicly, there is little doubt
that Hawaii has benefited from the apprehension of many Americans to
travel abroad after 9/11 and opting to visit Hawaii and other domestic destinations instead.

Figures 2-5 and 2-6 show the actual number of U.S. (domestic) and Japanese

tourist visits to Hawaii before and after 9/11 and forecasts of their visits to
Hawaii had 9/11 and other terrible global events not occurred.[89] The figures
show that after 9/11, far fewer Japanese but far more U.S. mainland residents
visited Hawaii compared to the numbers that would have come had 9/11 and
other terrible events not occurred. In Hawaii, the surge in domestic travel
more than offset the decline in Japanese travel, so that by year-end 2004
the industry had fully recovered—both in the headcount of tourists and in
tourism revenues—from 9/11 and other global shocks.[90] In 2005 the number
of visitor arrivals reached an all-time high of 7.45 million, an increase of 7.8
percent over 2004 and surpassing the previous peak of 6.95 million in 2000.[91]
In sum, tourism in Hawaii is booming despite the continuing decline in Japanese visitors.[92] For now, no one is talking about Butler's tourist destination
life cycle!

Tourism's Impacts on Hawaii:
The Good and the Not So Good

Exports have always been the engine of Hawaii's economy. In 1959, earnings
from U.S. defense spending in Hawaii ($316 million) were the largest exter-
nal source of revenue, followed by pineapple ($128 million), sugar ($123 million), and tourism ($109 million). By 1990, earnings from tourism exceeded
$9.7 billion, or 2.5 times the sum of the other three.[93] Tourism accounted for
more than one-quarter of total household (personal) income in Hawaii.[94]

The rise in tourism's importance in Hawaii's economy was not only because of the spectacular growth of tourism, but also because of the stagnation and the long-run decline of Hawaii's traditional exports of sugar
and pineapple. Thus tourism growth transformed what was once a sedate
economy dependent on commodity exports based largely on plantation agriculture into one based largely on the export of services. As Hawaii's economic base shifted from agriculture and agricultural processing to tourism
services and national defense, so did the structure of jobs and employment
in Hawaii. Hawaii's economy became even more service dependent than
the U.S. economy.

Incomes in Hawaii also rose in tandem with the growth in tourism. In
1959, income per person in Hawaii was 20 percent lower than the national
average. By 1970, income per person in Hawaii caught up with the national
average, and no doubt this convergence was largely due to the extraordinary
growth of tourism in Hawaii, which enabled the state's economy to grow
much faster than the nation's economy.[95]

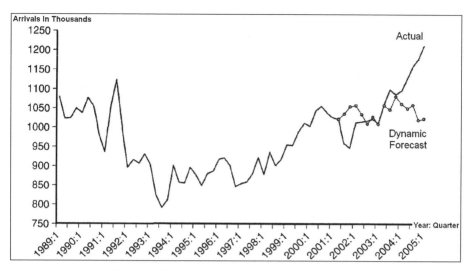

Fig. 2-5. U.S. visitors to Hawaii: Actual versus forecast.
Source: Bonham, Edmonds, and Mak (2006).

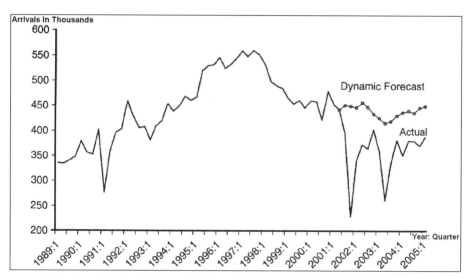

Fig. 2-6. Japanese visitors to Hawaii: Actual versus forecast.
Source: Bonham, Edmonds, and Mak (2006).

Tourism's detractors argue that tourism provides mostly low wages, low earnings, and menial jobs.[96] Household surveys consistently have found that while Hawaii residents appreciate the wide range of jobs tourism generates, the majority of the respondents believe that most tourism jobs do not provide much opportunity for advancement.[97] They also believe that the best jobs in tourism tend to go to outsiders.[98] How much of what people believe is true and what is actually true have not been carefully studied. On the matter of pay, data show that tourism industries are below-average compensation industries. In the United States, the average compensation of employees in the tourism industries in 1997 was $23,475, compared to $35,944 for all industries. Although tourism employment comprised 3.5 percent of total employment in all U.S. industries, employee compensation in the tourism industries was only 2.5 percent of that in all U.S. industries.[99] The same is true for Hawaii. For example, between 1992 and 1998, 26.1 percent of all the jobs in Hawaii were directly and indirectly generated by tourism, but earnings from tourism represented only 20.2 percent of all worker earnings.[100] Low earnings in tourism are mainly due to the prevalence in tourism of unskilled, seasonal, casual, part-time, transitory, and female employment.

The rapid growth of tourism had significant consequences for Hawaii's population (see chapter 3). Tourism growth induced massive in-migration to the state as tourism-driven demand for labor outstripped the available local labor supply. Influx of labor keeps real wages from rising and diminishes the economic benefit of tourism growth to residents.[101] Tourism's population impacts were particularly large on the sparsely populated Neighbor Islands, which had seen net population out-migration since the 1930s as plantations continued to shed workers (see chapter 8). Rapid tourism growth reversed the population decline on the Neighbor Islands after 1960. Population has since grown much faster on the Neighbor Islands than on Oahu.

Rapid population growth on the Neighbor Islands taxed the State and local governments' capacities to provide affordable housing and public facilities such as schools and roads for residents. Not infrequently, residents have fought against new tourism-related developments to maintain their area lifestyles (especially in rural areas), to preserve open space and protect the environment, or until infrastructure improvements were completed. In a highly publicized dispute in the early '90s, residents of Maui and Kauai resisted State efforts to lengthen the airport runways on their islands intended to better accommodate direct overseas flights by jumbo jets.[102] Their runways were not extended. The Kona Airport runway on the Big Island, however, was lengthened. In another high-profile and bitterly contested dispute on Kauai, residents fought over the permissible use of the Hanalei River by commercial boating companies offering sightseeing tours along the majestic Na Pali coast (see chapter 6). The State government banned all commercial sightseeing boats on the river in 2000. The proliferation of illegal vacation rentals and bed-and-breakfast establishments in residential neighborhoods has become the latest high-profile controversy. In 1989, the City and County of Honolulu stopped issuing new permits for vacation rentals and bed-and-breakfast establishments in residential neighborhoods. But the ordinance has been weakly enforced and County officials concede that it may be unenforceable.[103]

While Hawaii's residents welcome the higher incomes, more jobs and entertainment opportunities, and the generally higher standard of living tourism has given them, many also feel that the visitor industry has been a major contributor to the high cost of housing, congestion, and crime in Hawaii.[104]

Tom Hamilton, who was perhaps the most respected observer and student of Hawaii tourism during the '70s, once offered the notion that in places where tourism is or becomes the central or one of the central economic activities, there seems to be a three-stage natural history of local reaction. These three, he suggested, might be labeled periods of *enthusiasm,* *plateauism,* and *antagonism.*

Hamilton postulated that when tourism first begins to develop, there usually is a hearty welcome from almost all segments of society, particularly where unemployment or underemployment is high. Here appears to be a new source of income, of tax revenue, of jobs in a labor-intensive industry. Many of the local population now can see the possibility of rewards for skills they thought had little economic value. And in this period of enthusiasm, nothing is so cheered as the announcement that this year's batch of visitors exceeded last year's.

Then there comes the plateau. Now tourism is accepted as a part of the local social and economic life. The ebb and flow of the tourist trade is accepted philosophically. Visitors are not greeted ecstatically. On the other hand, it is generally recognized that treating them well is simply good business, and one learns to live with their presence.

The third phase of antagonism takes many forms. It may express itself in vocal and printed criticism of alleged harm to the environment, exploitation of local labor, cultural damage, overcrowding, and a drain on tax revenues. In a few instances, unfortunately, in parts of the world there has been violence.

In Hawaii, six similar household surveys were conducted between 1988 and 2006 to solicit residents' reactions to tourism development, and they clearly indicate that Hawaii has not entered the stage of antagonism.[105] Although an overwhelming majority (77 to 85 percent) of the residents agreed that "My island is too dependent on tourism," between 69 and 77 percent of the residents agreed that "Overall, tourism has brought more benefits than problems to this island."[106] Those with jobs in tourism were more likely to respond positively. Filipinos were most likely, while Native Hawaiians were the least likely, to give strongly favorable responses. But for the first time, in 2006, less than 50 percent (44 percent) of the respondents indicated that tourism "has been mostly good for you and the family."[107]

Between 34 to 40 percent of the respondents in the 1999, 2001, and 2002 surveys agreed with the statement that "Unless we are sure some other major industry will work here, we must support more tourism growth." Only 5 to 7 percent of the respondents agreed with the statement, "We should not support any more tourism growth, even if that means the economy will stay the same or get worse." Roughly half (45 to 52 percent) of the respondents agreed that "We should support more tourism growth in the short term, but we have to accept long-term limits even if we can't find other major industries that will work here."[108] In sum, Hawaii's residents are more pro- than antitourism growth, especially if there are no other economic alternatives.[109] Support for tourism growth weakens if there are other viable options. That is hardly surprising considering that most of the respondents already believe that Hawaii is overly dependent on tourism.

Is it likely that the residents' generally positive responses toward tourism were influenced by poor economic conditions in those five years? Indeed, 2001 and 2002 were poor years for tourism and Hawaii's economy, but 1988 and 1999 were relatively good years and 2005 was a boom year. Thus, the generally positive responses cannot be attributed to weak macroeconomic conditions.

The surveys uncovered one worrying trend: It is widely acknowledged around the world that in developing tourism, the well-being of destination residents should be paramount.[110] In Hawaii, there is a rising percentage of residents who believe that their island "is being run for tourists at the expense of the local people."[111]

Percent of respondents who agree with
the statement that their island is being
run for tourists

Year	Percent
1988	43
1993	45
1999	49
2001	48
2002	48
2005	55
2006	62

Beginning in the 1960s, some individuals and groups began to question the benefits of tourism growth. Even though they constituted a minority, their complaints were sufficiently articulate to receive considerable attention. Some of the criticism stemmed from the growing antibusiness, antiestablishment tenor of the times. There were, however, other more pointed questions raised. Some alleged that the taxes generated by the industry did not cover the cost of building and maintaining the necessary tourism facilities, and thus the local taxpayers were subsidizing tourism (see chapter 4). Others held that tourism produced too many jobs that were servile and low paying. Environmentalists of many persuasions were unhappy about the treatment of the beaches, the alleged pollution of the waters, and the elimination of views. Culturalists pointed to tourism as one of the destroyers of local lifestyles. Some of those who sympathized with tourism's contribution to the economy nonetheless were not happy with the density in Waikiki (see chapter 7), the design of hotel buildings, the middle-class and middle-aged tourist couples clad in matching aloha shirts and muumuus, and the substitution of rock for Hawaiian music. Even those who advocated tourism's growth, or at least were willing to accept it as necessary, had some doubts about the impact of tourism on population growth. How fast should tourism be permitted to grow? And how do you control it, even if you wanted to?

The following chapters examine Hawaii's public policy responses to tourism growth since statehood. They look at how public policies and planning responded to the concerns about tourism and how they shaped tourism's development in Hawaii. Chapter 3 begins by recounting the history of the development of the State government's policies on tourism.

Notes

1. For this early period, see Chong (1963).

2. In the 1980s the Armed Forces YMCA, which was listed on the Hawaii Register of Historic Places, was redeveloped by megaresort developer Christopher Hemmeter as the Hemmeter Corporation Building (currently the No. 1 Capitol District Building). Sadly, this once elegant and grandiose structure, which won a national award for historic preservation, now houses several State government departments.

3. Ebel, Mak, and Moncur (1977), p. 35.

4. Hoover (December 17, 2003), p. A6.

5. Actually, the first transpacific Clipper service took place in November 1935 when the *China Clipper*, a Martin M-130 flying boat, took twenty-one hours to fly from the West Coast to Hawaii. This was a mail service–only flight. Schneider's unpublished paper, "The Evolution of Mainland-Hawaii Air Travel" (December 15, 1978) provides a brief informative history of early commercial aviation in Hawaii.

6. Hoover (2003), p. A6.

7. Schneider (1978), p. 2.

8. Chong (1963).

9. Until the late 1990s, visitor arrival statistics were separated into "westbound" and "eastbound" visitors. Westbound visitors traveled to Hawaii in a westerly direction. Thus, in addition to U.S. mainland visitors, westbound visitors would also include Canadians, Latin Americans, Europeans, and so on. Eastbound visitors comprised visitors from the Asia-Pacific region, including Japanese, Australians, New Zealanders, Koreans, and so on. Historically, U.S. mainland visitors comprised most of the westbound visitors while eastbound visitors comprised largely visitors from Japan after the 1960s.

10. Ebel, Mak, and Moncur (1977), p. 35.

11. Schneider (1978), p. 7.

12. Ibid.

13. Still, as late as 1957, almost one-fourth of Hawaii's tourists came by surface. By 1975, it was less than 0.5 percent. Despite the resurgence of cruise tourism in recent years, the percentage of tourists coming to Hawaii by ship is still a puny 1 percent. State of Hawaii Department of Business, Economic Development and Tourism (DBEDT) (2005), Table 65, p. 106.

14. Ibid., Table 8, p. 12.

15. Ibid.

16. Actually, credit for the first passenger jet plane to land in Honolulu must be given to Australia's Qantas Airways; its Boeing 707 jet plane first arrived in Honolulu in July 1959. Schneider (1978), p. 10.

17. The total number of authorized airlines increased from three to nine in 1969 and to ten in 1970. Ibid, p. 14. The increase in competition was devastating

to Pan Am since it was not permitted to extend its routes to interior U.S. mainland markets. Ebel and Mak (1974), chapter 15.

18. For example, the average load factor on Hawaii–U.S. mainland flights was 46.8 percent in 1971 compared to 56 percent the year before. Ebel and Mak (1974), p. 36. One would have expected airfares to fall. Instead, real airfares (coach class) between San Francisco and Honolulu actually *increased* by 10 percent. Ebel, Mak, and Moncur (1977), p. 40.

19. Ebel, Mak, and Moncur (1977), p. 40.

20. Ibid.

21. *Honolulu Advertiser* (November 15, 2004), p. C3.

22. DBEDT (2005), p. 12.

23. Hawaii Visitors Bureau (1970), pp. 0–1 and Ebel, Mak, and Moncur (1977), fn. 30, p. 47. Between 1967 and 1971, the number of military personnel and their dependents who came to Hawaii on R & R due to the Vietnam War totaled nearly 1.8 million. At the peak of the war in 1969, nearly a quarter of a million U.S. military personnel and dependents spent R & R time in Hawaii. By 1970, the number had dropped to 90,000.

24. Bank of Hawaii Research Department (July/August 1988), p. 1.

25. Mak (2004), chapter 8.

26. A New River Media interview (circa 2002), reproduced in Mak (2004), p. 94.

27. Mak (2004), chapter 8.

28. Most of the benefits of airline deregulation in the United States stemmed from the entry of low-cost carriers such as Southwest Airlines. Mak (2004), p. 92. Discount air carriers did not make an entry into the U.S. mainland–Hawaii market until very recently.

29. By comparison, the state of Hawaii has had a poor record in supporting economic competition. Too often it has tended to shield incumbent local businesses from potential competitors. McClain (1992), pp. 7–13. I provide three examples here: (1) In Hawaii the motor carrier industry, which includes tour bus and limousine carriers, is regulated by the Hawaii Motor Carrier Law, which oversees entry and exit of motor carriers and tariffs. The law permits motor carriers to agree among themselves on rates to be charged and exempts their collusive price setting from the State's antitrust laws. Not surprisingly, tariffs were set higher than if there were competition. While other states have dismantled economic regulation of motor carriers, Hawaii has not. State of Hawaii Legislative Auditor (December 1975). (2) In 1991 when United Airlines wanted to enter the interisland air transportation market, it was sternly discouraged by State officials. McClain (1992). Paul Brewbaker, chief economist at the Bank of Hawaii (personal communication), surmised that the rebuff may have prompted United Airlines to reduce its presence in the Hawaii market. (3) After the terrorist attacks of 9/11, the State supported Aloha and Hawaiian Airlines' application to the U.S. Department of Transportation to permit them to collusively reduce capacity on the major interisland routes. Interisland airfares rose sharply after the agreement

went into effect. Blair, Mak, and Bonham (2007). The State's failure to encourage competition often has harmed consumers and impeded economic progress. In the examples presented here, most of the consumers turn out to be tourists.

30. Butler (1980), vol. 24, pp. 5–12.

31. Carlile (1996), p. 16. DBEDT was so unsure of the accuracy of these early estimates of visitor arrivals that its own published statistics on Japanese begin with visitor arrivals in 1983. The Japan Ministry of Transport, in *Tourism in Japan* (reproduced in Mak and White 1992, p. 18), reported 492,880 Japanese international departures in 1969, giving Hawaii a market share of 14 percent, if Carlile's figure of 69,000 is believable.

32. Carlile (1996), p. 13.

33. Mak and White (summer 1992), pp. 14–23; Carlile (1996), pp. 11–18; Mak, Carlile, and Dai (2005), pp. 151–162; and Mak (2004), pp. 39–40.

34. See also Tyrrell et al. (1991).

35. Japan Ministry of Transport, *Tourism in Japan,* reproduced in Mak and White (1992), p. 18.

36. Mak and White (1992), p. 17.

37. Mak (1993).

38. JATA-NET, at http://www.jata-net.or.jp/english/materials/2002/materials0203 .htm.

39. Shiraya (June 7, 1993), p. D1.

40. Ibid.

41. Still, in a 2001 survey conducted by Mainichi Newspapers, Japanese overseas air travelers considered Hawaii the safest destination. Hawaii was also considered the most friendly country/region in the same survey. At http://jin.jcic .or.jp/stat/stats/220PN4C.html.

42. In the late '80s and early '90s, after the signing of the Plaza Accord (1985), Hawaii became a very popular shopping destination among single female Japanese office workers to purchase expensive (and mostly European) name-brand goods. Mak (1996). A survey of Japanese overseas travelers conducted by the Mainichi Newspapers in 2001 found that Hawaii was still the fourth most "fun" place to shop, after France, Italy, and Hong Kong. http://jin.jcic.or.jp/stat/ stats/220PN4A.html.

43. DBEDT (2005), p. 6.

44. Ebel and Mak (1974), chapter 22; Downs (1991); and University of Hawaii Economic Research Organization (September 1998).

45. Rickard (1973). He also purchased the Surfrider, the Sheraton Waikiki, and the Royal Hawaiian Hotels in Waikiki. By the end of the 1970s, he owned 20 percent of all the hotel rooms in Waikiki. Allen (2004), p. 157.

46. Downs (1991), p. 1.

47. Heller and Heller (1973), chapter 23.

48. Ibid.

49. Ibid.

50. DBEDT (1978).

51. Ibid. Caucasians comprised the largest percentage of tourism employees. At the top echelons, Caucasians accounted for nearly half (46 percent) of managerial and professional employees.

52. Schaefers (October 16, 2005).

53. Ibid.

54. During the second investment boom, the mayor of Honolulu, Frank Fasi, announced that he would demand from Japanese golf course developers a $100 million development exaction for each proposed golf course on Oahu before county permits would be issued. Shortly after that, the golf course building mania subsided. Callies (1992).

55. Rose (1992).

56. Natarajan (2004), p. 35.

57. This section borrows heavily from Mak (1993).

58. Fujii, Im, and Mak (May 1992), pp. 185–195. Direct flights between Hilo and the mainland began in 1967 and ceased in 1987. United Airlines initiated direct flights from the U.S. West Coast to Maui in January 1983. Direct flights to Keahole-Kona Airport on the Big Island followed in June 1983. Direct flights to Kauai began in August 1984 but were terminated in September 1985 and replaced by one-stop service via Honolulu. Direct flights greatly increased the number of tourists visiting only the Neighbor Islands (and not Oahu).

59. Aguiar and Arakawa (June 5, 2005), pp. F1–F2.

60. Hawaii Visitors Bureau (1995).

61. In 1971, the average length of stay in Hawaii among westbound visitors was around eleven days. The average length of stay on Oahu was around six days and roughly three days for each of Maui, Kauai, and Hawaii. By contrast, in 2004 the average length of stay of "domestic" visitors to Hawaii was nearly ten days; the average number of days spent on Oahu was 7.6 days, 7.7 days on Maui, 7.1 days on Kauai, and 7.4 days on the Big Island. DBEDT (2005), p. 8.

62. Kindly supplied by Cy Feng (DBEDT).

63. Mak and Sakai (1992), pp. 185–200.

64. Mak (September 16, 1993).

65. Bonham and Gangnes (November 2001).

66. Bonham, Edmonds, and Mak (2006).

67. DBEDT (1996), pp. 1–5.

68. See, for example, DBEDT (2000), pp. 8–9.

69. DBEDT (1996), p. 3.

70. Mak (September 26, 1996).

71. Bonham, Edmonds, and Mak (2006).

72. Grandy (2002).

73. See, for example, Gee (September 20, 1993), p. C1; Shiraya (June 7, 1993), p. D1; and Wright (April 11, 1994), p. C1. See also DBEDT (July 1999), pp. 15–18.

74. Honolulu International Airport was shut down for two full days, and when

commercial flights were resumed on September 13, it took a week to catch up. See Ishikawa and Brannon (September 14, 2001), pp. B1 and B5.

75. DBEDT (2005), p. 12.

76. The ships were old and hardly competitive with the sleek and glamorous mega cruise ships that were being built. The company ordered two new ships from a U.S. shipyard, but construction was delayed and costs were far over initial estimates. The ships were not completed.

77. Magin (February 14, 2003), pp. A1 and A10.

78. Despite the repeal of England's Navigation Acts in 1849, cabotage laws such as the PVSA remain prevalent around the world. Mak (2003).

79. For additional details and the economic implications of the PVSA, see Mak (2004), pp. 88–89.

80. Senator John McCain of Arizona and other cruise ship companies objected to granting a monopoly to Norwegian Cruise Line. DePledge (February 23, 2003), pp. C1 and C6; Magin (February 14, 2003), pp. A1 and A10. A study done by the General Accounting Office (February 2004) concluded that the exemption would not grant substantial market power to Norwegian Cruise Line because "NCL will likely have little power to raise prices on these itineraries because of competition from other vacation options."

81. Magin (February 14, 2003), p. A10.

82. Ibid.

83. Arakawa and Dingeman (May 25, 2007).

84. Dingeman (February 27, 2007).

85. DBEDT (2006), p. 105.

86. Indeed, domestic pleasure travel in the United States increased yearly after 2001. Bonham, Edmonds, and Mak (2006).

87. Bonham, Edmonds, and Mak (2006) and Edmonds and Mak (June 22–23, 2005).

88. Bonham, Edmonds, and Mak (2006).

89. For a detailed explanation of the econometric methods used in generating these forecasts, see Bonham, Edmonds, and Mak (2006).

90. "Recovery" here refers not to getting back to the level of tourism in year 2000 (i.e., before September 11, 2001), but to where tourism would have been had 9/11 not occurred. See Bonham, Edmonds, and Mak (2006) for further explanation of this point. As of year-end 2004, the travel and tourism industry in the United States still had not fully recovered from the effects of 9/11 and subsequent events.

91. And 2004 saw an 8.3 percent increase over 2003.

92. The continuing decline in Japanese travel to Hawaii could be partly due to demographic change and changing consumer tastes in Japan. Japan's rapidly aging population means that there are fewer and fewer single females in their twenties, and this group comprises the largest cohort of Japanese visitors to Hawaii. Mak,

Carlile, and Dai (November 2005), pp. 151–162. See also Kobayashi (October 2003), p. 5.

93. Over $10 billion if airline purchases in Hawaii are included.

94. Direct, indirect, and induced. *State of Hawaii Data Book, 1995* (1996), pp. 208 and 348.

95. Income per person in Hawaii increased to 115 percent of the national average by 1985 before sliding down to the U.S. average in the late 1990s.

96. See, for example, Brown (2000), p. 57.

97. Residents indicating this numbered 65 percent in 2002 and 53 percent in 2005. Market Trends Pacific Inc. and John M. Knox & Associates (December 2005).

98. The numbers were 61 percent in 2002 and 51 percent in 2005. Ibid.

99. Kass and Okubo (July 2000).

100. DBEDT (July 1999), p. 7.

101. See, for example, R. M. Towill Corporation, Inc., et al. (2004), p. 28. Towill et al. simulated the effects of an increase in tourist spending on real wages in Hawaii and concluded that "residents are better off when visitor spending is not accompanied by a growth in the labor force" (p. 28).

102. Mak (1993), p. 21. The planes could easily land on the shorter runways but could not take off fully loaded with fuel. They had to take off partially fueled and then top the fuel tanks in Honolulu.

103. Arakawa (June 5, 2005), p. F2.

104. Nearly identical resident reaction surveys—with a few changes in the questions asked from year to year—were conducted in 1988, 1999, 2001, 2002, 2005, and 2006. For the latest study with comparative responses for all six years, see Market Trends Pacific, Inc., and John M. Knox & Associates (November 2006).

105. Market Trends Pacific, Inc., and John M. Knox & Associates (November 2006). There was also a limited survey in 1993.

106. John M. Knox & Associates (2004), p. 56; Market Trends Pacific, Inc., and John M. Knox & Associates (2006), pp. 13–17.

107. Market Trends Pacific, Inc., and John M. Knox & Associates (2006), p. 14.

108. Ibid., p. 57.

109. Curiously, respondents by sizable percentages do not want more hotels to be built even if more tourists were to come; the highest percentage (73 percent) was reported in 2005.

110. World Tourism Organization (1994), p. 8.

111. Market Trends Pacific, Inc., and John M. Knox & Associates (November 2006), p. 17.

References

Aguiar, Eloise, and Lynda Arakawa. 2005. "Unlawful Hospitality." *Honolulu Advertiser*, June 5: F1–F2.

Allen, Robert C. 2004. *Creating Hawaii Tourism.* Honolulu: Bess Press.

Arakawa, Linda. 2005. "1989 Ban Has Been Mostly Ineffective." *Honolulu Advertiser,* June 5: F2.

———. 2006. "Visitor Industry Still Growing." *Honolulu Advertiser,* June 29: C1 and C3.

Arakawa, Linda, and Robbie Dingeman. 2007. "NCL Cruiseline Changes Leadership in Hawaii." *Honolulu Advertiser,* May 25: C1 and C3.

Bank of Hawaii Research Department. 1988. "Hawaii's Visitor Industry in Transition." *Business Trends* (July/August).

Blair, Roger, James Mak, and Carl Bonham. 2007. "Collusive Duopoly: The Effects of the Aloha and Hawaiian Airlines' Agreement to Reduce Capacity." *Antitrust Law Journal* 74(2): 409–438.

Bonham, Carl, Christopher Edmonds, and James Mak. 2006. "The Impact of 9/11 and Other Terrible Global Events on Tourism in the U.S. and Hawaii." *Journal of Travel Research* 45(1): 99–110. See also University of Hawaii at Manoa Economics Department Working Paper No. 06-2, January 30, at http://www.economics.hawaii.edu/research/workingpapers/WP_06-2.pdf.

Bonham, Carl, and Byron Gangnes. 2001. *The Effect on Hawaii's Economy of the September 11 Terror Attacks* (November). At http://www.hawaii.gov/dbedt/uhero/index.html.

Brown, Frances. 2000. *Tourism Reassessed: Blight or Blessing?* Boston: Butterworth Heinemann.

Butler, Richard W. 1980. "The Concept of the Tourist Area Cycle of Evolution: Implications for the Management of Resources." *Canadian Geographer* 24: 5–12.

Callies, David L. 1992. "Why would anyone oppose the $100 million golf-course development fee proposed by Mayor Fasi?" In Randy Roth, ed., *The Price of Paradise: Lucky We Live Hawaii?* (Honolulu: Mutual Publishing): 169–173.

Carlile, Lonny E. 1996. "Economic Development and the Evolution of Japanese Overseas Tourism: 1964–1994." *Tourism Recreation Research* 21(1): 11–18.

Chong, Anson. 1963. *Economic Development of Hawaii and the Growth of Tourism before 1945.* New York: Erickson Enterprises.

DePledge, Derrick. 2003. "Cruise Exemption Bolstered." *Honolulu Advertiser,* February 23: C1 and C6.

Dingeman, Robbie. 2007. "NCL Sailing in Sea of Red." *Honolulu Advertiser,* February 27: A1–A2.

Downs, Anthony. 1991. *Japanese Real Estate Investment in Hawaii.* New York: Solomon Brothers.

Ebel, Robert, and James Mak. 1974. *Current Issues in Hawaii's Economy.* Honolulu: Crossroads Press.

Ebel, Robert, James Mak, and James Moncur. 1977. "The Future of Hawaii's Major Exports." In Moheb Ghali, ed., *Tourism and Regional Growth* (Leiden: Martinus Nijhoff Social Sciences Division): 20–48.

Edmonds, Christopher, and James Mak. 2005. "Terrorism and Tourism in the Asia Pacific Region: Is Travel and Tourism in a New World after 9/11?" Paper presented at the 2005 APEC Economic Outlook Symposium: The Economic Effects of Terrorism and Counter-Terrorism, June 22–23, East-West Center, Honolulu.

Fujii, Edwin, Eric Im, and James Mak. 1992. "The Economics of Direct Flights." *Journal of Transport Economics and Policy* (May): 185–195.

Gee, Chuck Y. 1993. "UH Dean Urges Improvements to Lure Tourists." *Honolulu Advertiser,* September 20: C1.

General Accounting Office (GAO). 2004. *Maritime Law Exemption: Exemption Provides Limited Competitive Advantage, but Barriers to Further Entry under U.S. Flag.* Washington, D.C.: GAO (February).

Grandy, Christopher. 2002. *Hawaii Becalmed: Economic Lessons of the 1990s.* Honolulu: University of Hawaii Press.

"Hawaii Tops in Dream Vacation Poll." 2005. *Honolulu Advertiser,* May 28: A1.

Hawaii Visitors Bureau (HVB). 1970. *1969 Annual Research Report.* Honolulu: HVB. (Also 1970, 1989, and 1994.)

Heller, H. Robert, and Emily E. Heller. 1973. *The Economic and Social Impact of Foreign Investment in Hawaii.* Honolulu: Economic Research Center, University of Hawaii.

Hoover, Will. 2003. "The Day Hawaii Really Took Off." *Honolulu Advertiser,* December 17: A1 and A6.

Ishikawa, Scott, and Johnny Brannon. 2001. "Security Tight at Hawaii Airports." *Honolulu Advertiser,* September 14: B1 and B5.

JATA-NET. 2002. Data files at http://www.jatanet.or.jp/english/materials/2002/materials0203.htm.

John M. Knox & Associates. 2004. *Sustainable Tourism in Hawaii, Socio-Cultural and Public Input Component, Volume I, Summary Report.* Prepared for the State of Hawaii Department of Business, Economic Development and Tourism. Honolulu: DBEDT.

Kass, David I., and Sumiye Okubo. 2000. "U.S. Travel and Tourism Satellite Accounts for 1996 and 1997." *Survey of Current Business* (July): 8–24.

Kobayashi, Hideyoshi. 2003. "Trends and Potential of the Japanese Outbound Travel Market." *JATA World Tourism Congress 2003.* Yokohama, Japan: JATA (October).

"Leadership Corner." 2004. *Honolulu Advertiser,* November 15: C3.

Magin, Janis L. 2003. "Congress OKs Cruise Exemption." *Honolulu Advertiser,* February 14: A1 and A10.

Mak, James. 1993. "Tourism and Hawaii's Economic Development." Presented to the Philippines Exchange Mission to Hawaii, Sheraton Waikiki Hotel. Honolulu: Department of Economics, University of Hawaii at Manoa (September 16).

———. 1996. "The Future of Hawaii as a Tourist Shopping Destination."

Unpublished paper. Honolulu: Department of Economics, University of Hawaii at Manoa (September 26).

———. 2003. "Economic Regulation of Waterborne Transportation." *Oxford Encyclopedia of World Economic History,* vol. 5. Oxford: Oxford University Press: 254–256.

Mak, James, Lonny Carlile, and Sally Dai. 2005. "Impact of Population Aging on Japanese International Travel to 2025." *Journal of Travel Research* 44(2) (November): 151–162.

Mak, James, and Marcia Sakai. 1992. "Tourism in Hawaii: Economic Issues for the 1990's and Beyond." In Zachary A. Smith and Richard C. Pratt, eds., *Politics and Public Policy in Hawaii* (Albany, NY: State University of New York Press): 185–200.

Mak, James, and Kenneth White. 1992. "Comparative Tourism Development in Asia and the Pacific." *Journal of Travel Research* (summer): 14–23.

Market Trends Pacific, Inc., and John M. Knox & Associates. 2005. *2005 Survey of Resident Sentiments on Tourism in Hawaii, Analysis and Report.* Prepared for the Hawaii Tourism Authority (December).

———. 2006. *2006 Survey of Resident Sentiments on Tourism in Hawaii, Analysis and Report.* November, at http://www.HawaiiTourismAuthority.org/documents_upload_path/reports/HTPLA-Report-11-30-2006.pdf.

McClain, David. 1992. "What Can Hawaii Do to Stay Competitive in the World Market and Keep Its Economy Strong?" In Randy W. Roth, ed., *The Price of Paradise: Lucky We Live Hawaii?* (Honolulu: Mutual Publishing): 7–13.

Natarajan, Prabha. 2004. "Japanese selling off assets, reducing Hawaii presence." *Pacific Business News,* December 10: 1 and 35.

Rickard, Robin. 1973. "The Japanese Influx: What Does It All Mean?" *Honolulu Advertiser,* January 4.

Rose, Louis A. 1992. "Is a Tax on Real Estate Speculators a Good Idea?" In Randy W. Roth, ed., *The Price of Paradise: Lucky We Live Hawaii?* (Honolulu: Mutual Publishing): 149–151.

Schaefers, Allison. 2006. "Hosting tourism." *Honolulu StarBulletin,* October 16. Accessed at Starbulletin.com.

Schneider, Bruce A. 1978. "The Evolution of Mainland-Hawaii Air Travel." Unpublished paper. Honolulu (December 15).

Shiraya, Kazuhiko. 1993. "Japan Tour Ideals Changing." *Honolulu Advertiser,* June 7: D1.

State of Hawaii Department of Business, Economic Development and Tourism (DBEDT). "Hawaii Tourism in Transition." *Hawaii's Economy* (First Quarter): 1–5.

———. 1996. *State of Hawaii Data Book, 1995.* Honolulu: DBEDT.

———. 1999. "Developing the Niche Markets." *Hawaii's Economy* (July): 15–18.

———. 1999. "The Economic Impact of Tourism: An Update." *Hawaii's Economy* (July): 7.

————. 2000. *1999 Annual Research Report.* Honolulu: DBEDT.

————. 2006. *2005 Annual Visitor Research Report.* Honolulu: DBEDT.

State of Hawaii Department of Planning and Economic Development (DPED). 1978. *State Tourism Study: Manpower.* Honolulu: DPED Office of Tourism.

State of Hawaii Legislative Auditor. 1975. *Management Audit of the Public Utilities Program, Volume 3: The Regulation of Transportation Services.* Honolulu (December).

"Travel Weekly Readers Choice Awards: World's Best in Travel." 2006. *Travel Weekly Daily Bulletin,* January 17: Article 49786.

Tyrrell, Brian, Cary Countryman, Gong-Soog Hong, and Liping A. Cai. 2001. "Determinants of Destination Choice by Japanese Overseas Travelers." *Journal of Travel & Tourism Marketing* 10(2 and 3): 87–100.

University of Hawaii Economic Research Organization (UHERO). 1998. *Japanese Investment in Hawaii: Past and Future.* Honolulu: UHERO (September).

World Tourism Organization. 1994. *National and Regional Tourism Planning.* New York: Routledge.

Wright, Walter. 1994. "New Rx for Tourism: Health Care Called Route to Recovery." *Honolulu Advertiser,* April 11: C1.

Chapter Three

Genesis of State Policy on Tourism

Since the beginning of the twentieth century, the Hawaii State government's stance toward tourism has been to encourage its growth. That stance has not changed. However, tourism has always been viewed in Hawaii as private business and allowed to operate largely by the rules of a market economy. In his recently published memoir, longtime Hawaii tourism executive Robert C. Allen recalled that "No other resort complex in the world ever came together under similar circumstances, created as it was by individuals of considerable skill who gathered together the elements of a sleepy exotic resort and created the booming Hawaii visitor mecca."[1] Having adopted a laissez-faire approach, the State government has tended to shun direct involvement in the development of tourism, unlike governments in many other destinations around the world.

For example, Hawaii's State government has not provided financing for private resort development, nor has it given (until very recently) generous fiscal incentives to induce private investment in tourism. It has not entered into the hotel business, either by outright or joint ownership. Nor has it set quality ratings for hotels and other tourist services. With the exception of tour bus and limousine service, it has not imposed economic regulation (i.e., regulation of prices, service levels, and entry and exit) on tourism suppliers. It has not passed legislation to regulate hotel overbooking—a chronic problem in the tourist industry—or to require tour bus drivers and guides to meet certification standards for competency. Virtually everywhere else, responsibility for destination tourism promotion is assigned to government agencies. In Hawaii, the first tourism promotion bureau—the Hawaii Promotion Committee, predecessor of the Hawaii Visitors Bureau—was founded by the Merchants' Association and the Honolulu Chamber of Commerce in 1903, both private entities.[2] In the mid-1990s, the industry founded the Visitor Aloha Society of Hawaii to assist tourists who became victims of crime or misfortune.[3] The industry also started the Visitor Industry Education Council on a shoestring budget to educate residents about the economic benefits of tourism.

One area in which the State played a direct role in launching tourism development in the early post–World War II years was in infrastructure development, which is a traditional function of state and local governments.[4] The State wanted to encourage the development of tourism on the Neighbor Islands to stem thirty years of population exodus and decline since 1930 (see chapter 8). The First State Legislature (1959) passed Act 18, directing the State Planning Office to submit a plan for the development of tourist destination areas in each county.[5] The Planning Office came up with a menu of public improvement projects that heavily targeted the Neighbor Islands. Between 1960 and 1970, the State's visitor-related capital improvement program (CIP) expenditures totaled $168 million, of which more than half was spent on the Neighbor Islands. Most of the money (83.5 percent) was spent on airports and roads, and the rest was spent on parks, historical sites, scenic lookouts, small boat harbors, water and sewer systems, golf courses, and so on. During the 1970s, $393 million more was allocated to visitor-related CIP projects, of which 63 percent were destined for the Neighbor Islands.[6] Governor John Burns' biographers, Dan Boylan and T. Michael Holmes, note that "One of the legacies of the Burns era [1963–1975] was the rapid development of the neighbor islands as tourist destinations."[7] Actually, the policy was in place from the very beginning of statehood under the watch of Hawaii's first elected governor, William Quinn.[8] The State has also supported human resource development for tourism by funding tourism education and manpower training programs at the University of Hawaii.

Roaring '60s and Reflective '70s

The decade following statehood saw spectacular growth in tourism in Hawaii. The number of visitors grew from less than 300,000 in 1960 to nearly 1.8 million in 1970, an average growth of 20 percent per year. The growth rate far exceeded all expectations. For example, the State Planning Office predicted in 1960 that visitor arrivals would increase to 764,000 by 1970.[9] In the same year, the Hawaii Visitors Bureau predicted visitor arrivals would reach 773,000 by 1968; the actual number was nearly twice that many, at over 1.3 million.[10] First Hawaiian Bank's chief economist predicted 700,000 visitor arrivals also for 1968.[11] The Economic Research Center at the University of Hawaii predicted even lower numbers.[12] Tourism's share of total export earnings rose from 14.3 percent in 1960 to 32.3 percent in 1970, and tourism revenues as a percent of Hawaii's gross state product rose from 7.4 percent in 1960 to 16.2 percent in 1970.[13] Some feared that tourism was creating another plantation economy with low-paying, menial jobs. In his second state of the State address, Governor Burns said that he did not see an economic future for Hawaii in sugar; instead, he argued that "From both a short and long term point of view . . . tourism shows the greatest promise of sustained growth."[14]

The late 1960s were prosperous years for the nation's economy. Fueled largely by the explosive growth of tourism, Hawaii's economy outperformed the rest of the country. The ensuing labor shortage induced massive population immigration to the state—the preferred term in Hawaii is "in-migration," as most of the newcomers came from other U.S. states rather than from foreign countries. Between 1960 and 1970, Hawaii's resident population grew to 770,000, a gain of 137,000 since 1960. Net civilian in-migration (excluding military dependents) averaged more than 5,200 persons annually between 1960 and 1970 and accounted for somewhat less than 40 percent of the growth in the state's population. These figures do not indicate the number of tourists present on any given day; the average daily census of tourists more than tripled from 12,000 in 1960 to nearly 37,000 in 1970.[15]

For many—and perhaps most—residents in Hawaii, the frantic pace of economic and population growth in the '60s was quite unsettling. Change was coming much too quickly. In the late 1960s, forward-thinking residents began to question whether unchecked growth was good for Hawaii. The 1970 Legislature created the Temporary Commission on Population Stabilization, which was replaced by the Commission on Population and the Hawaiian Future. In 1970, the Governor's Conference on the Year 2000, involving some 700 laymen, was convened. The *Sunday Star-Bulletin & Advertiser* noted that the conference was "essentially an educational undertaking to sensitize people to the view that they can have an impact on the future(s), rather than being passive and adapting to whatever happens."[16] John Griffin, the emeritus editorial page editor of the *Honolulu Advertiser*, recalled that the purpose of the conference was not to predict what the future of Hawaii might look like in thirty years but to bring a broad spectrum of the state's population together to examine alternative scenarios of future development. Griffin described the purpose as "brainstorm[ing] exciting possibilities." A State commission was later established to follow up, but nothing came of it, as "the momentum dwindled and died."[17] Tom Coffman, a scholar of modern Hawaii history, has observed that "such commissions often reflect an active concern but a lack of resolve or clarity."[18]

Another conference, this one on Alternative Economic Futures for Hawaii, was held in March 1973. Unlike the Governor's Conference on the Year 2000, this was a private affair funded by the Chamber of Commerce, private businesses, and labor unions. Following the one-day conference, task forces were appointed to continue with the real work. In late 1974, the task forces reported their findings. Based on what happened in the 1960s, the task force on tourism envisioned potentially huge increases in tourism growth in Hawaii between 1973 and 1985. Starting with a base of 2.6 million visitors in 1973, the task force assumed a "low" visitor estimate of 5 million in 1985, a "medium" estimate of 10 million, a "high" estimate of 15 million, and a "very high estimate" of 30 million (the actual number of visitor arrivals in 1985 was 4.8 million).[19] The chairman of the task force noted that tourism not only held the greatest potential for Hawaii's future economic growth, it also presented the greatest threat to Hawaii's lifestyle.

By the early 1970s, resentment toward tourism began to surface, especially among many Native Hawaiians.[20] But opinion polls showed that most residents still supported tourism. A survey of Oahu and Maui residents in 1972 commissioned by the Hawaii Visitors Bureau found that 69 percent of the respondents thought that tourism was "good," compared to 8 percent who thought that it was "bad" for Hawaii. Another 22 percent of the respondents said that tourism was both good and bad.[21] A similar statewide survey found that 73.7 percent of the respondents thought that tourism was "good" for Hawaii and only 5.3 percent thought that it was "bad."[22] Nonetheless, there were fears that unchecked growth could lead to the erosion of Hawaii's famous hospitality—the "Aloha Spirit."

In 1972, Citizens for Hawaii, a public interest group, published the widely circulated *Maximillion Report* (often referred to as the "Babbie Report"), urging the State to take steps to stabilize the growth of Hawaii's population at one million by the year 2000. University of Hawaii at Manoa sociology professor Earl Babbie authored the report. It noted that "in many ways, the quality of life has been declining in Hawaii in recent years—and . . . the observed decline is largely the result of population growth."[23] The report also argued that halting net migration was the key to stabilizing Hawaii's

population. Since people migrate primarily in search of jobs, halting migration means slowing the growth of jobs in Hawaii, which in turn means
slowing the growth of tourism. During his successful campaign for governor in 1974, George Ariyoshi argued that "It is irresponsible for public officials to discuss Hawaii's future in terms of unlimited growth."[24] But as an
American state and not a sovereign nation, Hawaii had virtually no direct
control over migration.[25]

As the most important driver of Hawaii's economy during this period,
tourism came under close scrutiny. Several important studies were completed. For instance, State lawmakers wanted to know whether tourism
generated more benefits than costs to Hawaii. The Department of Planning
and Economic Development (DPED) commissioned the highly regarded
consulting firm Mathematica, Inc., of Princeton, New Jersey, to do a study.
Because the study (released in February 1970) was directed by the eminent
Princeton University economist William Baumol, it was widely referred to
as the "Baumol Report." The content of the report, however, didn't quite
measure up to its grandiloquent title, *The Visitor Industry and Hawaii's
Economy: A Cost-Benefit Analysis.* Rather than a cost-benefit analysis of
tourism in relation to Hawaii's economy, the report compared public revenues generated by tourism against State government spending on tourism
—or, the benefit-cost ratio to the State treasury.

Despite its limitations, the Baumol Report was an important study. It was
the first careful study (anywhere) to attempt to ascertain whether tourists
through the taxes and fees they paid directly and indirectly (e.g., via the
suppliers of tourism services) pay back the costs they impose on the host
government. It was not a trivial question. To illustrate, the mayor of Honolulu testified (incorrectly) before the 1973 Legislature that Island residents
were "subsidizing the visitor industry to the tune of millions of dollars a
year."[26] The Baumol Report found that "Visitors to Hawaii easily pay back
their costs to the state government taking into account the direct and indirect revenues they provide and the direct and indirect public costs incurred
on their behalf." Although it was not the question that everyone would have
liked answered, the report produced important information. For many
years, the Baumol Report would also be cited (improperly) to help defeat
efforts to enact a hotel room tax in Hawaii (more on this in chapter 4).

Another study, *A Survey of Residents to Determine Attitudes, Awareness,
Familiarity and Opinions Regarding the Visitor Industry in Hawaii* (August
1972), commissioned by the Hawaii Visitors Bureau, asked several hundred

residents of Oahu and Maui what they thought about their visitor industry. Of the respondents, 71 percent answered that "economic benefits" were the "best feature" of the industry. The most common dislike of tourism was its contribution to overbuilding and crowding. Nonetheless, 69 percent of the respondents felt that, overall, tourism was "good" rather than "bad" for Hawaii. But when asked, "Taking all the good and bad features into consideration, would you say tourism: is just right, should grow, or should be cut back?" only 36 percent of the respondents said that they wanted more tourism growth, nearly 46 percent of the respondents said that it was just right, and 17 percent of the respondents indicated that it should be cut back. Thus, while most of the respondents liked tourism at the current level (i.e., about 1.8 million visitors), more than 50 percent of the respondents did not want to see any more tourism growth! Popular support was clearly swinging in favor of some form of State tourism management policy, though not everyone wanted it for the same reason.

For example, the International Longshore and Warehouse Union (ILWU) —the politically powerful union for the state's plantation and dockworkers —wanted the State to control the location of new hotels and the number of rooms to make sure that developers would build them where local labor could be found to minimize the need for imported labor. The union further urged the State to make sure that existing labor standards and benefits would not be depressed by labor in-migration.[27]

A two-volume study prepared by DPED (1972) entitled *Tourism in Hawaii: Hawaii Tourism Impact Plan* also urged a curb on uncontrolled tourism growth. The report recommended, among other things, to halt additional zoning for resort development, place all tourist facilities away from shoreline areas, initiate a program to buy beach properties and beach right-of-way access, enforce high design standards, and establish a design review board in each county to review all public and private construction projects.[28]

Even the Hawaii Visitors Bureau jumped on the growth management bandwagon. In a speech before the sales and marketing executives of Honolulu on August 29, 1973, the board chairman of the HVB, William G. Foster, urged that the State act to control the growth of tourism.[29] If tourism was not controlled, he argued, the erosion of the Aloha Spirit would cause tourism to go into a nosedive. He proposed that the way to control tourism was for the State and county governments to use their zoning powers to limit the number of hotel rooms. Thus, along with what should be controlled, Foster also named the parties that should be doing the controlling.

However, his proposal came too late. State and county zoning for resort development was far more progrowth than antigrowth in the '60s and '70s. Indeed, by 1971 the amount of land zoned for resort use totaled 3,641 acres; the amount actually used was just 484 acres. Far more land was zoned for hotel development than could be profitably used. In 1971, the inventory of hotel rooms in the state totaled 32,278 units; if all the land already zoned for resort development were fully developed at existing densities, the number of hotel rooms could rise to 105,000 units.[30] By comparison, the total number of hotel rooms in Hawaii in 2002 was only 70,783 units. University of Hawaii Law School professor David Callies notes that "Hawaii regulates the use of land more tightly than any state in the nation."[31] The statement is not offered as an endorsement of Hawaii's land use practices. Nonetheless, there was no shortage of land available for resort development. If anything, overbuilding, especially on the Neighbor Islands, has been a bigger problem than underbuilding.

The 1973 Temporary Visitor Industry Council, a broadly representative group created by Senate Concurrent Resolution No. 30 during the 1972 session, offered its own controlled tourism growth policy based on (1) the number of new jobs that the industry needed to provide for *local* residents; (2) the amount of public revenue tourism must provide as its share of future needed public services; (3) the "load-bearing" factor for each island and each area; and (4) the need for open space for both residents and tourists. The council also recommended the establishment of an office of "Tourism Coordinator" within the Governor's Office and a limit in the number of hotel rooms in Waikiki to about 26,000 units and approximately 11,500 residential housing units.[32] The council met its responsibility despite the fact that "no money was appropriated for its work, no professional staff was available, and secretarial assistance was almost non-existent."[33]

State lawmakers also looked for ideas and guidance in resort destinations elsewhere that were facing similar rapid growing pains. Throughout the Caribbean, there were also rising concerns about the effects of tourism growth.[34] In May 1975, a delegation comprising key members of the State Legislature, the State planning director, and several tourism industry leaders took a twenty-one-day inspection tour of nine resort destinations in Central and South America and the Caribbean to have a firsthand look at their governments' relationship to tourism. The editors-in-chief of Honolulu's two daily newspapers also went along on the trip to report on what the members of the delegation saw at each destination and to record their impressions. Curiously, there were no participants from the four counties. *Honolulu Advertiser* editor-in-chief George Chaplin observed that with the need for more cooperation between the State and the Honolulu City and County to improve Waikiki, the "flagship" of Hawaii tourism, the absence of a single Honolulu council member or the City's planning director on the mission was particularly "disappointing." Historically, State and county government relations in Hawaii have never been close, and getting them to work cooperatively on anything is a challenge. One reason, as Lowell Kalapa, president of the Tax Foundation of Hawaii, points out is that the State treats the four counties "like children."[35]

In his first report, Chaplin emphasized the potential significance of the mission: "One senses that 1976 may be a year of decision for State Government in terms of its role in developing a tourist growth policy and determining the standards of quality to keep the Islands appealing for both residents and visitors. Gaining information and insights first-hand into how other visitor destination resorts are seeking to cope with similar problems is the key objective of this 21-day project."[36] Senate President John Ushijima and House Speaker James Wakatsuki issued the following joint statement: "The 1976 legislative session will face some hard and basic decisions in the future course of tourism in Hawaii. How much or should the industry be taxed? Are greater government controls necessary? What have these tourist areas done, or plan to do, to control the growth?"[37]

In selecting resort destinations for study, members of the mission chose those that provided a diverse mix of government-private cooperation in tourism development, from "resort areas which have blended well the thoughts of the private and public sectors as well as the places that have completely ignored the private sector in the planning and controlling process." The destinations chosen were Guatemala, Acapulco, Rio de Janeiro, Caracas, San Juan, the Virgin Islands, Nassau (Bahamas), Bermuda, and Miami (Florida).

Of the destinations visited, Bermuda was the overwhelming favorite among the delegates. Chaplin concluded that careful planning and tight government control, combined with a pride in the product and a friendly and beautiful environment, had made Bermuda a "gem of a resort."[38] It was obvious that Bermudians had decided on what they wanted and were willing to allow the government to use its considerable clout to make it happen.[39] On the other hand, delegates also acknowledged that Bermuda's model of heavy-handed government involvement in nearly every facet of its tourist business was probably unworkable in Hawaii. Hawaii does not have a "command" economy. Bermuda and Hawaii have vastly different political, social, and economic cultures.

In sharp contrast to Bermuda, Puerto Rico was a struggling destination. Once a thriving resort destination, tourism was in deep trouble. Chaplin described its ominous situation as follows:[40] "This island is overbuilt on hotels. Some have been allowed to deteriorate. Service is poor, with a negative attitude and low productivity. Labor-management relations are explosive. And officialdom tries to meet problems with interim patching rather than long-range planning." Perhaps to keep up a positive image of a thriving industry, the government got into the tourist business by buying up hotels, providing generous fiscal incentives, and forgiving loans to failing hotels to keep them open. By getting into the tourist business, government became part of the industry's problem and not a solution to the problem. Puerto Rico demonstrates that government intervention does not necessarily make things better. It also demonstrates that once a tourist destination goes into a tailspin, it's very difficult to come back. As one delegate put it, "Puerto Rico is like a virgin who has lost her virginity and wants to be a virgin again. Hawaii should try to be a lady."[41]

All agreed that the most important lesson gained on this trip was that long-range planning was essential to maintaining a quality tourist destination. Respected Hawaii planner Thomas Creighton observed that this conclusion was obvious, but he generously added: "After all, there's nothing like seeing things for yourself and talking directly to those who have problems similar to yours. . . . If it took 17 people traveling 22,000 miles to discover that, the trip was certainly worthwhile."[42] The big question that remained was whether that lesson had really been learned. The tourist industry in Hawaii, Creighton surmised, doesn't want government controls, and long-range planning smacks of government interference. While more studies would be done and a plan might be formulated, he feared that no action would be taken. He cited the example of Act 182 of the 1969 Legislature that called for an "Open Space Plan"; the plan was completed in 1972 but had not been acted on by mid-1975.

Another delegation consisting of many of the same people went on a similar three-week study mission to the South Pacific in November of the following year, visiting Fiji, the New Hebrides (now Vanuatu), New Caledonia, Australia, New Zealand, Tahiti, Moorea, Bora-Bora, American Samoa, and Western Samoa.[43] Tom Hamilton provided his usual lively and astute observations of the places visited. From the trip, the importance of planning and execution was again stressed as a key ingredient to the development of a successful destination. Overall, there was far less to be learned from the South Pacific trip as tourism development was largely in its infancy in Oceania, and even in places such as Fiji and Australia, which since have become major international tourist destinations, there was not too much interest in it.

Act 133: The Interim Tourism Policy Act

Act 133 was passed by the 1976 session of the Hawaii Legislature and signed into law by the governor on May 27, 1976. In the history of tourism policy planning in Hawaii, this action was unique. In the past, when the Hawaii Legislature had wished to express itself on tourism in any comprehensive way, it had done so by resolution—House, Senate, Concurrent, or Joint. This was the first statute treatment that called for comprehensive planning for Hawaii's visitor industry. The law provided a directive for the development of an interim tourism policy that would be replaced by the policies of a broader and more inclusive State plan, when such a plan was approved by the Legislature.

There were other unique features of this action in addition to elevation to statute. The law called for the development of "a ten-year master plan for the growth of tourism for presentation to the 1978 session of the legislature." And it placed the responsibility for the development of this plan not on a citizen committee but directly on an official of State government: the director of the Department of Planning and Economic Development (DPED).

The act could not help but dismay somewhat those responsible for the preparation of the plan. For it at least implied that the following matters should be encompassed: (1) planned growth of tourism, (2) visitor satisfaction, (3) protection of Hawaii's natural beauty and attractions, (4) Hawaii's heritage, (5) resident requirements, (6) education and training, and (7) criteria for growth. Thus, it required a plan to guide future tourism development that would meet the needs of both tourists and residents and at the same time protect the environmental, social, and cultural resources of the state. In sum, the act directed DPED to craft a plan for "sustainable tourism"—a concept that would not be defined until 1992 (see chapter 9). For its time, Act 133 was quite a visionary piece of legislation.

In addition to the act's inclusiveness, the time for administrative compliance was short—perhaps too short, as something this ambitious had never been done anywhere else in the world. Hawaii would be the pioneer in policy planning for sustainable tourism, if it could be pulled off. The two years between the 1976 and 1978 legislative sessions shrank to fourteen months due to the time necessary to recruit personnel, hire consultants, appoint advisors, print the report, and so on. This is the usual pattern in these matters.

IMPLEMENTATION OF ACT 133

Act 133 called for the establishment of an interim tourism advisory council of thirteen members to "provide necessary advice and a means of citizen input." The law also emphasized that the council was to serve in an advisory capacity to the director of DPED, who was given the specific responsibility "to see that this plan is prepared."

The law specified that the governor should appoint nine of the members of the council—three representing the visitor industry, three organized labor, and three the public—one of whom the governor was to designate as chairman. Each of the four county governments was to have one ex-officio voting member. Thus, virtually all the important stakeholders were included. Despite the importance of the Aloha Spirit and Hawaiian culture to the state's tourist industry, the law made no specific provision for the appointment of at least one Hawaiian cultural specialist to the council.

The relationship between the council and the director of DPED at the outset was not well understood by the members of the council and probably never completely understood by the public—even many in the visitor industry. There was a good reason for this. Most earlier studies had been developed by citizen committees or councils. They were responsible for the results. It was not easy to shift to the solely advisory function and recognize that authority and responsibility rested with a department of the State government. For example, there was some bridling on the part of a few council members that they had not played a role in the selection of consultants to do the required studies. But in time, the council came to terms—if not always at peace—with its advisory role.

As had not been true of the two most recent reports on tourism, this time there was money available via appropriation to employ professional consultants, though the amount was not unlimited ($230,000). It first was necessary to determine what areas would be the subject of consultant study. Not all of the areas of interest—or even all of the ones mentioned in Act 133—could be the subject of professional analysis. Selectivity was necessary.

The Office of Tourism in DPED proposed areas, and after seeking and receiving the council's advice, five areas were selected for analysis: economic projections, public revenue cost analysis (i.e., an update of the earlier Baumol Report), manpower, social impact, and physical resources. The five studies used up all the money available for this purpose. Obviously, not all of the matters contained in Act 133 had received attention. Even had there been more money, time would not have permitted comprehensive coverage. Some things were going to have to be left for future years.

The council felt, however, that there were at least three additional matters that warranted immediate attention. Thus three members of the council were asked to chair subcommittees and were empowered to name members of the subcommittee from within and outside the council as competence dictated. In this fashion, reports were developed on Waikiki, the Aloha Spirit, and education and training.[44]

Six public information sessions were held by DPED in December 1977 to solicit comments on the summary of the draft consultant studies. Two meetings took place on the Big Island of Hawaii and one each on the islands of Maui, Molokai, Oahu, and Kauai. About 320 people attended. While these sessions needed to be held to satisfy the demand for public participation, the chairman of the advisory council (Tom Hamilton) opined that they produced little of substance. The benefits were largely therapeutic. Thus by the end of December, the findings of the consultants and limited public reaction to them were available. The plan still had to be prepared. And the Legislature was to convene on January 18, 1978.

The '80s: Planning for Tourism

A draft tourism plan was completed on time and submitted to the 1978 Legislature, but the Legislature wasn't ready to act on it because it wanted to consider the State Plan in its entirety, not just a piece of it. The State Plan was not finished. Moreover, several community groups and the industry wanted more time to offer input to the tourism plan. The Legislature instead created a sixteen-member Tourism Plan Advisory Committee to advise DPED on the formulation of the Tourism Functional Plan (or simply the Tourism Plan); its purpose was to "further define and implement the State Plan."[45] The Tourism Functional Plan was one of twelve State functional plans.[46] A revised Tourism Plan was submitted to the 1979 Legislature, but it was not until the following year that the State Plan was finally passed.[47]

The functional plans were not intended to be laws or statutory mandates; rather they identified areas of State concern and suggested strategies and budget priorities for the State and the counties. Thus, Hawaii's first Tourism Functional Plan was typical of most tourism plans around the world; for example, Emanuel de Kadt described Bali's tourism plan as "statements of intent without teeth—they cannot be enforced."[48]

Hawaii's State Plan identified nine goals to guide the development of tourism between 1980 and 1990:[49]

1. Assist in the overseas promotion of Hawaii's vacation attractions.
2. Ensure that visitor industry activities are in keeping with the social, economic, and physical needs and aspirations of Hawaii's people.
3. Improve the quality of existing visitor destination areas.
4. Encourage greater cooperation between the public and private sectors in developing and maintaining well-designed and adequately serviced visitor industry and related developments.
5. Ensure that visitor facilities and destination areas are carefully planned and sensitive to existing neighboring communities and activities.
6. Develop the industry in a manner that will provide the greatest number of primary jobs and steady employment for Hawaii's people.
7. Provide opportunities for Hawaii's people to obtain job training and education that will allow for upward mobility within the visitor industry.
8. Foster a recognition of the contribution of the visitor industry to Hawaii's economy and the need to perpetuate the Aloha Spirit.
9. Foster an understanding by visitors of the Aloha Spirit and of the unique and sensitive character of Hawaii's cultures and values.

Curiously, the "goals" made no specific mention of the natural environment. That was left to the 1990 update of the Tourism Plan.[50] Each of the nine goals was accompanied by "implementing actions." In developing the Tourism Functional Plan, State planners did not ignore work already completed by the counties, as they accepted the counties' designation of the areas where future resort development would be encouraged. Nonetheless, there were grumblings from county officials that the State would be taking over the control of their tourist industries.

Did the Tourism Functional Plan portend a fundamental change in the relationship between the industry and Hawaii's State and local governments? The plan stated clearly that it did not: "The initiative in the development of tourism belongs to the private sector; it is the role of government to support and regulate the visitor industry according to what is best judged to be in the public interest. The State and County governments each have a part in this role. The impact of the Tourism Plan will be significant only to the extent that they influence private sector activities and other State activities which themselves influence tourism development, such as the building of highways or the regulation of land use." In sum, the State's stance toward tourism is one of "market-friendly interventionism."

A central question raised in the Tourism Functional Plan was: How fast should tourism grow? It was determined that tourism should be encouraged to grow at a rate of 5 percent per year between 1980 and 1985 and 4 percent per year between 1986 and 1990. The numbers were based on statistical modeling exercises, which suggested that growth at these rates would minimize population in-migration and out-migration while keeping the State's unemployment rate at below 6 percent. If actual growth rates were below the desired rates, then the State should try to stimulate tourism growth; if actual growth rates were above the desired rates, the State should try to curb tourism growth. Exactly how that could be managed was neither specified nor well understood by the planners.

The truth is that the State has few available instruments to control tourism growth: It can raise or lower taxes on tourism, it can increase or decrease the amount of money for tourism promotion and tourism infrastructure development, and it can regulate land use within the State. But it is neither practical nor feasible to manipulate these instruments within a short period of time of five years and expect to achieve the desired growth target. First, lawmakers must recognize that the growth target will be missed and that recognition may not come until just before the end of the planning period; second, they must choose the right policy instrument; third, the responsible government agency must implement the change; and finally, the instrument has to work within the desired time period. Without the State's resources or its taxing powers, Hawaii's counties have even fewer policy instruments available to control tourism growth. Authors of the Tourism Plan acknowledged that experience with tourism planning at the State and county levels between 1960 and 1980 could not establish a cause-and-effect relationship between planning and tourism growth. The actual annual tourism growth rates turned out to be 4.34 percent per year between 1980 and 1985 and 6.84 percent per year between 1985 and 1990, for an average annual growth rate of 5.6 percent over the entire decade.

Implementing Actions

The Tourism Functional Plan recommended the following twenty-four implementing actions for the nine state tourism policies; each of the actions can be directly related to budget items:

Policy No. 1: Tourism Marketing and Promotion.
1(a) Budget funds to market the State including funds for an assessment of existing promotional efforts and a study to locate and evaluate potential markets.
1(b) Increase emphasis on marketing the convention and conference market.
Policy No. 2: Meeting the Social, Economic and Physical Needs of Hawaii's People.
2(a) Give preference to the development of full-service hotels over other types of visitor accommodations.[51]
2(b) Monitor the conversion of apartment/condominium units from residential to visitor use and vice versa, and study the impact of such conversions.
2(c) Monitor the public revenue-cost ratios of visitors every three years.
2(d) Establish a program to monitor and investigate both visitor and resident complaints related to the visitor industry and take appropriate actions as required.
2(e) Carry out scope of work for a social impact study of tourism.
2(f) Establish a Visitor Advisory Council fashioned after the Tourism Plan Advisory Committee.
2(g) Document annual progress on the Tourism Functional Plan; update the plan in 1985 and prepare a new plan for 1990.
Policy No. 3: Improve the Quality of Existing Visitor Destinations.
3(a) Appropriate funds for the improvement of Waikiki.
3(b) Recommend capital improvement expenditures for new and existing resort areas.
Policy No. 4: Encourage Greater Cooperation Between the Public and Private Sectors.

4(a) Expedite resort development approval systems at the State and County levels.

4(b) Encourage private development in areas where capital improvements are already in place or are projected to be made.

Policy No. 5: Ensure Visitor Facilities and Destination Areas Are Carefully Planned and Sensitive to Existing Neighboring Communities and Activities.

5(a) Update inventories of tourism resources in designated resort areas.

5(b) Encourage private developers, County governments and State agencies to consult all State Functional Plans to determine the impacts of development.

Policy No. 6: Provide the Greatest Number of Jobs and Steady Employment for Hawaii's People.

6(a) Foster favorable government and community attitudes toward tourism so as to provide steady employment in the visitor industry.

6(b) Give higher priority to resort development on the Neighbor Islands.

6(c) Investigate new means of maintaining targeted growth rates in tourism and use them in the event average tourism growth rates should exceed or fall short of targeted levels over five years.

Policy No. 7: Provide Opportunities for Hawaii Residents to Obtain Job Training and Education in Tourism.

7(a) Expand food service and other tourism occupational training programs in the State.

7(b) Provide research and teaching facilities at the University's travel industry management program.

7(c) Include tourism education in social studies curriculum in schools and tourism career development and guidance programs at all education levels.

Policy No. 8: Foster a Recognition of the Contribution of Tourism to the State's Economy, and the Need to Perpetuate the Aloha Spirit.

8(a) Support existing resident education programs on tourism and initiate new programs as needed.

Policy No. 9: Foster Understanding by Visitors of the Aloha Spirit and the Unique and Sensitive Character of Hawaii's Culture and Values.

9(a) Foster a better understanding among visitors of Hawaii's

uniqueness and a greater appreciation of the contribution
residents make to the enjoyment of their experience while
visiting Hawaii.

9(b) Provide public access to and information on significant
archaeological sites, and initiate a program to explain Hawaii's
history and values to visitors and residents.

As is often the case, development plans tend to sit on shelves and collect
dust. That did not happen to the Tourism Plan. A review of the two progress reports completed in 1984 and 1986 finds that most of the "implementing actions" were acted on or underway in some fashion.[52] Whether or not
in total the implementing actions made a significant difference in improving tourism for the benefit of residents and tourists is difficult to ascertain.
But much was learned from the planning process itself, and it would leave
a valuable template for future planning exercises. Most successful tourism
plans and initiatives invariably involve community participation and cooperation among the stakeholders. In Hawaii, a lot of people in the industry,
the public, and government participated in the planning process, and for
the first time, Hawaii's people got an opportunity to take in a full view of
tourism in the state—both the good and the bad. It was an extraordinary
exercise in tourism education for the public.

A Policy Fiasco

As tourism became a bigger player in Hawaii's economy, there was growing concern that the state would become too dependent on it. A statewide
survey conducted in 1988 found that 78 percent of Hawaii's residents agreed
that the state was indeed too dependent on tourism.[53] Many felt that Hawaii
had to elevate its efforts to diversify its economy in order to get it moving
again, despite the paucity of evidence that more diversified economies enjoy
more robust economic growth. In his 1990 state of the State address, Governor John Waihee emphasized the state's need for economic diversification.
In his speech, Waihee said,[54]

We must continue and strengthen our efforts to diversify our economy to avoid being overly dependent on any single industry and to
give our people choice in employment.
Hawaii has attracted substantial amounts of capital investment in

recent years. While such investments have contributed to our economic growth, they have not contributed as much to the diversification of our economy. Unfortunately, most investment has occurred in the resort and travel industry.

I am convinced that it will take more than promotion or incentives to change this investment pattern. Stronger action is needed if we are going to gain better control over our economic future. Accordingly, I have asked the Office of State Planning to prepare a policy for consideration by the Land Use Commission that will require creation of one non-tourism related job for every hotel room approved in future resort development.

Hawaii's unique land use law (Act 187) passed in 1961 directs all lands in the state to be classified under one of four categories: conservation, agricultural, rural, and urban.[55] If a developer wants to build a resort on a parcel of agricultural or conservation land, he has to petition the State's Land Use Commission (LUC) to change the parcel's designation to "urban."[56] This enormous regulatory power over land use enables the LUC to impose all kinds of requirements on developers as a condition for getting their petitions approved as long as the objectives conform to the goals of the State Plan. Chapter 226 of Hawaii Revised Statutes—the Hawaii State Plan—specifically mentions economic diversification as one of the State's goals. By directive of the governor, the Office of State Planning (OSP) came up with a policy that required a developer to either create one nontourism-related job (i.e., jobs not in hotels or apartment hotels) or pay its equivalent value in cash (estimated at $25,000 for each nontourism-related job) for each hotel room the developer wanted to build. The OSP allowed the nontourism-related jobs to be satisfied in a number of ways. For example, in the first agreement negotiated between the LUC and Haseko, Inc.—which had planned to build a $1 billion mixed-use project within ten to twenty years on 1,100 acres of land in Leeward Oahu—Haseko could receive one job credit for each twenty-five man-years of labor generated by the construction of residential, commercial, industrial, recreational, institutional, or other nontourism-related facilities. Haseko could also receive job credits using floor space in new nontourism-related construction projects; for example, 200 square feet of office space or 1,000 square feet of warehousing/storage space would qualify as one nontourism-related job. For large diversified developers like Haseko, Inc., the new requirement was not too onerous since it could satisfy the nontourism job requirements from its multitude of nontourism-related projects, including the redevelopment of an entire city block in town. The OSP policy would have been very burdensome for nondiversified resort developers. Thus, not only would the one nontourism job for one hotel room policy discourage hotel investment, it was also unfair because it favored large, diversified developers. Moreover, given the various ways of meeting the requirement, the new policy would not have done much to diversify the state's economy. Hawaii's weak economy ultimately convinced Haseko not to go ahead with its megaproject. While this poorly conceived policy is still on the books, it has not had much of an impact on the development of tourism in Hawaii.

The Troubled '90s

The decade of the 1990s was a very challenging one for Hawaii's tourist industry and the state's economy. During the decade, visitor arrivals grew at an anemic rate of 0.4 percent per year; in four of those ten years, visitor arrivals recorded negative growth. By comparison, there was only one year of negative tourism growth in the preceding thirty years. Tourism took a double hit in 1991 from the first Gulf War and a mild U.S. economic recession. Then Hurricane Iniki struck Kauai with a devastating blow in September 1992. The number of Americans visiting Hawaii declined for three consecutive years following the war. These external "shocks" are not the only factors that explain the declining growth trend in tourism. Others point to tourism's pathetic performance as evidence that Hawaii's tourist industry had finally reached the stage of maturity and could be headed toward decline if something was not done to rejuvenate it.

The state's economy was not doing much better, as it stagnated for seven straight years following the Gulf War, an "unprecedented" event in the state's history.[57] Since gaining statehood in 1959, Hawaii had never experienced two consecutive years of economic contraction until the 1990s. Tourism no longer appeared to be the engine that could continue to drive the economy.

By the mid-1990s public pressure mounted on the State administration to do something to revitalize the economy. Because tourism is so important to the economy, reviving it was a critical piece of the strategy. Acting on the recommendations of Governor Cayetano's Economic Revitalization Task Force (ERTF), the Legislature passed Act 156 in 1998. This act created a new government institution, the Hawaii Tourism Authority (HTA), with dedicated funding from the hotel room tax. The purpose of the act was to consolidate responsibility for the state's diverse tourism-related activities, except for tourism research, under a single institution, thus giving tourism more focus and attention. The mission of the authority is "to manage the strategic growth of Hawaii's visitor industry in a manner consistent with the economic goals, cultural values, preservation of natural resources, and community interests of the people of Hawaii."[58]

The authority's first (internal) strategic plan (June 1999), entitled *Ke Kumu —Strategic Directions for Hawaii's Visitor Industry*, outlined its three responsibilities: (1) to promote tourist travel to Hawaii; (2) to diversify Hawaii's visitors including the development of agri-, cultural, edu-, health and wellness, eco-, and techno-tourism; and (3) to increase visitor spending per person per day.[59]

Item 2 represents a policy departure from the State's earlier stance in that it places the State government in the role of picking "winners" for State support rather than allowing market forces to determine how and in what manner to diversify tourism. For example, it was the HTA that contacted a private firm in 2002 to develop a State plan and strategy to cultivate a health and wellness industry in Hawaii.[60]

Notably absent from Item 2 was any mention of gambling. Legalization of gambling has been a hugely controversial issue at the State Legislature since statehood. Currently, Hawaii is only one of two states in the nation that does not permit any form of gambling—the other is Utah.[61] Political pressure to legalize gambling in Hawaii—especially casino gambling (or "gaming," a term preferred by the industry)—heightened during the economic doldrums of the 1990s. Between 1983 and 1997, 187 gambling measures were introduced at the State Legislature, 77 of them between 1983 and 1989 and another 110 between 1990 and 1997.[62] The number of gambling measures introduced in any particular year was negatively correlated with the growth of general fund revenues in the previous year.[63] More measures were introduced when money was tight! Yet no one seriously believed that gambling was a solution to the state's growing fiscal woes. Likewise, no one believed that Hawaii could become another Las Vegas; indeed, William Eadington, the director of the Institute for Study of Gambling at the University of Nevada at Reno, surmised that "there is only going to be one Las Vegas in North America."[64] Hawaii could offer "casinos of convenience"—that is, casinos that would draw most of their customers from local residents or

Table 3-1. Per person daily visitor spending in Hawaii: 1999–2005

Year	Spending in current $	Spending in constant 1999 $
1999	171.27	171.27
2000	176.89	173.88
2001	159.19	154.70
2002	165.10	158.69
2003	169.80	159.50
2004	171.50	155.94
2005	174.40	152.79

Source: Calculated from data in DBEDT, *Annual Visitor Research Reports,* issues 1999 to 2005. Spending deflated by Honolulu CPI-U.

tourists who did not come to Hawaii primarily to gamble.[65] But that might not provide sufficient economic benefits to warrant the potential negative social costs associated with gambling.[66] Despite heavy lobbying by gaming interests, opponents of gambling—which include all the recent governors—have kept gambling from becoming legal in Hawaii.[67]

Item 3 represents a dramatic change from the previous State policy of maximizing the number of visitors; the new policy focuses instead on attracting higher spending visitors. HTA aims to achieve that goal through its marketing campaigns by targeting "active vacationers" (e.g., golfers) who are believed to spend more money per day than tourists who simply lounge on the beach. However, facts indicate that average visitor spending per day has declined since 2000 (Table 3-1).

Ultimately, attracting higher spending visitors requires Hawaii to produce a higher quality tourism product, which means developing luxury resorts instead of budget or standard quality hotels. To illustrate, DBEDT's 2002 Neighbor Islands' visitor expenditure surveys show the following relationship between per-person daily visitor spending on lodging and total daily spending:

	Maui	Molokai	Lanai	Kauai	Big Island
Lodging	$62.02	$28.41	$173.22	$51.71	$52.11
Total spending	$160.99	$83.28	$247.37	$142.66	$140.73

These numbers suggest that the kinds of visitors a destination attracts depends more on how you develop the destination than how you market it. From nearly the very beginning, Maui opted to go for quality (i.e., high-end) tourism. Maui attracts high-spending visitors because it has focused on developing high-end tourism and not because it has waged a more successful marketing campaign toward wealthy travelers than the other major Neighbor Islands.

Ultimately, action speaks louder than words. Governor Linda Lingle's vigorous efforts to persuade the federal government to ease visa rules on mainland Chinese travel to Hawaii—Chinese tourists are not big spenders— suggest that the State's policy on tourism growth—namely, to maximize the number of tourist visits—hasn't really changed.[68] Lingle has argued that easing Chinese travel restrictions to the United States could produce the next great tsunami of Asian visitors to Hawaii.[69]

The Legislature also changed the funding formula for tourism promotion by dedicating about $60 million per year from the hotel room tax revenues to tourism promotion, more than twice the amount that it had previously appropriated for that purpose.[70] The dramatic increase in marketing dollars prompted a lawsuit (filed in January 2000) by the Hawaii Chapter of the Sierra Club, which argued that State law required an environmental assessment be performed to evaluate the potential impact of the increased funding for tourism promotion on the environment. The State Supreme Court, by a 3-2 vote in December 2002, denied the Sierra Club's request, ruling that the Sierra Club did not have "standing" to challenge the HTA's decision not to perform an environmental assessment. Associate Justice Paula Nakayama further argued that the Sierra Club failed to show that "alleged adverse environmental impacts to land can be attributed to the expenditure of money on a marketing plan."[71] Nonetheless, partly because of the Sierra Club lawsuit, the 2001 Legislature appropriated $1.2 million to the Department of Business, Economic Development and Tourism to conduct a "sustainable tourism" study.[72] An even more important reason, according to Dr. Seiji Naya, director of DBEDT when the study was initiated, was that the jump in tourism in 2000 to nearly 7 million arrivals raised anew questions about how many more tourists Hawaii can accommodate. Naya explained that the real reason for the study was to find ways to accommodate more visitors.[73]

The goals of the sustainable tourism study are to (1) examine the impact of visitors on the economy, on the natural environment, on the cultural fabric of the community, and on the state's physical infrastructure, and (2) provide an information base, an analysis of potential consequences, and an analytical tool (more specifically, a computer model) for proactive policy responses to various tourism growth scenarios.[74]

The study was largely finished by the completion date of July 2004. But a study is not a plan. As tourism finally began to rebound in 2004 from the effects of the 9/11 terrorist attacks, the ensuing wars in Afghanistan and Iraq, and the SARS outbreak in 2003, public pressure again descended on the State to formulate a plan to guide future tourism development in Hawaii in a sustainable way.[75] In late 2004, the Hawaii Tourism Authority completed work on a new long-range Tourism Strategic Plan (TSP) to guide tourism development between 2005 and 2015.[76] Perpetuating the Hawaiian culture and protecting the state's natural environment play key roles in the new plan. The new TSP "outlines a shared vision for Hawaii tourism in the year 2015 by Hawaii's tourism stakeholders . . . and offers a roadmap . . . for achieving that vision."[77] An action plan for the TSP has yet to be completed; moreover, one wonders who will be asked to pay for the many initiatives recommended in the TSP—the industry, tourists, or resident taxpayers? HTA also provided funding for the counties to develop their own plans, which are to be consistent with the TSP. The county strategic plans for 2006–2015 were begun in 2005 and completed in 2006.[78]

Concluding Observations

Americans generally look upon development planning with a great deal of skepticism because we tend to associate planning with what goes on in poor developing countries with autocratic governments. Indeed, it is even seen as "un-American." Hawaii, by contrast, not only has developed plans for tourism, it is unique among the U.S. states in having a comprehensive State Plan. In 1997, *Forbes Magazine* dubbed America's Fiftieth State the "People's Republic of Hawaii."[79] It was not meant to be kind! Perhaps Hawaii's receptivity to development planning stems from its relatively simple government structure, which has only two levels of government—one State and four county governments—and a lengthy history of central government control.[80]

Tourism investors, on the other hand, see some value in having a stated long-term government policy/plan on tourism development, as it helps to reduce some of the uncertainty in decisions involving commitment of substantial investments that are notoriously risky. A clearly stated coherent tourism policy may also be necessary for local political reasons, as residents may want to know the government's stance and plans for future tourism growth.[81]

Hawaii's tourism plans were developed under very different circumstances. The first Tourism Plan was prepared in response to widespread public concern that tourism was growing too fast and needed to be reined in. That did not happen, at least not as a direct result of the plan. In contrast, the more recent tourism plans reflect concerns that tourism has not been growing fast enough, hence the need to diversify the state's sources of tourists. What has been a constant from very early on was the keen awareness among all the key stakeholders that tourism is a "fragile" industry that can be quickly damaged by irresponsible, shortsighted, opportunistic behavior. Tourism can also be a blessing or blight on the community. In many destinations, tourism planning is initiated to remediate damages that have already occurred. Emanuel de Kadt characterizes much of tourism planning as "shutting the stable door after the horse has bolted."[82] By contrast, in Hawaii residents and the visitor industry recognized the potential problems associated with tourism development relatively early and began a comprehensive planning process in the 1970s, just as mass tourism was beginning. As in most other tourist destinations, Hawaii's tourism plans still place more emphasis on maximizing gross returns from tourism (i.e., attracting more tourists and tourist receipts) than in maximizing net returns (i.e., net social benefit) to the state.[83] That's not likely to change soon.

It is widely acknowledged that sustainable tourism development requires comprehensive planning *and* tight government control. Hawaii's State government has planned for but *generally not* imposed tight control over tourism development. Longtime resort planners Charles Kaiser and Larry Helber observed that "there was little or no inhibiting legislation in existence at the time [major resort] developmental programs were launched" during the post–World War II tourism-driven development boom.[84] To be sure, the State's 1961 land use law probably screened out the most objectionable developments that required land reclassification from agricultural or conservation to urban uses.[85] But that is not enough to explain why Hawaii has developed itself into a dream destination—and has kept it that way.

David McClain borrowed Michael Porter's concept of sustainable competitive advantage to explain why Hawaii's tourist industry has been so successful.[86] Porter suggests that four interdependent forces—imagine a baseball diamond—influence a country or state's international competitiveness. The first is demand—the size and sophistication of the markets. Second is the sophistication and rivalry of the competitors. Third are the supply factors: land, labor, capital, natural resources, and so on. Fourth is the constellation of supporting industries. Two "outside" influences—the government and "chance"—can influence the outcome. McClain observed that Hawaii's tourist industry

> is competitive, vibrant and mutually reinforcing. On the demand side, the customers are sophisticated and world class, the potential market is large, and Hawaii enjoys the benefits of a diversified clientele in Asia and in America.
>
> As for supply, Hawaii's unique environment is a precious asset and America's political stability means that capital can flow into the islands freely. Related and supporting industries include the University of Hawaii's School of Travel Industry Management and its College of Language, Linguistics and Literature (one of only three U.S. National Resource Centers for the Study of Foreign Language), as well as an entire nexus of travel-related firms, including the airlines and an excellent telecommunication network.
>
> Competition in the travel and tourism industry is vigorous; government, through the Hawaii's Visitors' Bureau and other means, plays a supporting role.
>
> This is not to say the travel and tourism industry is immune from business cycles in America or Japan, or from overbuilding, as has occurred on the neighbor islands. But the travel and tourism diamond, most would agree, is relatively healthy.

McClain concludes that Hawaii generally has fared well for a long time, "but in many ways it has been despite governmental efforts rather than because of them."[87]

Add to McClain's analysis one other factor, thus far largely overlooked, that helps to explain why tourism in Hawaii has done so well: the state's concentrated pattern of land ownership. While comparative statewide data are unavailable, it would be unsurprising to learn that Hawaii has the highest concentrated ownership of land in the United States.[88] The pattern of land ownership in Hawaii in 1967—and it hasn't changed much since then—shows the following distribution: federal government, 9 percent; State government, 38 percent; seventy-two major private owners with 1,000 acres or more, 46 percent; all others, 6 percent.[89] One private owner had 9 percent of all the land in Hawaii; seven of them had nearly 30 percent; and eighteen private landowners had almost 40 percent. These shares would be roughly doubled if we counted only private landholdings. While this unusual pattern of landholding, especially in a highly developed country, has been much criticized for social and equity reasons, it has facilitated the development of attractive, large, master-planned, full-scale resorts, especially on the Neighbor Islands.[90]

Maui provides an excellent example. Eleven private landowners own 48 percent of the (most valuable) land on Maui; the State and federal governments own most of the rest. Major landowners account for three of the four major resort-related developments on Maui: Kaanapali (Amfac Inc.), Wailea (Alexander and Baldwin, Inc.), and Kapalua (Maui Land and Pineapple Co.).[91] Hawaii's first master-planned full-scale resort—the Kaanapali Beach Resort—was more than just another money-making idea. The first hotel—the Royal Lahaina (735 units)—was completed in 1962; since then Kaanapali has become " a standard which subsequent other large developments have sought to emulate."[92] On Lanai, one company owns 98 percent of the 141-square-mile island. Since the late 1980s, the company has converted what was once the "Pineapple Isle" into one of the world's most exclusive and secluded luxury resort destinations. (Microsoft's Bill Gates was married on Lanai on New Year's Day in 1994.) In Hawaii, owners of these large master-planned resort developments have produced high-quality resorts, and because the benefits from all the amenities they have created are largely captured privately, they also have the economic incentive and the ability to keep them that way. Thus, "tight control" of tourism development in Hawaii has been exercised to a significant degree by private resort developers. This is not to slight the efforts of the State and the counties, which have used their land use regulatory powers to impose numerous conditions on these developments to ensure that public interests are adequately protected before approvals are granted.

Where does all of this discussion place the contribution of the State's tourism plans in the development of tourism in Hawaii? Certainly it is not in the deciding role. The State's various tourism plans have definitely influenced State government budgets. But perhaps their biggest contribution has been in providing a wealth of information about the tourist industry and its impact on the community, in consensus building, and in developing shared visions of the preferred future(s).

Notes

1. Allen (2004), p. x.

2. Crampon (1976).

3. Founded by the Honolulu Rotary club in 1997 and now with funding from the Hawaii Tourism Authority as well as private contributions and volunteer help, it served over eight thousand visitors in its first five years and over nine thousand between 2002 and 2006.

4. In Hawaii, resort developers are often required to put in the on-site capital infrastructures such as streets, sewers, water and drainage systems, etc. Lowry (1977), p. 14.

5. State of Hawaii Department of Planning and Economic Development (DPED), *State Tourism Study, Executive Summary* (1978), pp. 5–6.

6. State of Hawaii DPED, vol. 1 (1972), p. 65.

7. Boylan and Holmes (2000), p. 197.

8. Indeed, the first general state plan in the nation was produced by the State of Hawaii's Planning Office in 1961, designating several areas in the state for tourism development. The plan argued that active participation by the State government in tourism development could increase tourism in Hawaii in 1980 by 20 percent over what might otherwise occur without active State participation. DPED, *State Tourism Study, Executive Summary* (1978), pp. 6–7.

9. Hawaii State Planning Office (1960), p. 3.

10. Craig (1963), p. 16.

11. Ibid.

12. Ibid.

13. State of Hawaii Department of Business, Economic Development and Tourism (DBEDT) (3rd quarter, 1995).

14. Quote from Boylan and Holmes (2000), p. 304.

15. Schmitt (March 24, 1973); Nordyke (1989), Tables 2-1 and 5-2.

16. *Sunday Star-Bulletin & Advertiser* (July 27, 1975).

17. Griffin (January 18, 2004), p. B3.

18. Coffman (2003), p. 242.

19. *Sunday Star-Bulletin & Advertiser* (July 27, 1975).

20. See, for example, Gray (1972), pp. 112–121 and Kent (1994), chapter 11.

21. Survey and Marketing Services, Inc. (August 1972).

22. State of Hawaii DPED (January 1976).

23. Babbie (1972).

24. Coffman (2003), pp. 241–244.

25. For example, at Ariyoshi's urging, the 1977 Legislature passed a measure establishing a one-year residency requirement for local government employment; the measure was invalidated by the federal district court. By contrast, the State of Oregon actually funded a campaign to encourage people to visit Oregon but not to move there.

26. Keir (February 24, 1973).

27. Cunningham (February 27, 1973).

28. State of Hawaii DPED, vol. 1 (1972), pp. 150–155.

29. Bone (August 30, 1973).

30. State of Hawaii DPED, vol. 1 (1972), p. 29.

31. Callies (1994), p. 7. For a political history of Hawaii's 1961 land use law, see Cooper and Daws (1985), chapter 3.

32. The 1973 Temporary Visitor Industry Council (1973), pp. i–ii.

33. Ibid., p. 2.

34. Goodsell (August 13, 1974).

35. Kalapa (1992), p. 47.

36. Chaplin (May 28, 1975), p. A11. The newspaper articles cited here are also available in a privately bound volume by Hamilton (1975) and housed in the Hamilton Library, University of Hawaii at Manoa.

37. Ibid.

38. Chaplin (June 23, 1975). See Manning (1979) for additional details on the development of tourism in Bermuda.

39. Limone (May 21, 2007). Not surprisingly, tight government control leads to high prices, making Bermuda an expensive place to visit. This may be what the Bermudians want — i.e., fewer but higher spending visitors.

40. Chaplin (June 18, 1975), pp. A15–16.

41. Ibid.

42. Creighton (July 6, 1975).

43. Hamilton (1976).

44. Because of quality issues, not all of these were published as final technical reports.

45. Department of Planning and Economic Development (October 1, 1979), p. I-3, hereafter referred to as the State Tourism Plan or Tourism Functional Plan.

46. These included separate functional plans for energy, transportation, water resources, historic preservation, recreation, health, conservation lands, education, housing, higher education, agriculture, and tourism. Of course, tourism interacts in varying degrees with all the other functional plans (See State Tourism Plan, Table 2, p. II-8).

47. All twelve functional plans were passed by the 1984–1985 Legislature. *The Hawaii State Plan, Tourism* (1990), pp. 1–2.

48. De Kadt (1979), p. 24.

49. State Tourism Plan (1979), p. I-4.

50. In the 1990 Tourism Plan, p. 13, Policy 1.A.1 states, "Identify and ensure a rate of industry growth that is consistent with the social, physical and economic needs of the residents *and the preservation of Hawaii's natural environment*" [italics added].

51. Apartment hotels provide fewer and less desirable jobs per room than

conventional hotels; conventional hotels offer more full-time and steadier jobs per room than apartment hotels. See also Fujii and Mak (March 1981), pp. 30–35.

52. State of Hawaii DPED (1984); also the September 1986 *Progress Report.*

53. State of Hawaii DPED (1988).

54. State of Hawaii Office of State Planning (1991). For a more detailed analysis of this policy, see Mak (1993), pp. 250–261.

55. Callies (1984); also Callies (1994).

56. Thus it is not necessary to petition the LUC if a resort is to be built on land already classified "urban." Cooper and Daws (1985, chapter 3) note that it was the coalition of Republicans and Oahu Democrats in the Legislature who pushed through the 1961 state land use law; Democratic lawmakers from the Neighbor Islands vigorously opposed the law because its impact on the rural outer islands would likely be the greatest.

57. Grandy (2002).

58. State Auditor (February 2002), chapter 1, p. 2.

59. See also Hawaii Tourism Authority (2002).

60. Global Advisory Services (May 31, 2004).

61. State of Hawaii DBEDT (April 1997), p. 2.

62. State of Hawaii DBEDT (July 1998), pp. 33–40.

63. Ibid., pp. 41–42.

64. Eadington (October 8, 1995).

65. Ibid.

66. Indeed, for the United States, Grinols (2004) found that for every dollar of benefits attributed to casino gambling, costs range from $3.90 to $6.30.

67. Titchen (November 3, 1999), p. 3; Zimmerman (January 23, 2002), p. 3; Zimmerman (January 30, 2002), p. 10.

68. University of Hawaii at Manoa School of Travel Industry Management (December 2003).

69. To date, the United States and Canada are the only two significant tourist destination countries that have not received approval from China to market prepaid package group tours to mainland Chinese. By contrast, China granted "Approved Destination Status" (ADS) to European Union countries in 2004. However, a recent study by the European Travel Commission (February 7, 2007) concluded that "it is proving difficult to generate sustainable and profitable business in a sector characterized by low-priced, low-yield, multi-destination tours."

70. For further details about the ERTF, see Grandy (2002), chapter 6.

71. Waite (December 7, 2002), pp. A1 and A9.

72. See www.hawaiitourismstudy.com/project.asp.

73. Seiji Naya, private conversation with the author.

74. Ibid.

75. For instance, the Department of Business, Economic Development and Tourism predicted the number of visitor arrivals in Hawaii would grow by 7

percent in 2004 over 2003, with total visitor days increasing by 4.5 percent and visitor expenditures increasing by 7 percent. HTA's forecasts were 5.1 percent for arrivals, 5.2 percent for visitor days, and 7.9 percent for visitor spending. HVCB Tourism Industry Update (August 23, 2004).

76. The plan was approved by the HTA board in October 2004.

77. Hawaii Tourism Authority, *Hawaii Tourism Strategic Plan: 2005–2015,* at www.hawaii.gov/tourism/tsp.html.

78. Plan available at http://www.hawaiitourismauthority.org/pdf/tsp2005_2015 _final.pdf.

79. LuBove (1997).

80. Meller (1992).

81. State of Hawaii DPED, *Physical Resources* (1978), pp. 348–349.

82. de Kadt (1979), p. 21.

83. For a discussion of this issue, see Mak (2004), chapter 11, and Mitchell (1970).

84. Kaiser and Helber (1978), p. 29.

85. Cooper and Daws (1985), p. 93. Overall, the Land Use Commission was quite permissive during the period of rapid tourism growth during the '60s and '70s; for example, between 1962 and June 1977 the approval rate to change land from agricultural to urban designation was 86 percent on Kauai, 80 percent on Maui, 80 percent on Oahu, and 75 percent on the island of Hawaii. The overall approval rate was 82 percent. Of the requests by petition to change 44,695 acres from agricultural to urban uses, 23,405 acres (or 52 percent) were approved, and another 13,158 acres were approved during the five-year boundary reviews in 1969 and 1974. Lowry et al. (1977), pp. 17–18.

86. McClain (1992), pp. 9–10. See also Ritchie and Crouch (2003), chapter 1.

87. McClain, p. 13.

88. Horwitz and Finn (1969).

89. Ibid.

90. State of Hawaii DPED, vol. 1 (1972); Kaiser and Helber (1978), p. 29; and Matsuoka and Shera (1990). Renaud (1972) suggests that high concentration of land ownership in Hawaii has also stymied the development of backward linkages between tourism and diversified agriculture in the state.

91. Farrell (1982), p. 77.

92. Ibid., p. 88.

References

Allen, Robert C. 2004. *Creating Hawaii Tourism: A Memoir.* Honolulu: Bess Press.

Arakawa, Lynda. 2004. "Farmers Embrace Agritourism." *Honolulu Advertiser,* November 14: F1–F2.

Babbie, Earl. 1972. *The Maximillion Report.* Honolulu: Citizens for Hawaii.

Bone, Robert W. 1973. "HVB Exec Elaborates on Controlled Tourism." *Honolulu Advertiser,* August 30.

Boylan, Dan, and T. Michael Holmes. 2000. *John A. Burns: The Man and His Times.* Honolulu: University of Hawaii Press.

Callies, David. 1984. *Regulating Paradise: Land Use Controls in Hawaii.* Honolulu: University of Hawaii Press.

———. 1994. *Preserving Paradise: Why Regulations Won't Work.* Honolulu: University of Hawaii Press.

Chaplin, George. 1975. *Honolulu Advertiser,* May 28, June 18, and June 23.

Coffman, Tom. 2003. *The Island Edge of America: A Political History of Hawaii.* Honolulu: University of Hawaii Press.

Cooper, George, and Gavin Daws. 1985. *Land and Power in Hawaii.* Honolulu: Benchmark Books.

Craig, Paul. 1963. *The Future Growth of Hawaiian Tourism and Its Impact on the State and on the Neighbor Islands.* Honolulu: University of Hawaii Economic Research Center (February).

Crampon, Jack. 1976. *Hawaii's Visitor Industry: Its Growth and Development.* Honolulu: University of Hawaii School of Travel Industry Management.

Creighton, Thomas. 1975. "Tourism Flaws Have Been Long Obvious." *Honolulu Star-Bulletin,* July 6.

Cunningham, J. F. 1973. "Greater Control over Tourism Seen Necessary." *Honolulu Advertiser,* February 27.

de Kadt, Emanuel. 1979. *Tourism: Passport to Development?* New York: Oxford University Press.

Eadington, William R. 1995. "Casino Gaming Activities Must Be Supported by Community First." *Honolulu Advertiser,* October 8.

European Travel Commission. 2007. *Market Insights: China.* At http://www.etc-corporate.org/modules.php?name=content8pa=showpage8pid=318ac=5, (February 7), p. 2.

Fujii, Edwin, and James Mak. 1981. "The Impact of Hotel Size on Staffing Levels in Hawaii." *International Journal of Tourism Management* (March): 30–35.

Global Advisory Services. 2004. "Healing in Paradise: A Strategy for Cultivating Health and Wellness Tourism in Hawaii." Presented to the Hawaii Tourism Authority, Honolulu: May 31.

Goodsell, James. 1974. "Caribbean Tourism on Trial." *Christian Science Monitor,* August 13.

Grandy, Christopher. 2002. *Hawaii Becalmed: Economic Lessons of the 1990s.* Honolulu: University of Hawaii Press.

Gray, Francine du Plessix. 1972. *Hawaii: The Sugar Coated Fortress.* New York: Random House.

Griffin, John. 2004. *Honolulu Advertiser,* January 18: B3.

Grinols, Earl L. 2004. *Gambling in America: Costs and Benefits.* New York: Cambridge University Press.

Hamilton, Thomas H. 1975. *Legislators Seaside Resort Study Mission, May 25–June 14, 1975.* Honolulu: Privately published.

———. 1976. *A Report on a Tourist Study Mission to the South Pacific Made by Representatives of the Public and Private Sectors of Hawaii, November 20 to December 9, 1976.* Honolulu: Privately published.

"Hawaii—1985?" 1975. *Sunday Star-Bulletin & Advertiser,* July 27.

"Hawaii Named Best Destination." 2004. *Honolulu Advertiser,* December 16: C1.

Hawaii State Planning Office. 1960. *Structure and Growth Potential of Tourism in Hawaii.* Honolulu: State Planning Office (September).

Hawaii Tourism Authority. 2002. *Ke Kumu: Strategic Directions for Hawaii's Visitor Industry.* Honolulu: HTA.

———. *Hawaii Tourism Strategic Plan 2005–2015,* at www.hawaii.gov/tourism/tsp.html.

Hawaii Visitors Bureau. 1972. *A Survey of Residents to Determine Attitudes, Awareness, Familiarity and Opinions Regarding the Visitor Industry in Hawaii.* Honolulu: HVB (August).

Horwitz, Robert H., and Judith B. Finn. 1969. *Public Land Policy in Hawaii: Major Landowners.* Legislative Reference Bureau Report No. 3. Honolulu: University of Hawaii.

Kaiser, Charles, Jr., and Larry Helber. 1978. *Tourism Planning and Development.* Boston: CBI Publishing.

Kalapa, Lowell. 1992. "Why Is It That the State Seems to 'Bully' the Counties?" In Randy Roth, ed., *Price of Paradise* (Honolulu: Mutual Publishing): 47–51.

Keir, Gerry. 1973. "Burns, Fasi Not So Divided." *Honolulu Advertiser,* February 24.

Kent, Noel J. 1993. *Islands under the Influence.* Honolulu: University of Hawaii Press.

Limone, Jerry. 2007. "Pink Beach has the ingredients to keep guests coming back." *Travel Weekly Daily Bulletin,* May 21.

Lowry, Kem, Marvin Awaya, Kathy Higham, Ted Luke, Abe Mitsuda, Phil Olsen, Harold Sonomura, and Gail Uchida. 1977. "Analysis of Alternative Land Use Management Techniques for Hawaii." In Kimura, Hubert S. (project coordinator), *Growth Management Issues in Hawaii* (Honolulu: Hawaii State Department of Budget and Finance, Hawaii Institute for Management and Analysis in Government): 7–92.

LuBove, Seth. 1997. "The People's Republic of Hawaii." *Forbes,* June 16.

Mak, James. 1993. "Exacting Resort Developers to Create Non-Tourism Jobs." *Annals of Tourism Research* 20: 250–261.

———. 2004. *Tourism and the Economy: Understanding the Economics of Tourism.* Honolulu: University of Hawaii Press.

Manning, Frank E. 1979. "Tourism and Bermuda's Black Clubs: A Case of Cultural Revitalization." In Emanuel de Kadt, *Tourism: Passport to Development?* (New York: Oxford University Press): 157–176.

Mathematica, Inc. 1970. *The Visitor Industry and Hawaii's Economy: A Cost-Benefit Analysis.* Princeton, NJ: Mathematica, Inc. (February).

Matsuoka, Jon K., and Wes J. Shera. 1990. *Lanai: A Community on the Threshold of Change.* Honolulu: University of Hawaii, School of Social Work (April).

McClain, David. 1992. "What Can Hawaii Do to Stay Competitive in the World Market and Keep Its Economy Strong?" In Randy Roth, ed., *The Price of Paradise* (Honolulu: Mutual Publishing): 7–14.

Mitchell, Frank. 1970. "The Value of Tourism in East Africa." *Eastern Africa Economic Review* 2(1): 1–21.

Nordyke, Eleanor C. 1989. *The Peopling of Hawaii,* 2nd ed. Honolulu: University of Hawaii Press.

Renaud, Bertrand M. 1972. "The Influence of Tourism Growth on the Production Structure of Island Economies." *Review of Regional Studies* 2(3): 41–56.

Ritchie, J. R. Brent, and Geoffrey I. Crouch. 2003. *The Competitive Destination.* Cambridge, MA: CABI Publishing.

Schmitt, Robert. 1973. "Changing Hawaii: Implications for the Future." Presented at conference on Alternative Economic Futures for Hawaii, Honolulu, Mid-Pacific Institute (March 24).

State Auditor. 2002. *Management Audit of the Hawaii Tourism Authority: A Report to the Governor and the Legislature of the State of Hawaii.* Report No. 02-04. Honolulu: State Auditor (February).

State of Hawaii Department of Business and Economic Development (DBED). 1988. *1988 Statewide Tourism Impact Core Survey: Summary.* Honolulu: DBED.

———. 1990. *Hawaii State Plan: Tourism.* Honolulu: DBED.

State of Hawaii Department of Business, Economic Development and Tourism (DBEDT). 1995. "Changing Structure of Hawaii's Economy." *Hawaii's Economy* (3rd quarter).

———. 1997. *The Economic Impacts of Shipboard Gaming and Parimutual Horse Racing in Hawaii.* Honolulu: DBEDT (April).

———. 1998. *Hawaii's Dilemma: The Benefits and Costs of Gambling.* Paper No. 3. Honolulu: DBEDT (July).

State of Hawaii Department of Planning and Economic Development (DPED). 1972. *Tourism in Hawaii: Hawaii Tourism Impact Plan,* vols. 1 and 2. Honolulu: DPED.

———. 1976. *What Hawaii's People Think of the Visitor Industry: Results of a Public-Opinion Poll Taken October 5–15, 1975.* Honolulu: DPED (January).

———. 1978. *State Tourism Study: Executive Summary.* Honolulu: Office of Tourism.

———. 1978. *State Tourism Study: Physical Resources.* Honolulu: Office of Tourism.

———. 1979. *State Tourism Functional Plan.* Honolulu: DPED (October 1).

————. 1984. *Hawaii Population and Economic Projection and Simulation Model.* Honolulu: DPED (July).

————. 1984. *Progress Report on Implementation of the State Tourism Functional Plan.* Honolulu: DPED; also the September 1986 *Progress Report.*

State of Hawaii Office of State Planning. 1991. *Requesting a Report about Tourism Jobs: Report to the Legislature on H.C.R. 73-90.* Honolulu: Office of State Planning.

The 1973 Temporary Visitor Industry Council. 1973. *The Report of the Temporary Visitor Industry Council.* Honolulu (November).

Titchen, Kathy. 1999. "Gambling: Is It Our Future?" *MidWeek* 16(15): 3.

Tourtellot, Jonathan B. 2004. "Destination Scorecard: 115 Places Rated." *National Geographic Traveler* (March): 60–67.

University of Hawaii at Manoa School of Travel Industry Management. 2003. *Identifying and Analyzing the Chinese Outbound Market for Hawaii.* Prepared for the Hawaii Tourism Authority. Honolulu: HTA (December).

Waite, David. 2002. "High Court Won't Order Tourism Impact Study." *Honolulu Advertiser,* December 7: A1 and A9.

"World's best island." 2003. *Honolulu Advertiser,* November 30: E1.

Zimmerman, Malia. 2002. "Just Say No to Isle Casinos." *Midweek* 18(27): 6.

————. 2002. "Gambling Man, James Boersma: Leading the Effort to Bring Legalized Gambling to Hawaii." *MidWeek* 18(28): 10.

Chapter Four

State Tax Policy on Tourism

There are over eighty-seven thousand subnational governments in the United States. Hawaii has only five: the State and the four counties. In Hawaii there are no governments with separate taxing powers below the county level. Honolulu is both a city and a county, and a single government—the City and County of Honolulu—serves both. The state has one of the most centralized fiscal systems among the fifty states, with the lion's share of the responsibility for providing public services and taxation resting with the State government and not with the counties.[1] It has been suggested that this high degree of fiscal centralization is a legacy of the Hawaiian Monarchy. Until 1893, Hawaii was a kingdom.

The State government guards its taxing powers jealously. Hawaii has seventeen separate tax laws, of which fourteen are administered by the State; the counties administer only the real property tax, the motor vehicle weight tax, and the public utility franchise tax.[2] While the State government uses just about every tax mentioned in a public finance textbook except for the real property tax, it denies the counties the same flexibility and prefers instead to dole out money to the counties. The caravan of county mayors trekking to the State Legislature to plead for money is played out annually.[3] Thus the four county governments in Hawaii must depend much more heavily on the real property tax than most other local governments in the nation to pay their expenses.[4] It was the 1978 State Constitutional Convention that ruled the State should turn over the real property tax to the counties, but it also inserted an additional provision delaying the complete transfer for another eleven years (thinking perhaps that the next constitutional convention possibly in ten years would revisit the issue before the final transfer took effect; voters, however, did not approve another constitutional convention). Thus the counties could not even set their own property tax rates until 1989.[5] Any analysis of tax policy on tourism in Hawaii must look to the State government.

Taxing Tourism

We take it as evident that no one likes to pay taxes. Oliver Wendell Holmes Jr. once said, "Taxes are what we pay for civilized society,"[6] so most of us pay our share grudgingly. That does not mean that we do not complain or debate vigorously amongst ourselves whenever new taxes or changes to the tax system are proposed. It is no different when it involves formulating tax policy on tourism. Some might disagree and suggest instead that governments find it easy to single out tourism for special taxation because tourists don't stay around to vote, hence it is better to tax them than local residents. Evidence indicates otherwise.[7] A tourist tax—it turned out to be a hotel room tax—would eventually be passed by the Hawaii State Legislature in 1986, but it wasn't because the industry simply laid down and didn't put up a good fight.[8]

The tourist tax long had been debated with heat in Hawaii. Seldom had it been discussed rationally. For years the smart, entrepreneurial, and often feisty mayor of Honolulu, Frank Fasi, was the most vocal proponent of the room tax—nineteen years, according to an interview with him in 1973.[9]

The need for a hotel room tax was far less urgent in the early 1960s when Hawaii's economy was booming and the state's cupboard was full. That all began to change after 1968. Tax revenue growth leveled off due to a variety of factors, most of them external to Hawaii: A major shipping strike by the International Longshore and Warehouse Union on the West Coast and in Hawaii; the end of a hotel construction boom in Honolulu induced partly by developers building ahead of the enforcement of a tougher Comprehensive Zoning Code; a national economic recession (1971); and the Arab oil embargo (1973) all contributed to the revenue slowdown. After seven consecutive years of general fund surpluses, the State projected a large deficit by the end of fiscal year 1971. At prevailing service levels, budget deficits were projected to rise upward to $200 million in fiscal year 1975.[10] The powerful chairman of the Senate Ways and Means Committee proposed a large menu of potential tax increases in 1973 to stave off looming deficits.[11] Taxation of tourism became a more urgent issue.

Governor John Burns was not so much against levying a tourist tax as much as he was opposed to levying a hotel room tax, which he considered to be discriminatory and unfair to tourists.[12] He made it clear that he would veto a room tax bill but would be willing to accept a broad-based tax increase —i.e., an across-the-board increase in the 4 percent general excise tax—that would be paid by both tourists and residents, if the fiscal situation required it. He noted that Hawaii's visitors were already taxed directly by the broad-based excise tax when they purchased goods and services and indirectly by the corporate income tax and property taxes levied on tourist businesses. A hotel room tax, he feared, would only fuel visitor resentment. However, proposing an increase in the general excise tax would probably ensure its political defeat since the burden of the tax would fall largely on residents.[13] Indeed, a careful study done by three economists at the University of Hawaii at Manoa in 1989 showed that almost the entire burden of the hotel room tax levied in Hawaii fell on tourists; by contrast, only 22 percent of Hawaii's broad-based general excise tax, 16 percent of the taxes levied on corporations, banks, and other financial institutions, 9 percent of the real property tax, and none of the State's personal income tax fell on tourists.[14] A poll of Hawaii residents in 1975 found that 51.7 percent of the respondents were in favor of a hotel room tax and 31.2 percent were opposed.[15] Sentiment in favor of the room tax was strongest on Oahu (55.3 percent in favor versus 27.6 percent against), while on the Big Island more people were opposed (49.2 percent) than were in favor of the room tax (34.1 percent).

The visitor industry offered other reasons why a hotel room tax would be a bad idea. It would increase the cost of a visit to Hawaii and drive significant numbers of tourists away. Citing the 1970 Baumol Report, industry lobbyists also argued that tourists already were paying more taxes than what the government spends to provide services to them; hence there was no economic justification to ask tourists to pay more than what they were already paying.

However, the Baumol Report made a point to emphasize that the "report was not undertaken with the visitor tax issue before it. . . . This report does not and cannot lead to the conclusion that a visitor tax is either desirable or undesirable."[16] While it is reassuring to discover that tourists pay more than their own way from the perspective of the public treasury, it is not the only reason to tax tourists.

Mayor Fasi countered that "No one quarrels with the right and logic of government to demand royalties such as for oil in Alaska. A hotel room occupancy tax is no more than a request for royalties from entrepreneurs and businessmen who are mining our natural resources—our beautiful climate, our sun and surf, our flora and fauna. . . . Even if tourists are paying a 'fair share of expenses' there is nothing wrong in charging the tourist who enjoys the cream of our resources a little bit more for that privilege."[17] Economists who study these matters would generally agree with Fasi.[18]

Indeed, strong evidence exists that across the country states intentionally design their tax structures to export taxes to nonresidents in order to subsidize the cost of public services they provide to their own residents.[19] Nevada, for example, generates most of its tax revenues from the gaming industry, and Nevada residents enjoy public services subsidized by tourism.[20]

If any pricing practice is clearly discriminatory that might fuel visitor resentment, it is the two-tier price system—referred to as "kamaaina rates," with tourists paying a higher price than locals—practiced (openly!) by tourist businesses and the State and local governments in Hawaii. A survey of five hundred North American visitors to Hawaii in 1999 found that 23 percent of the respondents were "annoyed by seeing things that are priced higher for tourists than for residents"; a separate survey of six hundred Japanese visitors found that 56 percent were similarly annoyed.[21]

Lawmakers still had questions about the magnitude of the potential negative impact of a room tax on visitor demand. Two economics professors at the University of Hawaii opined in their regular biweekly column in the *Honolulu Advertiser* that a modest tax would not deter tourist visits since it would have an insignificant impact on the total cost of a visit to Hawaii.[22] No one had proposed seriously a tax high enough to affect Hawaii's tourism in any drastic way. Still, no formal study had been done. Eventually, a study was commissioned as part of the Public Revenue–Cost Analysis authorized under Act 133, although it was unclear at the time whether the law actually mandated such a study. Representatives of the industry and some labor groups were opposed to such a study. Most of the other members on the advisory council seemed to feel that whether or not Act 133 called for such a study, there was sufficient legislative and public interest in the matter that it should be done. The finished study concluded that a modest hotel room tax was unlikely to have a significant negative impact on demand for Hawaii visits.[23] It would take nearly another decade before a hotel room tax would be enacted by the Legislature. There was, however, a growing sense of inevitability on this issue.

The 1980s witnessed the proliferation of tourist taxes around the world. In the United States, just about every state raised their tourist taxes or imposed new ones on hotels, car rentals, amusement and entertainment attractions, and food and drink at bars, nightclubs, and restaurants.[24] The hotel room tax (or "bed tax," as it is referred to in many countries) became the most widely employed tourist tax. The 1984 Hawaii Tax Review Commission conducted a survey of state hotel room taxes and discovered that hotel tax revenues were most often used for tourism-related activities such as tourism promotion and convention center financing.[25] Yet another study authorized by the commission, using different data and methodology, reached the same conclusions as an earlier study: A room tax is unlikely to have a significant negative impact on tourist travel to Hawaii; and a room tax is also preferable to some other leisure taxes (e.g., amusement tax, restaurant tax, and so on) because it is more easily exported to nonresidents.[26]

At some point in the debate over the merits of a room tax, even a majority of the members of the Chamber of Commerce when polled favored a tourist tax. The leadership of the chamber, however, continued to oppose it. There was a good reason why some people in the business community were switching over to the pro-tax camp. In the discussion over the issue, it was suggested that the revenues from the tax would be used to finance a world-class convention center, give more money to the Hawaii Visitors Bureau for promotion, and pay for other tourism-related projects.[27]

The 1986 Legislature enacted a transient accommodation tax (TAT) of 5 percent on the price of an occupied room. The 5 percent was in addition to the 4 percent general excise tax (which usually showed up on a bill as 4.166 percent) levied on the gross receipts (inclusive of the tax) on all final sales in Hawaii. Subsequent analysis showed that the new tax did not have a significant negative impact on demand for Hawaii travel.[28] However, the Legislature did not dedicate the tax to any specific use; instead it kept control over the money by allocating the revenues from the TAT to the General Fund. It gave more money to the Hawaii Visitors Bureau to promote tourism, but the convention center still had not been built. If the intent of the TAT was also to finance a world-class convention center, then the State clearly gained a windfall.

The 1989 Tax Review Commission, following the advice of the U.S. Advisory Commission on Intergovernmental Relations (ACIR), recommended that the TAT be transferred to the counties, including the power to set their own rates. The ACIR's reasoning was that since the counties bore the larger share of the cost of providing public services to tourists, it was only natural that the unit of government that is responsible for providing a service should be responsible for raising the money to pay for it. Economists call it the "accountability principle."[29] As well, the Public Revenue–Cost study prepared under Act 133 found that public revenue–cost ratios from tourism were much higher for the State treasury than for the county treasuries.[30] The State refused to give up the TAT. Instead, the 1990 Legislature (via Act 185) decided to divide 95 percent of the TAT revenues as a grant-in-aid among the counties by an "arbitrary" formula, keeping the remaining 5 percent to pay for collection costs.[31] The Hawaii Conventional Center was finally completed in October 1997, but the money from the 5 percent TAT had already been allocated; unless the State took back the TAT revenues from the counties, additional sources of money would have to be found. The Legislature elected to increase the TAT first to 6 percent as of July 1, 1994 (with 1 percent of the amount collected dedicated to the Convention Center Capital and Operations Special Fund) and finally to 7.25 percent effective January 1, 1999. With the increase, the combined TAT and general excise tax levied on occupied hotel rooms in Hawaii rose to 11.416 percent. Hawaii still didn't have the highest room tax rate in the country—the average effective hotel room tax rate among fifty major U.S. cities in the mid-1990s was 12.03 percent—but it was slightly above the average among the nation's resort destinations (10.8 percent).[32]

The Legislature also made major changes in the way money to support tourism is allocated. Acting on the recommendations of the Economic Revitalization Task Force (ERTF), formed by Governor Ben Cayetano in 1997 to look for ways to "revitalize" a stagnant economy, the Legislature (via Act 156) created a new institution, the Hawaii Tourism Authority (HTA), with dedicated money from the room tax.[33] The Legislature retained the power to set the formula used to allocate TAT revenues among the counties, tourism promotion, and the convention center. In fiscal year 2003, the State collected nearly $171 million from the TAT, or about 4.6 percent of total State government tax collections, and it allocated the revenues by a fixed formula as follows:[34]

Allocated to	Amount (million $)	Percent of the total
Convention Center Enterprise Fund	$29.6	17.3
Tourism Special Fund	63.3	37.0
Counties	76.5	44.8
State General Fund	1.5	0.9
Total	$170.9	100.0

Source: State of Hawaii Department of Taxation, *Annual Report 2002–2003.*

Is Hawaii a High-Tax Tourist Destination?

The World Travel and Tourism Council (WTTC), an organization of chief executives of the biggest tourism businesses in the world, releases annual tax indexes comparing tourist taxes among fifty-two leading tourist destinations around the world. The WTTC Tax Barometer calculates the amount of car rental, hotel, meal, and air passenger taxes and user fees for a standard trip. Not all the taxes are strictly "tourist" taxes; for example, most of the tax revenues collected on food and drink are probably paid by local residents rather than tourists. One of the tax barometers is based on the amount of taxes paid on a standard trip as a percentage of the total bill—or the "tax effort" (Table 4-1). For 2002, the average tax effort was 13.95, meaning that these four taxes paid represent about 14 percent of the expenditures; the median tax effort among the fifty-two destinations was approximately 15 percent. Honolulu averaged 15.51 percent and ranked twenty-sixth among the fifty-two cities.[35] On the WTTC scale, Hawaii is about average among the leading tourist destinations around the world when it comes to taxing tourism.

Clearly, taxes are not the only factor—or even the most important—in determining where people choose to visit. On the WTTC Tax Barometer, Tokyo has a tax effort rating of 6.27, placing it forty-seventh among the world's leading destinations in hitting up tourists for taxes. While Tokyo's tax burden is comparatively low, everything else there is expensive, making Tokyo a very expensive city to visit. The Baumol Report advises that it is not whether a tax is a tourist tax or how high the rate is but whether it serves most effectively the goals of the community.[36] Consider two objectives: (1) Reduce the growth rate of visitors to Hawaii; and (2) maximize tax revenues collected from visitors. Each of these two goals may have their own supporters. But to achieve the first goal may require a hefty tourist tax that will drive substantial numbers of potential visitors away; to achieve the second goal may suggest a modest tourist tax. The two goals imply very different tax policies.

Hawaii's visitor industry wanted more money for tourism promotion, and both the industry and the State wanted to build a world-class convention center to diversify the sources of visitors and to help fill empty hotel rooms during the slack periods (or at least that was the professed intention). The room tax made it possible for the industry to have both. Without a tourist tax it is unlikely that resident taxpayers would have agreed to spend

Table 4-1. Tax effort among leading tourist destinations: 2002

Destination	Tax effort (%)	Destination	Tax effort (%)
Copenhagen	24.25	Amsterdam	15.16
London	21.66	Toronto	15.09
Vienna	20.65	Rio de Janeiro	14.79
Brussels	20.17	Paris	14.46
Miami	19.51	Sao Paulo	14.03
Johannesburg	18.76	Mumbai	13.90
Buenos Aires	18.73	Auckland	13.39
Chicago	18.23	New Delhi	13.18
Stockholm	17.99	Rome	13.11
Frankfurt	17.94	Cairo	12.50
Tel Aviv	17.77	Madrid	11.17
Istanbul	17.71	Jakarta	10.72
Montreal	17.63	Barcelona	10.69
Munich	17.45	Manila	10.49
Los Angeles	17.16	Prague	10.20
Santiago	17.11	Seoul	10.14
Boston	17.08	Zurich	9.98
San Francisco	16.81	Geneva	9.45
Nairobi	16.80	Bangkok	7.80
Sydney	16.65	Kuala Lumpur	6.46
Vancouver	16.64	Tokyo	6.27
Athens	16.59	Osaka	6.21
Mexico City	16.33	Taipei	5.54
Helsinki	16.32	Singapore	4.98
New York City	15.62	Hong Kong	2.18
Honolulu	15.51	Beijing	0.97

Source: WTTC Tax Barometer, at http://www.traveltax.msu.edu; also in Mak (2004), p. 147.

more of their own tax dollars on tourism promotion or to build a convention center. Moreover, by earmarking a specific percentage of the money from the TAT for tourism promotion, the industry no longer has to go hat-in-hand each year to the Legislature to beg for money. Skipping this annual ritual also saves the industry and the State government a lot of time and money. Earmarking also provides greater assurance that money for tourism promotion will be not be drastically cut and diverted when there is a general budgetary crisis. Christopher Grandy opines that changing the way tourism promotion is funded "is one of the areas in which the Cayetano administration can claim to have successfully enacted meaningful economic reform."[37] Finally, the counties were given an additional source of revenue without having to lobby for it each year. Everything considered, Hawaii's hotel room tax has delivered on what it was asked to do. It has been good for the industry and residents.

A perennial problem remains. County governments still do not have the flexibility to design their own tax systems to meet their needs. Assigning them a fixed percentage of the TAT and dividing the money among them using an "arbitrary" formula does not solve the fiscal problems of the individual counties. Too often the counties do not have the resources to pay for large projects, such as refurbishing Waikiki or beautifying the Nimitz Highway between the airport and Waikiki, unless the State is willing to provide financial help. Though the counties finally have total control of the property tax, it is not necessarily the best tax to finance every public service. The property tax is also the most unpopular tax among voters in the United States. Without the flexibility to design their own fiscal systems, the counties cannot achieve their economic potential, and their residents end up being the losers. The situation in Hawaii cries out for greater fiscal decentralization. The new governor of Hawaii was a former mayor of Maui County, and she has expressed sympathy for fiscal "home rule." But a recent survey of State legislators revealed strong opposition to giving additional taxing powers to the counties.[38] The problem of fiscal imbalance between the State and the counties is likely to stay around for a long time.

Fiscal Incentives

Hawaii's State government historically had shunned the use of fiscal incentives to stimulate or attract private tourism investment. This all changed in 1981. In that year, the State granted American Hawaii Cruises an exemption from the State's public service company tax (PSC), a 4 percent tax levied on the revenues derived from the sale of passenger tickets, for interisland cruises on its cruise ship, the S.S. *Independence*.[39] The exemption was supposed to kick-start the development of a locally based, U.S.–flagged cruise ship industry in Hawaii in competition with established cruise tourism markets such as Alaska and the Caribbean, and it was supposed to last only five years. At the end of the five years, the Legislature extended the exemption twice more for a total of fifteen years, expiring on June 30, 1996. The tax

break, however, did not keep American Hawaii Cruises from going bank-
rupt; the company was acquired by American Classic Voyages, also owner
of the United States Lines, and emerged from bankruptcy in 1993. While it
is difficult to justify a fifteen-year tax break to help a start-up company get
on its feet, for Hawaii taxpayers the cruise ship tax exemption did not add
up to a huge amount of money. In testimony before the House Committee
on Finance on February 25, 2000, American Hawaii Cruises revealed that
it paid annual public service company taxes of about $2.86 million.[40] Hence
the annual value of the exemptions during the fifteen years that the fiscal
incentive was in effect was less than $3 million. But that money was largely
wasted.

Hotel Tax Credits

Beginning in 1997, the State Legislature passed several tax credit laws to
stimulate hotel remodeling and construction in Hawaii. The first of these
(Act 108) provided a *refundable* income tax credit of up to 4 percent of
renovation cost for each qualified hotel facility located in Hawaii, with the
amount of the income tax credit capped at 10 percent of the hotel room tax
(TAT) paid by the taxpayer in the preceding year.[41] Act 108 was designed
to encourage hotel owners to "refurbish, repair and renovate their facilities," because Hawaii's hotels—especially those in Waikiki—were aging and
in need of refurbishing. In the following year the Legislature passed Act
306, which removed the TAT cap. In 2000, the Legislature passed Act 195,
granting a 4 percent refundable credit for hotel construction and renovation costs for taxable years beginning after December 31, 1998, and before
January 1, 2003. Thus, Act 195 expanded the hotel credit base by allowing
new hotel construction as well as remodeling expenditures to qualify for
tax credits. The act further allowed the credit to be claimed retroactively on
hotel construction expenditures incurred after December 31, 1998.

Following the September 11, 2001, terrorist attacks, the Hawaii Legislature wanted to stimulate the economy and passed Act 10, which converted
the 4 percent refundable hotel construction and renovation credit (Act 195)
to a 10 percent nonrefundable credit for qualifying expenditures incurred
on or between November 2, 2001, and July 1, 2003; thereafter the 10 percent
nonrefundable credit reverted to a 4 percent refundable credit until the
law sunset on December 31, 2005.[42] In sum, the Legislature sweetened the
incentive by raising the tax credit from 4 percent to 10 percent on money

spent on hotel remodeling between November 2001 and July 2003; the stipulation was that the hotel could claim the credit only if it owed that much in taxes to the State. The tax credit is an offset against the hotel's pre-credit tax liability.

In 2003, the Legislature passed Senate Bill 1410, extending the life of Act 10; the bill sought to lower the tax credit from 10 percent to 8 percent and extend its life from 2003 to 2006. The credit would then fall to 4 percent and expire in 2010. The credit would also apply to "commercial buildings and facilities" located in an area zoned for resort use. The *Honolulu Advertiser* urged the State to "wean the hotel industry from state tax credits." The paper argued, "While we appreciate that these breaks are intended to stimulate the economy, we'd prefer to see them used to foster fledging industries. It's imprudent for the state to keep subsidizing tourism projects that are part of what is, after all, a well-established industry." [43] Governor Linda Lingle vetoed the bill for two reasons. First, she objected to the inclusion of "commercial buildings and facilities." Second, given the tight fiscal situation facing the State following September 11, she argued that the tax credit might be too costly since there was no cap on the total dollar amount that could be claimed. [44]

But she signed another tourism-related tax credit bill into law (SB2907) to benefit the developer of the Ko Olina Resort, located on the Leeward Coast of Oahu. The bill offered tax credits to develop a world-class aquarium, marine and mammal science research facilities, international sports training facilities, and a travel industry management training program. The bill capped the total credit at $75 million between June 2003 and May 2009, with an annual ceiling of $7.5 million. It also stipulated that the State would receive one-half of future net income from the aquarium and marine research facility after seventeen years. In an abrupt break from past State policy, the Ko Olina profit-sharing provision makes the State a codeveloper of the facilities. Moreover, there was no assessment of how the tax credit might affect the financial viability of the State's own small but widely acclaimed Waikiki Aquarium, the privately owned Sea Life Park, or another private proposal to build an aquarium in town.

The Ko Olina Resort and Marina—or at least the original idea behind it —was the brainchild of developer Herbert Horita during the late 1960s and early 1970s. Initially dubbed the "West Beach Resort," the idea was that it would be a master-planned, full-scale resort destination similar to those on the Neighbor Islands. [45] With Waikiki reaching its sustainable capacity to accommodate more tourist facilities, the West Beach Resort would allow further expansion of tourism on Oahu. It would not be a competitor to Waikiki. But Horita's dream of a fully developed West Beach Resort (with ten hotels containing seven thousand rooms and thousands of homes) was never realized. By the early 1990s, only one hotel, four lagoons, a golf course, and 280 townhomes were finished.[46] The idea was a hard sell when other rural Oahu resorts like Makaha and Turtle Bay were struggling. For some inexplicable reason, tourists either wanted to be in the middle of the action in urban Waikiki or out in the country on the Neighbor Islands; what they didn't want was to be on the outskirts of the metropolis. First Hawaiian Bank chief economist Tom Hitch described it as the "either-Waikiki-or-the-neighbor-islands" orientation.[47] West Beach was left to others to complete. In 2000, the Ko Olina Resort community contained only one hotel (owned by Japan Airlines) operating at an estimated 40 percent occupancy, a golf club, some townhomes, and Paradise Cove, home of the famous luau on Oahu.

In 2002, developer Jeff Stone came up with the proposal for a world-class aquarium and other educational and training facilities to rekindle momentum for the development of Ko Olina. The developer claimed that the aquarium would spark "over $700 million of hotel, timeshare and commercial development, would create over 10,000 construction jobs, over 2,000 permanent jobs, and over $186 million of new tax revenues over a ten-year period."[48] Proponents of the "Ko Olina tax credit" bill (SB2907) argued that it also would serve a legitimate public purpose because it would provide training and employment to residents in an area plagued by chronic high unemployment.[49] SB2907 was passed by the 2002 Legislature, but it was vetoed by lame-duck governor Ben Cayetano. In his veto message, Cayetano explained that he did not believe that the developer had proved its merits, and he opposed giving an incentive to one project rather than something that would benefit the entire community.[50] During her gubernatorial campaign to succeed Cayetano, Linda Lingle remarked that she would have signed the Ko Olina bill had she been governor. She said in a statement, "He had a chance to help the people of the Leeward Coast by relieving the chronic unemployment, poverty and social problems that have plagued the area for decades and he blew it."[51] So, it came as no big surprise that she signed the reintroduced bill into law after she became governor in 2003. But in January 2007, developer Jeff Stone announced that he would return the $75 million tax credit. His explanation was that the objective of the credit—to stimulate economic development at the resort and in the surrounding community—had been achieved by market forces. He noted that $500 million worth of condominium and time-share projects were already underway. He explained, "You don't need an attraction (at Ko Olina) anymore."[52]

Critics of tax incentives argue that they (1) reduce the tax base and result in less revenues for government programs; (2) distort resource allocation by favoring some activities over others; and (3) encourage corruption. Incentives given on a case-by-case basis such as the Ko Olina tax credit can also unfairly favor some businesses over others. Economists who study such matters generally argue against giving tax incentives. For example, when asked whether government should ever subsidize private investment in tourism, University of Toronto economist Richard Bird responded that "The correct answer is almost certainly 'no.' If private investors are not willing to risk their own funds in the tourist business, it is not clear why public money should remove the risk and leave them the profit."[53] Christopher Grandy argues that such tax breaks tend to encourage poor investment decisions; they also violate "good policy principles because they interfere with private arrangements."[54]

Despite these negatives, fiscal incentives are widely used around the world by governments to attract private investment. In the United States, tax incentives have become the "weapon of choice" among states in the battle for business investment.[55] Whether tax incentives are cost effective in inducing the desired investment remains "highly inconclusive."[56]

In principle, a 4 percent tax credit on hotel construction and remodeling is defensible. In 1988 Hawaii enacted legislation allowing businesses that purchase capital goods to claim a 4 percent refundable tax credit.[57] The capital goods excise tax credit offsets Hawaii's broad-based 4 percent general excise tax. In essence, the credit exempts qualifying capital goods purchases from paying the excise tax. The purpose of the credit was to reduce business costs and enhance the state's competitiveness. Even critics of tax incentives might agree on the merit of exempting intermediate goods from taxation. Hawaii's capital goods excise tax credit applies only to tangible "personal"—but not to "real"—property. Thus a hotel, for instance, can claim a 4 percent refundable credit for the purchase of a new computer but not the cost of remodeling a hotel or building a new one. The disparity in the treatment of these two types of capital goods—equipment versus structures—is curious in that capital employed in the state's leading export—tourism—consists mostly of structures rather than equipment.[58] Raising the tax credit from 4 percent (Act 195) to 10 percent (Act 10) is another matter.

Why then did Hawaii lawmakers do an about-face in 1997 and begin giving tax incentives to spur hotel investment? First, following the first Gulf War in 1991, Hawaii's economy stagnated for seven years.[59] Since gaining statehood in 1959, Hawaii had never experienced two consecutive years of economic contraction. After half a decade of denial that the state's economic malaise was more than cyclical in origin, Hawaii's new governor and lawmakers embarked on a major effort to identify and implement far-reaching policy changes to revitalize the sagging economy. Giving tax incentives was one of the economic remedies.

Second, since the 1950s, study after study had indicated that Waikiki was deteriorating, but not enough action was taken to stem its decline (see chapter 7). In 1988, Duty Free Shoppers' CEO in Hawaii, John Reed, described Waikiki as "a tired and old product."[60] Then Japanese travel to Hawaii took a steep plunge after 1997 and declined every year between 1997 and 2003. The number of Japanese visitors to Hawaii reached a peak of 2.15 million in 1997 and fell to 1.32 million in 2003. While the huge numerical decline was alarming, even more alarming were data that showed that Hawaii's share of Japanese overseas travel fell from 12.8 percent in 1997 to 9.3 percent in 2001 and 9.1 percent in 2002. It was apparent to everyone that Waikiki—the flagship of Hawaii's tourist industry since statehood and the favorite destination among Japanese visitors to Hawaii—was losing its appeal relative to other newer destinations. Christopher Grandy noted that "while everyone 'knows' that Waikiki must be refurbished, curiously, this has not happened."[61] Act 108, the first hotel renovation tax credit passed in 1997, was regarded by the State administration "as a way of jump-starting investment at a reasonable cost."[62]

One can only speculate on the reasons why hoteliers neglected their properties. It has been suggested that hotel room caps imposed in Waikiki by the City Council in the 1970s and then again in 1992 discouraged hotel renovations.[63] Another reason given for the deterioration of Waikiki was the enactment of the Waikiki Special Design District zoning ordinance in 1976 that was aimed at reducing new building density in Waikiki; the new ordinance left most of the existing buildings "nonconforming" and thus—it was argued—would require them to conform to the more stringent building requirements if they were remodeled.[64] Remodeling did not make any economic sense until the Waikiki Special District ordinance was amended in 1996. Whatever the merits of these arguments, it is clear that during the 1970s and 1980s demand for visitor lodgings in Waikiki was growing faster than capacity, which led to high hotel occupancy and room rates, reducing the incentive by hotel owners to renovate their properties. Indeed, until the mid-1990s, hotel occupancy rates in Waikiki were the highest in the state.[65] Why bother to renovate if you can rent a standard room at a deluxe room price? Moreover, when occupancy rates are high, taking rooms out of service means losing revenue while the rooms are being renovated. Not surprisingly, much of Waikiki's hotel inventory was left to depreciate.

In the 1990s, the hotel room cap in Waikiki (32,800 units) was generally not a problem, as hotel occupancy rates declined along with travel to Waikiki.[66] Rising vacancies should have provided additional incentive to hoteliers to renovate their properties. That did not happen for several reasons. First, Japanese owners of a number of major Waikiki hotels, acquired at inflated prices during the Japanese economic "bubble" of the late 1980s, found themselves unable to service their debts after the bubble burst in 1991, and they fell behind in the maintenance of their properties.[67] Second, high real estate prices fueled by the surge in Japanese investments in Hawaii during the "bubble" years followed by sudden market collapse in the early 1990s complicated ground rent renegotiations for hotels built on leasehold land. Negotiating parties found it difficult to reach agreements on future ground lease rents when land values were trending downward, but landowners demanded rents that were based on inflated real estate values observed during the "bubble" period. In some cases, disagreements were resolved through time-consuming binding arbitration, and hotel renovations were deferred until future ground rents were renegotiated and uncertainty was removed. Finally, in response to rising vacancy rates and increased geopolitical risks following the 9/11 terrorist attacks, a few hotel owners found it more profitable to withdraw aging (off-beach) hotel units from the vacation rental market and convert them into residential condominiums and apartment units.[68] A few were converted into "condotels."[69] Selling the less attractive off-beach hotel units rather than renting them got the investor's money returned sooner, and that made a lot of business sense in a world of increased risk and uncertainty combined with a hot local housing market fueled by low interest rates. Thus, several factors converged to discourage hotel renovation expenditures in the 1990s.

Between 1997 and 2003, the Honolulu City and County government spent $50 million to improve Kalakaua Avenue, the main thoroughfare through Waikiki. The president of the Waikiki Improvement Association noted that

the $50 million in public investment spurred $500 million in private investment in the area, with plans to spend another $600 million in the next five
years.[70] In the next phase of beautifying Waikiki, the City spent $19 million
to improve Kuhio Avenue, hoping this public investment would spur a renaissance of the second most important thoroughfare in Waikiki. Finally,
another $2.4 was spent to beautify the Ala Wai Boulevard.[71] In early 2004,
the State announced plans to spend up to $700,000 to replenish sand to
increase the width of Waikiki Beach, which has been eroding every year.[72]
Hospitality consultant Joe Toy observed that "We're seeing momentum returning to Waikiki. There is more to be completed but it is well on its way."[73]
Thus, tax credits may not have been needed to rejuvenate Waikiki.

Did the Hotel Tax Credits Work?

Table 4-2 summarizes the number of claims under the various tax credit
legislations and their dollar amounts for the tax years 1997–2004. For 2001,
two separate credits applied to hotel remodeling and construction spending; expenditures incurred before November 2 must file under Act 195, and
the rest under Act 10. Of the 259 claims (filed by 201 different taxpayers)
in 2001 totaling $7.4 million, 196 claims for $5.7 million were filed under
Act 195 and 63 claims for $1.65 million were filed under Act 10.[74] As most of
those who filed for the 10 percent credit (Act 10) also filed for the 4 percent
credit (Act 195), the full impact of Act 10 on investment decisions did not
kick in until at least 2002. In fiscal year 2002 (July 1, 2001 to June 30, 2002),
the Tax Department reported $6.2 million in claims filed under the hotel
tax credits and $14 million in FY 2003, the last year under Act 10. The lion's
share of the claims were on Oahu (i.e., primarily Waikiki), where it was
most needed.

It is clear that tax cuts of the magnitudes displayed in Table 4-2 (i.e., roughly
$7 to $14 million each year) could not provide much economic stimulus to
an economy with a gross domestic product in excess of $40 billion. The tax
credits were far too small for an economy that size. Thus, tax credits cannot
be defended as an effective short-term economic stimulus tool to remedy
cyclical economic downturns.

Did the hotel tax credits spur hotel renovation and construction? Table 4-3
presents estimates of hotel construction and remodeling expenditures between 1997 and 2004 (unfortunately data for earlier years are not available).

Different people looking at the same numbers might come to different conclusions. Indeed, the state director of taxation concluded, "Tax

Table 4-2. Hotel tax credits claimed: 1997–2004

Tax year	Number of claims	Amount
1997	56	$929,000
1998	118	1,810,000
1999	21	1,174,000
2000	127	7,100,000
2001	259	7,400,000
2002	147	3,700,000
2003	261	5,300,000
2004	292	12,700,000

Source: State of Hawaii Department of Taxation, *Tax Credits Claimed by Hawaii Residents* (annual since 1997), at http://www.state.hi.us/tax/a5_4credits.htm.

Table 4-3. Total hotel construction and remodeling expenditures: 1997–2004

Tax year	Expenditures (million $)
1997	at least $23.2
1998	45.3
1999	29.4
2000	177.5
2001	at least 159.0
2002	?
2003	?
2004	317.5

Note: Computed by dividing the value of the credits in Table 4-2 by the applicable tax credit rates. Actual hotel construction expenditures for 2002 and 2003 cannot be estimated in the same way, as the 10 percent credit could only be claimed if there was a (precredit) tax liability.

incentives, alone, cannot be credited with increasing total renovation and construction investment."[75] He noted that more than half of the large increase in 2000 is attributable to one large Waikiki hotel project (i.e., Hilton Hotel's Kalia Tower) begun in 1999 before the passage of Act 195. In other words, that hotel would have been built anyway without tax credits. However, Governor Ben Cayetano, who signed Act 195 into law in 2000, explained that Hilton had counted on the passage of the tax credit (and hence the act's retroactive provision covering projects that began after December 31, 1998) when it committed to build the Kalia Tower in 1999.[76] Nor can we point to low interest rates as the reason for the huge increase in hotel investment between 1997 and 2001 since total construction (of all types) grew at a slower pace than hotel construction and renovation—from $2.94 billion in calendar year 1997 to $3.77 billion in 2001.[77] Hospitality consultant Joseph Toy found that renovated hotels began paying back the State almost immediately, as they were able to charge higher room rates and thus generate higher tax revenues.[78] Some critics argue that the hotel construction and renovation tax credits only accelerated the timing of investment, not the total amount of investment in the economy; even if that were true, if redevelopment of an area is the objective, timing is everything.

Given the multiplicity of factors that influence hotel investment, it is difficult to pinpoint exactly how much additional capital spending was induced by the tax credits alone. Therein lies the problem. It is difficult enough to try to ascertain the benefits and costs of these incentives *after the fact,* much less try to figure out what they might be *before the fact.* Moreover, whether tax credits are the best way to spend taxpayer dollars is another matter. Grandy argues that it is "only if you can know that refurbishing Hawaii's hotels is the best use of investable funds in the state—a big 'if.'"[79] It is interesting to note that when residents were asked in a sample survey in 1999 whether or not they supported tax incentives to renovate or to build new hotels, 54 percent of the respondents said "yes," but the support fell to 34 percent in 2001 and 39 percent in 2002.[80] Looking at the total history of tourism fiscal incentives in Hawaii, the tax incentives provided by Hawaii's State government to tourism are hardly earthshaking when contrasted with the generosity seen elsewhere around the world. Hawaii demonstrates that generous tax subsidies are not necessary to develop a dream destination.

Notes

1. See, for example, Kalapa (1992b), pp. 47–51; Meller (1992); and U.S. Advisory Commission on Intergovernmental Relations, vol. 2 (1989).

2. Revenues from both the vehicle weight tax and the public utility franchise tax go into the counties' highway funds and not into their general funds. Public utilities do not pay county property taxes; instead they pay the franchise tax based on a percentage of their "gross income."

3. Kalapa (1992a), pp. 41–44. For a brief history of fiscal relations between the State and the counties, see Kalapa (1992b), pp. 47–51.

4. See Tax Review Commission, vol. 1 (1989), p. 14; and Tax Review Commission (1996), Appendix B.

5. Kalapa (1992b), pp. 47–51.

6. Mak (2004), p. 143.

7. Mak (2004), chapter 12.

8. In addition to the hotel room (transient accommodation) tax, the State levies two other minor tourist taxes: a daily rental motor vehicle tax and a tour vehicle surcharge tax (HRS Chapter 251). Revenues from both taxes are distributed to the State's highway fund and not into the General Fund.

9. Keir (February 24, 1973), pp. A1 and A11.

10. Ebel and Mak (1974), p. 65; Keir (February 24, 1973), pp. A1 and A4.

11. Ebel and Mak (1974), p. 68.

12. Keir (February 23, 1973), pp. A1 and A11.

13. See Fujii, Khaled, and Mak (1985); Miklius, Moncur, and Leung (1989).

14. Miklius, Moncur, and Leung (1989), Table 4, p. 10.

15. State of Hawaii Department of Planning and Economic Development (January 1976), p. 12.

16. Mathematica, Inc. (1970), p. 14.

17. Keir (February 23, 1973), pp. A1 and A11.

18. See, for example, Gray (1974), pp. 386–397; Tisdell (1983), pp. 3–20; and Mak (2004), Chapter 11.

19. See, for example, Gade and Adkins (1990), pp. 39–52.

20. Ebel, ed. (1990), chapter 6.

21. Market Trends Pacific Inc. (2000), p. 4.

22. Ebel and Mak (1974), pp. 13–14.

23. Mak and Nishimura (1979), pp. 2–6.

24. U.S. Advisory Commission on Intergovernmental Relations (1994); Loyacono and Mackey (1991), pp. 21–24.

25. Mak (1988), pp. 10–15.

26. Fujii, Khaled, and Mak (1985), pp. 169–178.

27. Mak (1993).

28. Bonham et al. (1992), pp. 433–442.

29. U.S. Advisory Commission on Intergovernmental Relations, vol. 2 (1989), pp. 139–314.

30. State of Hawaii Department of Planning and Economic Development (1978).

31. Kalapa (1992a), pp. 41–47.

32. State of Hawaii Tax Review Commission (1996), Appendix B-5 and B-6.

33. For further details about the ERTF, see Grandy (2002), chapter 6.

34. Arakawa (January 3, 2007). Currently, revenues in excess of $33 million are deposited into the State General Fund. In FY 2007, the State is expecting to collect $231.7 million from the TAT, and $7 million of that would go into the General Fund.

35. Mak (2004), pp. 146–148, or at http://traveltax.msu.edu/barometer/index
.htm. The WTTC Tax Barometer was discontinued after 2002.

36. Mathematica, Inc. (1970), p. 16.

37. Grandy (2002), p. 54.

38. *Honolulu Advertiser* (2004), "The 2004 Hawaii State Legislature: Where
Legislators Stand on the Issues" (January 18).

39. The PSC is in lieu of the 4 percent general excise tax levied on nearly all
final sales.

40. Testimony of American Hawaii Cruises, United States Lines, and American Classic Voyages (February 25, 2000), p. 2.

41. Refundable tax credits "are any qualified amounts of credit regardless of
tax liability." In other words, the State would send a refund check to the qualifying hotel for renovation expenses even if the hotel did not otherwise have a tax
liability.

42. Nonrefundable credits "may be claimed against the taxpayer's net income
tax liability for the taxable year." In most cases, excess credits—above the claim-
ant's income tax liability—may be claimed against the taxpayer's future income
tax liability until the qualifying credits are exhausted.

43. Editorial (May 5, 2003), p. A8.

44. The Tax Department estimated that SB1410 would generate claims of $32.9
million per year. Hao (August 24, 2003), p. F2.

45. State of Hawaii Department of Planning and Economic Development, vol.
1 (1972), pp. 202–203.

46. Gomes (January 23, 2005), p. F1.

47. Hitch (1992), p. 197.

48. *Ko Olina Resort, Honolulu, Hawaii* (2003), a brochure distributed by the
company.

49. The bill, however, did not include a provision that would give employment
preference to residents from that area.

50. Lynch (June 26, 2002). The veto triggered a lawsuit against Governor Cayetano by Leeward Coast senator Colleen Hanabusa, who had introduced the Ko
Olina bill.

51. Ibid.

52. Gomes (January 18, 2007).

53. Bird (1992), p. 1155.

54. Grandy (2002), p. 94.

55. Brunori (2001) and Buss (2001).

56. Zee, Stotsky, and Ley (2002); see also Buss (2001).

57. The goods must be depreciable and have a useful economic life of at least
three years.

58. McGuckin and Stiroh (2002), pp. 42–59.

59. Grandy (2002).

60. Takeuchi (1998), p. 26.

61. Ibid., p. 87.

62. Ibid.

63. Rosen (1998), p. 21.

64. Ibid.

65. City and County of Honolulu Planning Department (February 1996), pp. 2–3.

66. Pang (April 2, 1996).

67. Mr. Joe Toy, principal of Hospitality Advisors, LLC (Honolulu), personal conversation with author.

68. Yamanouchi (February 1, 2004), pp. F1 and F2; Yamanouchi (March 10, 2003), pp. C1 and C2; Gomes (November 2, 2003), pp. F1 and F6.

69. Natarajan (January 21, 2005), pp. 1 and 5.

70. Shapiro and Brannon (January 30, 2004), pp. A1 and A12; see also Sunderland (February 14, 2007), pp. 34 and 41; and Seiden (2006).

71. Gonser (December 15, 2004), pp. B1 and B10.

72. Gonser (January 19, 2004), pp. A1 and A5.

73. Yamanouchi (February 1, 2004), p. F2; see also Hao (August 23, 2003), p. F2.

74. Letter from Kurt Kawafuchi, director of taxation, to Representative Dwight Takamine, chair, House Finance Committee, dated April 28, 2003.

75. Ibid., p. 2.

76. Grandy (2002), p. 89.

77. Laney (2004), pp. 62–64.

78. Toy (April 2003), pp. 36–40.

79. Grandy (2002), p. 89.

80. Market Trends Pacific/John M. Knox & Associates (2003), p. 44. It is unclear what accounts for the big turnabout in sentiments.

References

American Hawaii Cruises, United States Lines, and American Classic Voyages. 2000. *Testimony before the House Committee on Finance H.B. 2212, H.D. 1, Relating to Harbors.* Honolulu (February 25).

Arakawa, Linda. 2007. "Tourism Rescue Fund Proposed." *Honolulu Advertiser,* January 3: A1–A2.

Bird, Richard. 1992. "Taxing Tourism in Developing Countries." *World Development* 20(8): 1145–1158.

Bonham, Carl, Eric Im, Edwin Fujii, and James Mak. 1992. "The Impact of the Hotel Room Tax: An Interrupted Time Series Analysis." *National Tax Journal* 45(4): 433–442.

Brunori, David. 2001. *State Tax Policy.* Washington, D.C.: Urban Institute Press.

Buss, Terry F. 2001. "The Effect of State Tax Incentives on Economic Growth and Firm Location Decisions: An Overview of the Literature." *Economic Development Quarterly* 15(1): 90–105.

City and County of Honolulu Planning Department. 1996. *Waikiki Planning & Program Guide*. Honolulu (February).

Ebel, Robert, ed. 1990. *A Fiscal Agenda for Nevada*. Reno: University of Nevada Press.

Ebel, Robert, and James Mak. 1974. *Current Issues in Hawaii's Economy*. Honolulu: Crossroads Press.

Editorial. 2003. "Wean Hotel Industry from State Tax Credits." *Honolulu Advertiser*, May 5: 8.

Fujii, Edwin, Mohammed Khaled, and James Mak. 1985. "The Exportability of Hotel Occupancy and Other Tourist Taxes." *National Tax Journal* 38(2): 169–178.

Gade, Mary, and Lee C. Adkins. 1990. "Tax Exporting and State Revenue Structures." *National Tax Journal* 43 (March): 39–52.

Gomes, Andrew. 2003. "From Hotels to Condos." *Honolulu Advertiser*, November 2: F1 and F6.

———. 2005. "Is 2005 Ko Olina's Big Year?" *Honolulu Advertiser*, January 23: F1–F2.

———. 2007. "Ko Olina Says It Doesn't Need Aquarium after All." *Honolulu Advertiser*, January 18: A1 and A3.

Gonser, James. 2004. "State Will Replenish Sand at Waikiki." *Honolulu Advertiser*, January 19: A1 and A5.

———. 2004. "Waikiki Beautification Complete." *Honolulu Advertiser*, December 15: B1 and B10.

Grandy, Christopher. 2002. *Hawaii Becalmed: Economic Lessons of the 1990s*. Honolulu: University of Hawaii Press.

Gray, H. Peter. 1974. "Towards an Economic Analysis of Tourism Policy." *Social and Economic Studies* 23(3): 386–397.

Hao, Sean. 2003. "For Waikiki, Not the Best of Times." *Honolulu Advertiser*, August 23: F2.

Hitch, Thomas Kemper. 1992. *Islands in Transition: The Past, Present, & Future of Hawaii's Economy*. Honolulu: First Hawaiian Bank.

Honolulu Advertiser. 2004. "The 2004 Hawaii State Legislature: Where Legislators Stand on the Issues." January 18, at the.honoluluadvertiser.com (last accessed on January 21, 2004).

Kalapa, Lowell. 1992a. "Do Neighbor Islanders Get Their Fair Share of Benefits from the State?" In Randall W. Roth, ed., *The Price of Paradise: Lucky We Live Hawaii?* (Honolulu: Mutual Publishing): 41–44.

———. 1992b. "Why Is It That the State Seems to 'Bully' the Counties?" In Randall W. Roth, ed., *The Price of Paradise: Lucky We Live Hawaii?* (Honolulu: Mutual Publishing): 47–51.

Kawafuchi, Kurt. 2003. Letter from Director of Taxation to Representative Dwight Takamine, Chair, House Finance Committee (April 28).

Keir, Gerry. 1973. "Burns Would Veto Room Bill." *Honolulu Advertiser,* February 23: A1 and A11.

———. 1973. "Burns, Fasi Not So Divided." *Honolulu Advertiser,* February 24: A1 and A4.

Ko Olina Resort, Honolulu, Hawaii. 2003. (Developer's brochure.)

Laney, Leroy. 2004. "Hawaii's Economy to Stay Healthy in 2004." *CP 2004:* 62–64.

Loyacono, Laura, and Scott Mackey. 1991. "The Taxidental Tourist." *State Legislatures* (October): 21–24.

Lynch, Russ. 2002. "Ko Olina Plans Not Dead, Backers Say." Starbulletin.com, June 26.

Mak, James. 1988. "Taxing Hotel Room Rentals in the U.S." *Journal of Travel Research* 27(1): 10–15.

———. 1993. "The Economics of the Convention Center." Presented to the Hawaii Association of Public Accountants Annual Conference. Honolulu (June 23).

———. 2004. *Tourism and the Economy: Understanding the Economics of Tourism.* Honolulu: University of Hawaii Press.

Mak, James, and Edward Nishimura. 1979. "The Economics of a Hotel Room Tax." *Journal of Travel Research* 17(4): 2–6.

Market Trends Pacific. 2000. *North America Bulletin.* Honolulu (May).

Market Trends Pacific and John M. Knox & Associates. 2003. *2002 Survey of Resident Sentiments on Tourism in Hawaii.* Honolulu: Hawaii Tourism Authority (April).

Mathematica, Inc. 1970. *The Visitor Industry and Hawaii's Economy: A Cost-Benefit Analysis.* Princeton, NJ: Mathematica, Inc.

McGuckin, Robert H., and Kevin J. Stiroh. 2002. "Computers and Productivity: Are Aggregation Effects Important?" *Economic Inquiry* 20(1): 42–59.

Meller, Norman. 1992. "Policy Control: Institutionalized Centralization in the Fiftieth State." In Zachary A. Smith and Richard C. Pratt, eds., *Politics and Public Policy in Hawaii* (Albany: State University of New York Press): 13–26.

Miklius, Walter, James E. T. Moncur, and PingSun Leung. 1989. "Distribution of State and Local Tax Burden by Income Class." In *State of Hawaii Tax Review Commission Working Papers and Consultant Studies,* vol. 2: 7–19.

Natarajan, Prabha. 2005. "Waikiki Hotels Going from Tired to Trendy." *Pacific Business News,* January 21: 1 and 5.

Rosen, Mark J. 1998. *Waikiki Developments: Streamlining the Regulatory Process.* Report No. 4, State of Hawaii Legislative Reference Bureau (December).

Seiden, Allan. 2006. "Hawaii Renovates." Waikiki Special Report. *Travel Weekly,* November, at http://www.travelweekly.com/Multimedia/ waikiki20061113/p03.html.

Shapiro, Treena, and Johnny Brannon. 2004. "Mayor Won't Rule Out Tax Hike." *Honolulu Advertiser,* January 30: A1 and A12.

State of Hawaii Department of Planning and Economic Development (DPED). 1972. *Tourism in Hawaii: Tourism Impact Plan,* vol. 1. Honolulu: DPED.

———. 1976. *What Hawaii's People Think of the Visitor Industry: Results of a Public-Opinion Poll Taken October 5–15, 1975.* Honolulu: DPED (January).

———. 1978. *State Tourism Study: Public Revenue-Cost Analysis.* Honolulu: DPED.

State of Hawaii Department of Taxation. 2003. *Annual Report 2002–2003.* Honolulu.

State of Hawaii Tax Review Commission. 1989. *Report of the Tax Review Commission.* Honolulu (December 1).

———. 1996. *Report of the 1995–1997 Tax Review Commission.* Honolulu (December 16).

Sunderland, Susan K. 2007. "The Making of the New Waikiki." *Midweek,* February 14: 34 and 41.

Takeuchi, Floyd. 1998. "Tough Talk." *Hawaii Business* (February): 24–26.

Tisdell, Clem A. 1983. "Public Finance and the Appropriation of Gains from International Tourists: Some Theory with ASEAN and Australian Illustrations." *Singapore Economic Review* 28: 3–20.

Toy, Joseph. 2003. "From Renovations to Revenues." *Host* (April): 36–40.

U.S. Advisory Commission on Intergovernmental Relations (ACIR). 1989. "Intergovernmental Fiscal Relations in Hawaii." In *State of Hawaii Tax Review Commission Working Papers and Consultant Studies,* vol. 2: 139–314.

Yamanouchi, Kelly. 2004. "Hotel—or Condo?" *Honolulu Advertiser,* February 1: F1 and F2.

———. 2004. "Oahu Sees Drop in Hotel Rooms." *Honolulu Advertiser,* March 10: C1 and C2.

Zee, Howell, Janet Stotsky, and Eduardo Ley. 2002. "Tax Incentives for Business Investment: A Primer for Policymakers in Developing Countries." *World Development* 30(9): 1497–1516.

Chapter Five

Tourism Promotion, the Hawaii Convention Center, and the Hawaii Tourism Authority

This chapter examines the promotion of tourism in Hawaii, the development of a convention center, and the role of the Hawaii Tourism Authority.

Tourism Promotion

With few exceptions, governments all over the world use public funds to promote tourist travel to their destinations. In sharp contrast, the famous Florida orange juice television commercials are paid for by industry self-assessment of the state's citrus growers and not by money from the State treasury. Using public money to pay for tourism promotion is not always popular among voters. In 1993, voters in Colorado closed the State Tourism Board by refusing to fund it. In 1995, the California Legislature passed SB156, the California Tourism Marketing Act, directing the tourist industry to come up with a formula to self-assess the state's travel companies to fund tourism promotion. The State promised to appropriate about $7.5 million a year to the Division of Tourism for promotion, but the industry was expected to raise at least $25 million per year from its own assessments.[1] In 1996, Congress also discontinued funding for tourism promotion to attract foreign visitors to the United States. With few exceptions, government funding of destination tourism promotion has become so widespread that the tourist industry takes it for granted that promoting tourism—or at least paying for it—is the responsibility of the government and not the industry.

It did not begin that way in Hawaii. The first organization to promote tourism to Hawaii—the Hawaii Promotion Committee (HPC)—was founded by the Honolulu Chamber of Commerce on August 1, 1903.[2] The Territorial Legislature appropriated $15,000 to match the $15,000 raised from private sources. Article IV, Section 12 of the By-Laws of the Honolulu Chamber of Commerce states, "The Hawaii Promotion Committee shall advertise the attractions of the Territory of Hawaii, promote tourist travel, disseminate literature and, by correspondence with tourist agencies, steamship and railroad companies, endeavor to enlist their aid and assistance in directing travelers and tourists to the Territory."

In 1919 the name of the Hawaii Promotion Committee was changed to the Hawaii Tourist Bureau, to Hawaii Visitors Bureau (HVB) in 1945, and finally to Hawaii Visitors and Convention Bureau (HVCB) after the Hawaii Convention Center was built in late 1997 and the bureau was given the contract to promote it. In 1959, the HVB was separated from the Chamber of Commerce and reorganized as a nonprofit corporation. A major reason for the separation was that organizers felt the new State government would be less reluctant to help fund a quasi-public entity than an obvious business organization. Over the years, the predecessors of HVB came to rely increasingly on government appropriations. In 1918, the Territorial Legislature accounted for 22 percent of the HPC's annual budget, and during the 1920s the government's share rose to over 35 percent of the budget. The Territorial government's share exceeded 50 percent only twice in the first forty years. In 1959, State government appropriations to the HVB comprised 50.8 percent of its budget, and private contributions (described as "membership dues") accounted for the remaining 49.2 percent. State appropriations to the HVB rose from $442,000 in 1959 to $26.05 million in 1994. By the early 1990s, private contributions to the HVB budget comprised less than 10 percent of its annual budget (Fig. 5-1). Private contributions to the HVB totaled only $2 million annually, and that modest amount, considering that tourism was already a $10 billion business, was collected at great expense— around $500,000.[3] More recently, private contributions to the HVCB have averaged about $2.5 million per year from approximately 3,600 members, while it has received about $48 million of "taxpayer money" generated from the hotel room tax.[4]

Economists who study voluntary membership trade associations like the HVCB would have predicted that there was never any hope that the HVCB could possibly raise an adequate amount of money to fund tourism promotion through voluntary contributions alone. Why would any travel business want to make a voluntary contribution to promote Hawaii travel other than

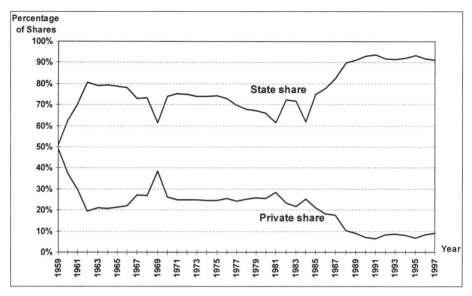

Fig. 5-1. State government and private contributions to
the Hawaii Visitors Bureau annual budgets.
Source: Grandy (2002), p. 53.

to be (or be seen as) a "good citizen"? If someone else foots the bill, the
business that did not pay could still benefit from (hopefully) the increased
numbers of tourists enticed by promotion to visit Hawaii. One business can
free ride on other businesses' contributions, but if all the businesses choose
to be free riders, there would not be enough money available to promote
travel in the manner that all of them want.

To illustrate the seriousness of the problem, around 1990 the HVB promoted membership in the organization by pushing the theme of "community responsibility" or "fair share." The annual membership fee was based
on a sliding scale depending on the size of the business and whether or
not it was a "tourist-oriented" business. The general guideline for annual
membership dues for tourist-oriented businesses was 0.1 percent of gross
receipts, with a minimum of $500; for nontourist businesses, the suggested
annual membership fee was 0.01 percent of gross receipts, with a minimum of $300. With twenty-eight thousand businesses in Hawaii (1989), if
every business paid the $300 minimum, the total amount collected would
have been six times the amount actually collected by the HVB. Moreover,

because membership was voluntary, each year around 10 to 15 percent of the HVB members failed to renew their memberships.[5] In some years, the nonrenewal rate was much higher.[6] Indeed, some of the largest travel companies in Hawaii didn't give a dime to the HVB. One study found that in 1985, 78 percent of the airlines, 66 percent of the hotels, 32 percent of the lending institutions, 24 percent of the restaurants, and only 4 percent of the retail establishments in the state belonged to the HVB.[7]

The main reason for the low contribution rates is that the incentive structure in most voluntary membership organizations encourages free riding. Thus, organizations like the HVCB are chronically plagued by shortage of money. By contrast, in funding agricultural promotion such as Florida orange juice, free riding is minimized because of legislation enabling their associations to levy assessments on every grower in the industry. The money collected belongs to the industry and not to the State treasury.

The agricultural promotion funding model does not work very well when it is applied to tourism. It is easy to spot who is a citrus grower in Florida when you want to assess that business to help pay for the orange juice television ads; it is not so easy to identify who is in the tourist business or how assessments should be set among restaurants, hotels, ground transportation companies, and so on. Not surprisingly, California's attempt to adopt the Florida orange juice funding model to pay for tourism promotion has not been very successful. California expected the travel industry to raise at least $25 million via self-assessment, but in 2003 it raised only $6.8 million.

The only effective way to mitigate free riding and raise enough money to pay for destination promotion is to tax the industry and return the proceeds to them (minus a collection fee, of course). That is exactly what the District of Columbia Convention and Visitors Association (DC-CVA) did in the early 1980s; it went to the City Council and asked it to impose a daily flat tax on all occupied hotel rooms and allocate the revenues to the DC-CVA for tourism promotion.[8] But in most destinations, money for tourism promotion comes from the general fund as a direct taxpayer subsidy.

Act 300 of Hawaii Session Law 1980 stipulated that $500,000 in supplementary funds would be allocated to the HVB in FY 1981 only after the bureau agreed to become less dependent on State funding, and that after 1984, the State's share would not exceed 50 percent of its annual budget.[9] Act 300 was destined to fail. Rather than falling, the State's contribution to tourism promotion from the General Fund continued to rise. With the enactment of the 5 percent hotel room tax in 1986, any hope of revenue matching evaporated. Nonetheless, the money for the HVB each year still had to be secured by hard lobbying at the Legislature.

That changed with the passage of Act 156 in 1997. This act established the Hawaii Tourism Authority (HTA), with dedicated funding from the hotel room tax; tourism promotion received a percentage of the room tax receipts administered by the HTA. There is still a cap placed on the amount available for tourism promotion in any given year. The industry did not want a cap, but it remains. There is, however, a provision to allow additional money to be spent from a reserve fund in the event of an emergency, such as right after the September 11 terrorist attacks. While the industry did not get all that it wanted, it got most of what it wanted—a big increase in the tourism promotion budget from a dedicated source of funding. Clearly, using a dedicated tax levied on the industry to fund tourism promotion is preferable to the old scheme of annual lobbying for subsidies from the State treasury.[10]

Unlike the District of Columbia, the money raised in Hawaii from the room tax that goes toward tourism promotion is considered the State's (i.e., taxpayers') money—not the industry's—to do with as it pleases. The State can still call the shots on how the money is spent, which opens the door to continued government interference. In 2003, Lingle's office and the HVCB agreed to pay the travel costs of a reporter and cameraman from KITV Television accompanying her on a promotional visit to Japan. The ensuing public outcry over the use of public funds to subsidize KITV persuaded the television station to refund the travel money.[11]

One can only speculate on what might have happened if the visitor industry had gone to the Legislature first to ask for a dedicated room tax to fund tourism promotion rather than having the funding proposal come from Governor Cayetano's Economic Revitalization Task Force. Perhaps it would not have made any difference. As long as the money comes from a tax, that money may always be considered "public funds." As it turned out, HVCB's spending of "taxpayer money" is constantly second-guessed by the media, lawmakers, and the public.[12] In 2004, the bureau returned over $20,000 to the HTA for inappropriate expenditures identified in a highly critical 2003 State audit.[13]

The media hype following the State audit—which revealed that the bureau president, who was already under the gun at the Legislature, had spent about $2,000 on such things as parking fines and in–hotel room movies —finally prompted the generally well-regarded president to resign. The usually critical Rees wrote in his column, "The HVCB lost a strong leader when Vericella resigned."[14]

The creation of the HTA also led to HVCB's losing its monopoly in marketing destination Hawaii tourism around the world. While the HVCB retained contracts to market leisure travel to North America and to corporate meetings and incentive travel (and for support of its Neighbor Island chapters) worth $24.2 million, beginning in 2004 the HTA distributed the rest of its former marketing responsibilities among four other firms. The HVCB had become just another vendor. Until then, a legislative budget provision required the Department of Business, Economic Development and Tourism (DBEDT) to give the money to HVCB; DBEDT had no other option. Thus, the one hundred-year marriage between the State and the HVCB finally came to an end.[15] With the creation of the HTA to oversee all aspects of tourism in Hawaii, their breakup was probably inevitable as the HTA was expected to hold open competition for its marketing business. The real surprise was that the exclusive arrangement between the HVCB and the State lasted so long. Under the new regime, HTA selected Dentsu—Japan's largest advertising agency—to market to Japan ($7.3 million), Marketing Garden to market to the rest of Asia ($950,400), the Magnum Group for Europe ($768,000), and the Walshe Group for Oceania ($600,000).[16] The Legislature had earlier (2002) passed legislation taking away the responsibility for marketing the convention center from the HVCB and assigned it to the center's operator, SMG. The Legislature wanted the same organization that managed the center to market it as well.

To be sure, as life is now more complicated, there remained a few unanswered questions about the change. "One of them," noted Governor Lingle, "was how do we maintain Hawaii branding if you split it up into five different organizations. We worked for 100 years to create the image of Hawaii that we want, that conjures up certain images in people's minds. How do you maintain that consistency of image now that you've broken this up into five contracts?"[17]

But experts in "branding" work argue that it really does not matter who delivers the message or what tactical messages are sent; that should not necessarily change the brand. Gloria Garvey and Brook Gramann, principals of the Brand Strategy Group in Honolulu, write about the Hawaii "brand" as follows:[18]

A brand is not a logo or a name. It is not advertising or public relations. It is not even a product or a place. A brand is a promise that you make to your customer. The other side of that coin is the experience that your customer has of you. If they don't match, then you are in trouble.

Brand promises are intangible, they meet needs and solve problems, they are emotionally based and, most importantly, they belong to your customers.

This true definition of a brand is especially fitting in Hawaii's case. Hawaii is a place the whole world knows and loves. A place of staggering beauty and extraordinary gentleness. A place that offers rest and restoration. A place of unique heritage and culture. A place of Aloha. A place that is American, and yet it is not.

This is what most people believe about Hawaii, and this is Hawaii's brand promise. And Hawaii certainly belongs to the people who love her.

The proof of Hawaii's strong brand is that those who experience it come back again and again. . . .

While advertising agencies might craft different messages about Hawaii . . . they should never be in control of Hawaii's brand.

Garvey and Gramann note that when there was no HTA, the Hawaii Visitors Bureau was the keeper of the Hawaii brand. The question now is, Who is responsible for communicating Hawaii's brand? For now, it appears that the torch has been passed from the HVCB to the Hawaii Tourism Authority.

The breakup of the promotional budget raises other questions that remain to be answered. How much more costly will it be for the HTA to monitor five contracts instead of one? How do you structure contracts with organizations when some of them are for-profit firms and others are not-for-profit organizations?[19]

HVCB's Performance

Tom Hamilton once said that the HVCB did two things well: research and marketing tourism.[20]

RESEARCH

As an organization whose primary mission is to sell a dream, the importance of HVCB as a tourism research organization was often overlooked. However, HVCB's research—or more accurately, data collection and generation—made a huge contribution to Hawaii.

Not many years after the founding of the Hawaii Promotion Committee (around 1911), it began compiling first-class ship passenger statistics. Until the data collection program was transferred to the Department of Business, Economic Development and Tourism in 1998 under the directive of Act 156, the HVB was noted for producing some of the best tourism statistics in the world. The 1973 Temporary Visitor Industry Council observed that one of the reasons why Hawaii's tourism statistics were regarded as being so good was because everyone else's was so bad.[21] But that was still early in the evolution of HVB's research program; tourism research at the bureau would become increasingly sophisticated and more comprehensive in coverage.

To be sure, there are definite advantages to being an island destination when it comes to counting visitor arrivals, since just about everyone coming to Hawaii has to come on a commercial ship or plane; passenger statistics are tabulated by the carriers and, in the case of foreign visitors, also by the U.S. Immigration and Naturalization Service. Even if not everyone leaving a ship or a plane is a tourist, the total number of passengers provides a reliable control count of the potential number of visitors. A supplemental survey of disembarking passengers to ascertain the typical proportion of visitors, transit passengers, returning residents, and immigrants allowed the bureau to identify how many of the disembarking passengers are tourists.[22] By comparison, some destinations have to estimate their visitor arrivals by tabulating vehicle counts on major highways. Las Vegas uses hotel occupancy data to estimate its visitor count. One small community valiantly tries to estimate the number of tourists by counting the number of times toilets are flushed by measuring pressure changes in the community's water system. Having a geographic advantage is not enough to produce quality statistics, however; it was still necessary for the bureau to make a commitment to fund a quality research program. Airlines must also agree to provide data on disembarking passengers, access to their customers, and even have their own staff hand out and collect surveys on their planes. Hotels must agree to distribute diaries to selected guests so they can keep a running tally of their daily spending. A lot of people and businesses cooperate to make it work.

Throughout its history, the bureau made a conscientious effort to produce the highest quality tourism statistics its shoestring research budgets would allow. Beginning in 1950, the HVB formed a Research Committee "to direct the collection, dissemination and improvement of visitor statistics." The Research Committee met regularly (several times) each year. The

members, except for the HVB staff, served pro bono and were drawn from
the diverse expertise available in the community. HVB's tourism data not
only supported the bureau's marketing program, it was an invaluable resource to the State and county governments in economic and tax revenue
forecasting and for planning purposes. The public benefits of HVB's research program spilled over beyond government work, as its massive data
resources were also shared with serious researchers, both in business and
in academia. To teach its largely small business members how to use its
data, the Research Committee occasionally conducted research workshops.
Table 5-1 provides a time line of HVCB's statistical output.

As the saying goes, "If it ain't broke, don't fix it." Why, then, was the
HVCB's research program transferred to the Department of Business, Economic Development and Tourism? To be sure, not everyone in the industry
was happy about the bureau's research program. Some complained that
the bureau did not collect data for their own (narrowly defined) industry.
Others griped if the sales trend for their company did not agree with the
overall trend indicated by the HVCB's industry-wide data, the HVCB data
must be wrong. Some people were concerned that the bureau might have
the incentive to collect and present data that would make itself look good.
However, the members of the Research Committee came from outside the
bureau and served pro bono. From my own experience serving on the Research Committee, I am convinced that the members were not corruptible.
Who could corrupt the legendary State statistician, Robert Schmitt? There
were concerns that research might be shortchanged at the bureau when
push came to shove in the competition for money between research and
marketing; when that time comes, some parts of the research program less
valuable to the bureau's marketing program but essential for State planning
might be sacrificed. For example, the HVCB may not value information
(contained in its passenger surveys) on the number of in-migrants arriving
from the U.S. mainland to Hawaii, but the State and the counties do. In
time, HVCB's tourism data became more valuable to the community than
they were to its own Marketing Department; indeed, at times the marketing
people in the bureau were criticized for not paying more attention to their
own research. Thus, many in the community felt that the State government
with its deeper pocket could do a better job in the long run by taking it over.
For the bureau, the transfer was a mixed blessing because creating original
data was a highly labor intensive activity requiring a lot of (though low-
paid) data entry and processing employees, which demanded some explanation whenever lawmakers—and even bureau administrators—questioned

Table 5-1. HVCB tourism research time line

1911 (about)	HPC begins compilation of first-class ship passenger statistics.
1915	Split passenger arrivals between those in transit and those coming specifically to Hawaii.
1920 (about)	HTB begins monthly and annual reports.
1921	Passenger statistics are refined to distinguish between tourists and residents.
1928	Initiates survey of visitor expenditures.
1950	The Basic Data Survey (BDS) and Visitor Reaction (i.e., Satisfaction)–Expenditure Survey programs begin.
1951	The use of eastbound and westbound visitor classifications begins.
1963	Begins official counts of convention visitors.
1964	Annual survey of *Visitor Plant Inventory* begins.
1974	The frequency of the *Visitor Expenditure Report* is increased to triennial and in 1986 becomes an annual publication.
1977	Survey of Japanese visitor expenditures begins.
1982	Definition of "visitor" changed to include nonresidents staying at least overnight in Hawaii.
1989	The Visitor Expenditure Survey includes an additional category for visitor spending related to meetings, conventions, and incentive travel (MCI). In addition, greater use of random sampling is initiated. Immigration and Naturalization Service reports become the basis for eastbound visitor counts and country of origin.
1990	A new basic data survey design is implemented that can be optically scanned. This enables all the passenger survey forms to be used instead of a fraction of them.
1998	Act 156 transfers the official state visitor statistics program to the Department of Business, Economic Development and Tourism (DBEDT).

Source: DBEDT (February 2001), p. 13; First Hawaiian Bank (June 1972), p. 1.

why the research department had so many employees. Finally stripped of its data collection responsibility, HVCB could conduct more market research—finding out what's going on in tourism in the rest of the world and identifying changes in market trends—things it didn't do enough of before the transfer.

MARKETING

Among its peers, the HVCB has received many awards for excellence in tourism marketing. In 2003, the Hospitality Sales & Marketing Association International awarded the HVCB four Adrian Awards, recognizing the bureau for excellence in travel advertising and public relations.[23] In 2004—for the fourteenth straight year—the *Successful Meetings* magazine awarded the bureau a Pinnacle Award, one of the "most credible and prestigious symbols of excellence among meetings planners and hoteliers."[24] In the same year, HVCB received its third straight Award of Excellence from *Corporate & Incentive Travel* magazine.[25]

Summarizing his observations from an inspection trip to several tourist destinations in Central and South America and the Caribbean as a member of a high-ranking Hawaii delegation in 1975, Tom Hamilton wrote, "There is no doubt that Hawaii's marketing program is a great deal more efficient than any of those areas. HVB spends a great deal less per visitor."[26] However, another person looking at the same numbers might come up with a totally different interpretation—that is, Hawaii is not spending enough money on tourism promotion.[27]

Hawaii received a lot of free publicity until the early 1960s through its exposure in literature, World War II, and (especially) statehood, but that could not go on indefinitely. Eventually, Hawaii had to pay for advertising and promoting its tourist attractions. How much money should be spent on promotion and how effectively the monies are being spent remain difficult questions to answer once we leave the abstract realm of economic theory.[28]

One rule of thumb often used to determine promotion budgets is that you need to spend about as much money as your closest competitors.[29] This is tourism's corollary to a military arms race. As part of its strategic tourism plan development, the Hawaii Tourism Authority commissioned a study of Hawaii's competitor destinations, and the following is what Hawaii's closest competitors spent on destination promotion in 1998 and the number of visitor arrivals (in 1997):[30]

California: $11.7 million	46,125,100 arrivals
Florida: $23 million	52,294,879
Las Vegas: $78 million	30,464,635
Mexico: $40.2 million	19,351,027
Caribbean: $160.4 million	15,881,400 (land based)
Australia: $81.8 million	4,317,900
Thailand: $66.6 million (1997)	7,293,957
Guam: $14 million	1,381,513
Fiji: $5 million	359,441
Bali: $9.5 million	1,230,316
Cruise lines: $400 million (1997)	5,051,000 passengers

Looking at these comparative numbers, it is difficult to advise whether Hawaii should have spent more than the $28 million it spent in FY 1998 (6,761,135 arrivals in CY 1997). In the following year, Hawaii's promotional budget more than doubled to $60 million. The Travel Industry Association (TIA) 2004–2005 survey of U.S. states and territories reported that Hawaii's budget of $69 million was the highest promotional budget, $21 million more than the next biggest spender, Illinois.[31]

An alternative rule of thumb employed by many businesses is to budget a fixed percentage of gross revenues on promotion. A dedicated hotel room tax based on a fixed percentage of the rental price of an occupied room complies (approximately) with that rule. But neither of the two rules informs us whether the money spent at the margin on promotion actually induced tourist visits in sufficient numbers to justify the expense.

Since it is the public's money that is being spent in most cases, the public everywhere is increasingly demanding that government tourist bureaus supply hard evidence that their money is well spent.[32] First, the money should be spent on things that were intended, and second, the money spent persuaded more tourists to come than would have otherwise.[33] The 1987 State of Hawaii legislative auditor's report criticized the HVB for failure to conduct follow-up studies to measure the effectiveness of its promotional expenditures.[34]

HVCB is not alone in its failure to verify substantive outcomes. Rarely are rigorous studies done to measure the quantitative effects of promotional expenditures on what really matters to taxpayers: How much additional sales did they generate? When evidence is supplied, they usually consist of "conversion studies" (e.g., how many coupons are returned from a magazine insert), the number of "hits" on the advertiser's Web site, the estimated number of "impressions" (i.e., how many times a message or an image had the potential to reach consumers from newspapers, television, and magazines), and so on, but not how many additional sales were made. For example, in 2003 HVCB organized Governor Lingle's promotional mission to Japan—a nation of 127 million people—which purportedly produced "136 million impressions worth more than $759,000 in media exposure for Hawaii."[35] The trip cost the HVCB $231,000. Lingle herself candidly admitted that she was more interested in how many additional Japanese visitors were persuaded to visit Hawaii in the months following her visit rather than how many Japanese and the number of times each one of them might have been exposed to the news of her visit. The *Honolulu Advertiser* acknowledged that trying to measure the real impact of her visit "is like corralling cats."[36] The Hawaii Tourism Authority's *Hawaii Marketing Effectiveness Study*, prepared by its consultant, *tnsintersearch*, has an impressive title but contains no estimate on the impact of promotional expenditures on visitor arrivals or spending.[37]

Relationship between Promotion and Visitor Arrivals

Figures 5-2 and 5-3 illustrate the difficulty of measuring the impact of promotion spending on tourist arrivals. Figure 5-2 shows Hawaii's promotional budgets between 1997 and 2005 and Figure 5-3 shows the corresponding visitor arrivals. Did the sharp increase in the tourism budgets after 1999 increase the number of visitors to Hawaii? It is difficult to say, because there are factors—such as the state of economic conditions in the United States and Japan, the yen/dollar exchange rate, the Asian financial crisis in 1997 and 1998, 9/11, and so on—besides promotional spending that may have influenced people's decisions to travel for leisure.

Without hard evidence on the effectiveness of marketing, everyone substitutes opinion for analysis. Not surprisingly, the HVCB and the HTA have caught a lot of criticism for perceived poor marketing decisions.[38] And the heat is not about to go away soon. In marketing, just about everyone can have an opinion about what works and what does not.

To its credit, in FY 1995 the HVB commissioned Longwood International, a Canadian research firm, to conduct a careful study of the effectiveness of its advertising campaigns on the U.S. mainland and provide an estimate of the return on investment on its marketing expenditures.[39] Longwood selected a national sample of participants, showed them ads

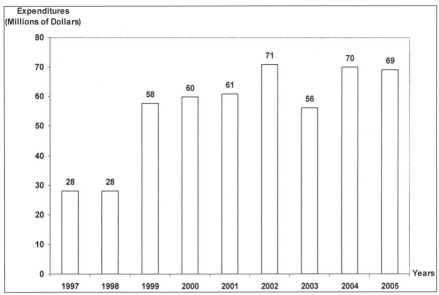

Fig. 5-2. Tourism promotion and Hawaii Tourism Authority expenditures: FY 1997–2005.
Source: Hawaii Tourism Authority (HTA), published in the *Honolulu Advertiser,* June 2, 2002,
for 1997 and 1998; HTA, *Annual Report to the Hawaii State Legislature,* October 31, 2006,
at www.hawaiitourismauthority.org. *Note:* Fiscal years are used for tourism promotion
budgets and calendar years are used for visitor arrivals.

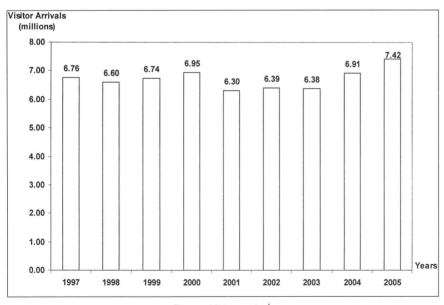

Fig. 5-3. Visitor arrivals.
Source: HTA, published in the *Honolulu Advertiser,* June 2, 2002, for 1997 and 1998; HTA, *Annual Report to the Hawaii State Legislature,* October 31, 2006, at www.hawaiitourismauthority.org. *Note:* Fiscal years are used for tourism promotion budgets and calendar years are used for visitor arrivals.

(including a couple of bogus ones to keep them honest), and tried to ascertain whether those who recognized these ads were more likely to actually visit Hawaii than another group of participants who had not seen the ads. This very complicated study demonstrated the impressive drawing power of HVB's ads. But complicated studies are not immune from flaws. For example, Longwood's study could have been tainted by self-selection in the responses, since those who were already interested in visiting Hawaii might have been looking for information and thus more likely to have seen the ads. And even if the study showed that the return on money spent was positive, it could not be used to justify allocating either more or less spending for tourism promotion.

Ultimately, as keeper of Hawaii's brand for a hundred years, it is safe to assume that the bureau's promotional activities must have shaped consumer expectations about the kinds of experiences they will likely get when they visit Hawaii. If the promise greatly exaggerates what is delivered, visitors will leave unhappy and won't come back. The evidence is that only a small percentage of Hawaii's visitors indicate that their Hawaii vacations did not meet their expectations (and some of those may have encountered a few rainy days that spoiled their vacations). Some 97 percent of visitors from the mainland United States, 93 percent from Japan, 98 percent from Canada, and 96 percent from Europe indicated that their vacations exceeded or met their expectations.[40] And nearly two-thirds of them had visited Hawaii before (4.43 trips on average).[41] By this measure of success, HVCB can claim to have done a very good job.

Is Hawaii spending too much or too little on tourism promotion? It is impossible to say without first performing careful benefit-cost analysis of Hawaii's promotional spending. Geoffrey Crouch finds that in international travel, demand is not very responsive to the promotional and marketing expenditures of national tourist offices.[42] Despite more than a doubling of the tourism promotion budget since 1999, the industry and Governor Lingle want to have even larger budgets on tourism promotion.[43] Hawaii is not India, which has to be promoted to be noticed. Hawaii Tourism Authority's *Hawaii Tourism Product Assessment* study (1999) notes that "Hawaii is the strongest brand in the world, with global recognition and far less negatives than other destinations."[44] While travel companies such as airlines have been trying hard to cut their distribution costs, tourism bureaus have little incentive to pare costs, perhaps because they are government-run and/ or -financed organizations. It is not likely that the budgets for tourism promotion (by anyone) will be falling any time soon.

The Hawaii Convention Center

The Hawaii Visitors Bureau was interested in attracting conventions to Hawaii as early as the 1960s. It began offering convention services in 1962 and in the next year began counting the number of convention visitors (23,334). But with tourism growing at 20 percent per year, there was no urgency to put the convention business high up on its priority marketing list. In February 1971, the bureau created its Convention Division and began soliciting convention business in a systematic way. The division set its first goal at half a million convention visitors within five years. In the same year, the bureau was granted full membership in the International Association of Convention Bureaus, a significant achievement since memberships were typically conferred on cities and not on tourist bureaus.[45] By the 1980s, tourism growth had slowed down dramatically. The double-digit annual rates of growth had become single digits. Visitor spending, adjusted for inflation, had been flat for about a decade. In the early 1980s, Hawaii was hosting nearly 90,000 convention visitors per year.[46] The Legislature felt that it was time to earnestly develop this market—the convention and meetings market.

The twelfth Legislature appropriated $50,000 to the Department of Planning and Economic Development (DPED) to conduct a feasibility study for a convention center in Honolulu, and the consulting firm of Pannel Kerr Forster (PKF) was contracted to do the study.[47] PKF noted that existing facilities in Honolulu were able to host meetings and conventions for groups with less than five thousand attendees but could not accommodate larger groups. It recommended that the State build a "mid-sized" convention center at an estimated construction cost of $170 million. PKF projected annual operating revenues of $3,383,000 (from 133,450 delegates and exhibitors per year) and annual operating expenses of $3,809,000, for a deficit of $426,000 per year (in 1985 dollars). At 10 percent interest, the annual debt service (over thirty years) on the construction loan would be $18 million.[48] To pay for the annual operating loss and debt service, PKF suggested that the State raise the excise tax on hotel room rentals (i.e., impose a hotel room tax) by 1.5 percent. Since the tax was expected to raise only $16 million per year, PKF recommended that the State impose the tax increase immediately so that it could accumulate a reserve to pay for future shortfalls. In response, the Legislature enacted a 5 percent hotel room tax in 1986.

In 1986, the visitor industry formed the nonprofit Hawaii Convention Park Council to lobby for the convention center. Two years later, the State created the Convention Center Authority to oversee the development and completion of a convention center.

While the State was moving ahead with crafting its proposal, the City and County of Honolulu had already issued a request for proposal to develop a private convention center at the former Aloha Motors site (the site of the current Hawaii Convention Center). In 1989, a private developer submitted its proposal, which included a convention center, hotel, two apartment condominium towers, an office building, and retail space. The City Council approved it in 1990, but the proposal fell through when the developer sold the land to another private party in 1993. The new owner, Indonesian businessman Sukamto Sia, put forth his own proposal of four hotels and a convention center that would be built and operated at no cost to the City in exchange for zoning variances that would allow higher density use of the site. Since the convention center was expected to be operated at a loss, the only way a private entrepreneur would build and operate it was if he got something in return—in this case, it was higher density development at what was already one of the most congested locations in Honolulu.[49] Clearly, it would not be a "free" convention center if density concessions had to be made. Others criticized the proposal because the convention center would not be "world class" and it would not have sufficient exhibition space.[50]

Once this proposal was rejected, the City was no longer a serious contender to develop a convention center. Without the power to levy its own hotel room tax or excise tax, the City could not possibly pay for a convention center and the expected annual operating deficits. Convention centers being built in the United States were being paid for largely by using hotel room tax revenues supplemented by excise/sales taxes.[51] Since the Hawaii Convention Center would also benefit the Neighbor Islands, as convention delegates would be encouraged to travel to the outer islands either before or after the meetings, the State was in a better position to compel the Neighbor Island visitor industries to help pay for a convention center in Honolulu by levying a statewide hotel room tax.

In a special session in 1993, the Legislature approved HB No. S7-93, which set in motion the State's plan to develop the Hawaii Convention Center, including the purchase of the former Aloha Motors site from its owner. The Legislature budgeted $350 million for the center—$200 million for construction and the rest for site acquisition. To pay for it, the Legislature raised the hotel room tax from 5 percent to 6 percent as of July 1, 1994. Since revenues from the 5 percent room tax had already been allocated to the counties, unless the State had undisclosed plans to take the money back, the 1 percent rate increase clearly wouldn't be enough to pay for the center, even though that possibility was never discussed publicly. Nordic/PCL was selected as the design/build team on August 31, 1994.

The Hawaii Convention Center (HCC) was completed in October 1997, on time and under budget—an extraordinary feat for a major government construction project. On June 30, 2000, the Convention Center Authority expired and the management of the convention center was turned over to the Hawaii Tourism Authority, and the HTA then contracted with the HVCB to market the convention center.[52]

Other than some complaints from neighborhood residents about excessive noise spilling over from the rooftop garden when it first opened in 1998, the HCC was widely praised as a beautiful structure with a "Hawaiian sense of place." The center was named "the most attractive convention center" in North America in a 2003 study of forty major convention centers by Gerard Murphy & Associates, a market research and consulting firm for the travel and meeting industry.[53] It boasts 1.1 million square feet of building space, a 200,000+ square-foot exhibition hall, nearly 150,000 square feet of total meeting space, a 35,000 square-foot ballroom, forty-seven meeting rooms plus two theaters with tiered seating, a 2.5-acre landscaped rooftop garden, and ten thousand hotel rooms nearby, among other desirable attributes.[54] Attendees wrote glowingly of their warm reception and exceptional experiences in Hawaii. The only problem was that not enough of them came. The number of bookings and attendees fell far short of expectations.

Most of Honolulu's disadvantages as a convention/meetings city have been known for a long time.[55] Honolulu is an expensive place to get to, and the great distance and the amount of travel time required between the U.S. mainland and Hawaii also pose a disadvantage. Additionally, Hawaii has never been able to shake the perception that attending a convention or corporate meeting in Honolulu is a "boondoggle"—unlike attending the same function in New York City. Indeed, in 2005 the national media severely criticized the National Association of Counties for holding its annual meeting in Honolulu.[56] The mayor of Detroit canceled his planned trip to attend a public pension conference in Honolulu in 2007 after he found out that Michigan television stations were planning to send crews to follow him.[57] The State had become a victim of its own too-successful marketing campaigns. After a hundred years of cultivating a leisure image, it has been difficult to convince people that Hawaii is also a good place to meet for business. Finally, just about every other midsized to large city in the United States was building or had plans to build a convention center or to expand an existing one. In 1970, U.S. convention centers provided 6.7 million square feet of total meeting space; by 1990, total square footage of meeting space had increased to 40 million square feet, and the figure increased to 50.7 million square feet by 1998 when the Hawaii Convention Center came on line, with projections of 11 million additional square feet to be completed by 2003.[58] Even as the amount of convention space was increasing, business and convention travel was declining: between 1998 and 2003, business and convention travel fell by more than 14 percent.[59] Competition was definitely getting stiffer. The boom in convention center construction across the nation was predicated on the assumption that creating more space would lead to more visitors. Build it and they will come! Feasibility studies performed by high-priced national accounting and economic consulting firms never concluded that a new convention center or expanding an existing center was unnecessary.[60] Convention centers became the largest tourist infrastructure construction movement during the last century.[61] Even if they didn't pay off in dollars and cents as predicted in the feasibility studies, they became the symbol of a modern, revitalizing city and a "feel good" public investment. John Tierney, op-ed columnist for the *New York Times*, likened urban politicians' obsession with convention centers, sports stadiums, aquariums, and museums to the Roman emperors before them, as having succumbed to the Circus Maximus syndrome.[62]

The 9/11 terrorist attacks in 2001 and the ensuing war against terrorism dealt tourism around the world a crippling blow; in the United States, business and convention/meetings travel were hurt more severely than leisure travel.[63] None of this was foreseen. For Hawaii, the total number of meetings, convention, and incentive (MCI) visitors (not just those who used the convention center) fell by nearly 160,000, from 574,916 to 416,236 (or 27.6 percent) between 2000 and 2002.[64] The number of offshore events held at the center fell from thirty-one in FY 2000 to twenty-eight in FY 2002 (delegate counts were not available before 2003).

The unexpectedly low bookings can also be blamed on the Convention Center Authority (CCA) for fostering unrealistic expectations of future convention attendance at the planning stage. To illustrate, the final version of the environmental impact statement (dated July 1995) expected the center to operate at 90 percent capacity by 2003 and host fifty-two events (each lasting about three days in duration) that would use the center approximately 156 days of the year.[65] The center would reach its operating capacity by 2004–2006, hosting sixty events per year, with an average attendance "projected" to range between 6,200 to 7,500 delegates and exhibitors per event. That would mean 372,000 to 450,000 delegates each year, minus 20,000 MCI visitors who might have come to Hawaii even without the center. Adding spouses and others would raise the total to 633,600 to 774,000 out-of-state people at capacity utilization. However, there was no supporting information to show how this projection was made. By comparison, in 1993, the International Association of Convention and Visitors Bureaus surveyed sixty-seven U.S. and six non–U.S. cities with questionnaire responses from more than seventeen thousand meetings delegates, associations, exhibitors, and exposition service contractors. In that year, the number of delegates attending international, national, and regional conventions averaged two thousand attendees per event. If it is reasonable to assume that Hawaii would be targeting that group for its business, the CCA's 6,200 to 7,500 delegates per event projection was much too high, an observation that was pointed out to CCA's consultant at the draft stage a couple of months before the final version of the EIS was issued.[66]

The CCA had projected thirty bookings for 1998; the actual number of bookings was fifteen.[67] In FY 2003, HCC had thirty-eight bookings (instead of the projected fifty-two) totaling 132,356 delegates, or an average of 3,483 delegates per event.[68] The HTA then (2003 Annual Report) scaled down its goals for fiscal years 2003–2008 to forty bookings and 122,500 delegates per year, or approximately three thousand delegates per event.[69] In the next year the number of bookings was scaled down again to thirty-four but retained the same number of delegates. Table 5-2 displays the latest available performance data and goals for the convention center.[70]

These numbers suggest that the convention center has exceeded its goals in most years since it was built. But the goals have changed drastically from those initially envisioned.

Cynics might conclude that the initial inflated attendance figures used by the CCA were intended to make the proposed convention center look financially more attractive in order to garner public support for the project. Another possible motive might be that a high average attendance figure would be less threatening to hotels and other existing meetings facilities that already were hosting smaller MCI groups and did not want to see them lured away. Indeed, HTA initially refused to allow local events to be held in the center, but it eventually relented after a public outcry.[71] Today the

Table 5-2. Hawaii Convention Center offshore events

Year	1998	1999	2000	2001	2002	2003	2004	2005	2006
Bookings:									
Goal	—	17	24	22	30	34	34	34	34
Final	19	17	31	22	28	40	39	46	37
Delegate count:									
Goal	—	—	—	—	—	122,500	122,500	122,500	122,500
Final	43,480	72,430	108,600	51,950	69,200	112,196	152,015	176,130	97,170

Source: Robbie Dingeman, "Who Will Fill These Seats?" *Honolulu Advertiser,* May 27, 2007, pp. F1–F2; data for 1998–2000 from the Hawaii Visitors and Convention Bureau; 2003–2006 from the Hawaii Tourism Authority. "Goals" are from the HTA, *2005 Annual Report to the State Legislature,* p. 14.

overwhelming majority of the bookings at the HCC are local events.[72] What is clear is that the difference in average attendance from over six thousand to three thousand delegates per event has huge implications for HCC's financial balance sheet. The Convention Center Authority didn't conduct sensitivity analyses to ascertain how the fiscal impacts might change if its "projections" were off the mark. Apparently the CCA wasn't too interested in getting the numbers right; its mandate was to get the convention center built.

Does HCC Pay Its Own Way?

Like other publicly owned and financed convention centers around the country, HCC was never expected to break even as a stand-alone facility.[73] It was intended as a loss leader. In FY 2003, rental income for the use of the $350 million facility came to only $1.3 million, of which $.516 million came from thirty-eight conventions and the rest from other community events:

Operating revenues	
Food and beverage	$5,128,604
Rental income	$1,309,563
Event revenue	$1,014,357
Other	$50,928
Total	$7,503,452
Expenses (excluding purchase of fixed assets)	$11,243,726
Net Loss	$3,740,274

Source: Hawaii Tourism Authority, *Report to the Twenty-Second Legislature, Regular Session of 2004, FY 02–03 and FY 03–04,* December 18, 2003.

The net operating loss totaled $3.7 million, excluding $215,579 for purchases of fixed assets. Moreover, the reported operating expenses do not include several million dollars of marketing expenses to promote corporate meetings, conventions, and incentive travel.[74] Including that as part of the operating expenses would raise the deficit to nearly $6 million. Then there is the annual debt service of $26.4 million.[75] It's obvious why no private entrepreneur would want to build it!

Supporters of the convention center argue that the case for having it must be made on the additional income, employment, and tax revenues that would be generated by convention-related spending in the state. Assuming an average attendance figure of three thousand delegates and exhibitors, the Department of Business, Economic Development and Tourism estimated that it would take seventy-one bookings per year for the State and local governments to break even, taking into account both the additional tax revenues that would be generated and the additional indirect public costs, such as road repair, police, fire protection, and so on to service more tourists. That's eleven bookings above its estimated operating capacity. At forty bookings per year—HTA's goal for FY 2004 and beyond —the estimated annual loss to the government treasuries would be $16 million in 1999 dollars.[76] The "break-even" level, however, is extremely sensitive to assumptions about the number of delegates per event. For example, the break-even point could be reached at thirty-seven events if the average attendance rose to five thousand delegates or at 222 events (an unlikely situation) if average attendance fell to fifteen hundred.[77] What is apparent is that the convention center will not likely be breaking even soon for the State treasury, even after taking into account the tax revenues that additional convention-related induced spending would generate in the economy.

Nonetheless, DBEDT argues that the Hawaii Convention Center is still a good investment for the economy as a whole because spending by the attendees will generate millions of dollars in additional household income in Hawaii each year. Indeed, DBEDT claims that just eight conventions with an average attendance of three thousand delegates and exhibitors will generate enough additional income to offset the losses to the government treasury. At five thousand delegates, the center needs only four bookings per year to offset the public sector red ink.[78] This argument, however, is not widely accepted by economists.[79] Feasibility studies for other capital projects do not usually include the multiplier income effects as a benefit.[80] If the convention center had not been built, the site would have been used to build other commercial facilities that might also generate additional income, employment, and tax revenues to the state, but without the subsidy.[81]

Moreover, DBEDT's estimates of the additional number of delegates attracted by the new convention center and their economic contributions are probably far overstated, because they assume that all of those attending events at the center would not have come to Hawaii if it had not been built, and attendees do not displace other (leisure) travelers even when there are very large conventions in town. To illustrate, Figure 5-4 displays the number of meetings, convention, and incentive visitors to Hawaii between 1990 and 2006. It also displays separately the number of convention visitors.

It is obvious that there was a spike in the number of MCI and convention visitors to Hawaii right after the HCC opened in October 1997; then the numbers fell sharply, no doubt due in large part to the effects of 9/11. However, it is difficult to tell simply by looking at the numbers how many additional MCI and convention visitors came to Hawaii because of the HCC. Figure 5-4 indicates that the number of MCI visitors to Hawaii averaged 445,706 per year before HCC was opened for business and 489,541 per year after it was opened for business; the difference is less than forty-five thousand additional MCI visitors per year. The difference in the number of convention visitors was less than thirty-five thousand. One might argue that the post–HCC averages were depressed by the effects of 9/11 in 2001 and the Iraq War and SARS in 2003; but the pre–HCC average was similarly influenced by the effects of a national recession and the first Gulf War in 1991 and Hurricane Iniki in 1992. In this business, you have to expect a lot of ups and downs. The thirty-five and forty-five thousand figures are far smaller than the actual annual delegates attending events at the convention center between 2003 and 2006 (see Table 5-2).[82] The new convention center probably diverted some events that previously were held at other Hawaii venues.

The Hawaii Convention Center was not born out of a sudden fit of "irrational exuberance."[83] The State went into it after years of deliberation. The growth of leisure travel in Hawaii was slowing down and economic diversification became the buzz phrase of the day. What better way to diversify Hawaii's economy than within its demonstrated core area of competence—tourism? The convention center was expected to create a new market to help revitalize Waikiki and to elevate Honolulu to the position of a premier urban tourism destination distinct from the Neighbor Island destination resorts. Convention tourism was seen as a natural complement to pleasure

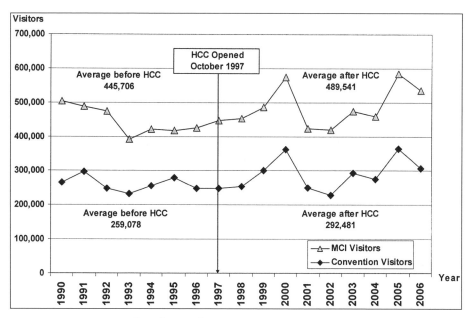

Fig. 5-4. Number of MCI and convention visitors to Hawaii: 1990–2006.
Source: State of Hawaii DBEDT, *State Data Book* (2000–2005); State of Hawaii
tourism records; DBEDT, *Monthly Visitor Statistics,* December 2006, at
http://www.hawaii.gov/dbedt.

tourism, and Hawaii was already a master of the latter. The convention center's slogan is "Where Business and Aloha meet."[84] But Gloria Garvey and Brook Gramann argue that to date Hawaii as a "business brand" has not been a believable promise.[85] Consultants who prepared HTA's 1999 *Hawaii Tourism Product Assessment Report* concluded that the convention center is "underutilized and undersold."[86]

Everything considered, the convention center/meetings business is a very expensive business to operate. Table 5-2 shows that it is also a very volatile business, with potentially large annual swings in attendance. The Hawaii Tourism Authority spent about $60 million in 2003 and attracted about 6.3 million visitors, or roughly an average of $10 per visitor. By contrast, it cost the State $32 million in convention center subsidy to attract about 132,000 delegates to the HCC in FY 2002–2003. Even if we assumed that all of it represented additional business that would not have materialized if the convention center was not built and each delegate was accompanied by an additional 0.8 visitors,[87] the cost per visitor would have been $135, or more than thirteen times what it cost to attract a leisure visitor to Hawaii. To be generous, suppose it is assumed that HCC generated an additional hundred thousand delegate visits per year and each delegate brought an average of 0.8 visitors along, then the $32 million annual subsidy to the convention center figures out to be $178 per visitor brought to Hawaii.

Even more devastating to its original planners, HCC can't be expected to be much of an economic generator for the state in the future. Today it is criticized for not having reached its operational capacity. But if it did reach its capacity, there is no further room for expansion at its present location. In an ideal world, the convention center reaches its economic potential very quickly. Peter E. Tarlow, publisher of *Tourism & More, Inc.*, surmises that continuing advances in technology in teleconferencing and interactive Web conferences will displace personal travel to meetings and conventions in the future. Not only will the new information technologies be cheaper, they will also allay fears of kidnapping and terrorist attacks. Hence, cities that depend heavily on the convention business will suffer financially.[88] A recent study by Heywood Sanders of the Brookings Institution notes that while the amount of exhibition space in the United States has expanded steadily, the demand for such space has plummeted.[89]

Yet not every convention center is doing poorly. While the HTA has had to drastically scale back the original goals for the Hawaii Convention Center, the Jacob Javits Convention Center in New York City, by contrast, turned away almost six hundred meetings between 2001 and 2004 due to a lack of space. New York City planned to expand the center's exhibition space by 340,000 square feet (bringing the total to 1.1 million) and increase the amount of meeting space from 30,000 square feet to 265,000 square feet at a cost of $1.4 billion.[90] Competition to the Hawaii Convention Center became stiffer beginning in 2005 as San Juan, Puerto Rico, opened its new convention center.[91] Indeed, around the country forty-four new or expanded convention centers were being planned or under construction as of 2005, adding to the already intense competition.[92] Act 143 passed by the Legislature in 2002 mandated that the HTA develop a strategic marketing plan to market Hawaii as both a leisure and business destination. The burden now falls on the HTA to do everything it can to make the convention center work. In April 2004, SMG—the convention center operator and marketer—announced that the first ten events that generate a minimum of 2,500 hotel room nights on at least one night during the event and booked before the end of the year would be given a 50 percent discount on the rent at the convention center plus $50,000 to offset expenses such as ground transportation and other services at the center.[93] In March 2004, SMG announced that it would give free rent to delegates attending the Professional Convention Management Association meeting in Honolulu who book events at the HCC between 2005 and 2010 by the deadline of January 31, 2005.[94] SMG reported that the free rent offer secured eleven bookings.[95] While providing incentives may attract more meetings and conventions to the center, it could also divert more events from hotels and other meeting venues. In the long run, SMG hopes to build up bookings by developing repeat business.[96] For now, future bookings look bleak.[97]

Some industry leaders now speak openly about their disappointment with the performance of the HCC and call for a new marketing strategy. There is a suggestion to return the job of marketing the center to the Hawaii Visitors and Convention Bureau. The senior vice president of Starwood Hotels in Hawaii suggests that the center is focusing too much on booking local events and should instead be bringing groups of five thousand–plus business travelers to Hawaii.[98] Old debates have resurfaced.

In reviewing the history of the Hawaii Convention Center, one cannot escape the conclusion that the potential economic benefits of the HCC were greatly exaggerated. Hawaii's experience is not unique. Economist Heywood Sanders reviewed thirty convention center feasibility studies done by major national accounting and economic consulting firms and found systematic inflation of the number of attendees and/or their lengths of stay.[99]

The Hawaii Tourism Authority

Act 156 signed into law by Governor Ben Cayetano on July 9, 1998, established the Hawaii Tourism Authority with dedicated funding from the transient accommodation (hotel room) tax. The law raised the hotel room tax from 6 percent to 7.25 percent effective January 1, 1999, broadened its base to include time-shares, and set aside 37.9 percent of the money to go into a Tourism Special Fund to pay for tourism promotion. A board consisting of thirteen private and public sector members (including representation from each of the four counties) would manage the fund, create a vision and long range plan for tourism, and oversee statewide tourism activities. While still attached to the Department of Business, Economic Development and Tourism for administrative purposes, the HTA reports directly to the governor and the State Legislature. Virtually all State government tourism responsibilities except for research that were previously assigned to DBEDT were transferred to HTA. There could be obvious credibility concerns if the HTA were to produce data that were then used to evaluate itself.[100]

The idea behind the creation of the HTA initially came from recommendations by the 1997 Governor's Economic Revitalization Task Force, which was formed by Governor Ben Cayetano to seek bold solutions to address Hawaii's prolonged economic stagnation.[101] As important as tourism was to the state's economy, many felt that it deserved more focused attention than it received as just another responsibility of DBEDT.

From the very beginning, HTA was embroiled in controversy.[102] In January 2000, the Sierra Club sued the HTA for failure to perform an environmental impact assessment of the potential environmental consequences of more than doubling the State's annual tourism promotion budget.[103] In 2002, the Legislative auditor issued a scathing report on the HTA, finding that "the Hawaii Tourism Authority is plagued by an alarming array of management deficiencies."[104] In March 2002, one board member resigned from the HTA apparently because the process used to search for a new executive director was a "mockery."[105] And when a new executive director was finally appointed, there were various complaints that he didn't have a professional background in tourism and his salary was too high. In the same year, Governor Cayetano exercised his power of line-item budget veto by cutting the HTA's marketing budget by $5 million (or 8 percent of the total) because he was displeased by the way the request for a reappointment to the board was allegedly "set up" by the board member and the Speaker of the House.[106] There is continuing controversy over whether the authority should have more board members with tourism experience. The HTA was the target of much criticism by members of the visitor industry at Governor Lingle's closed-to-the-public second tourism summit in 2003. As well, some saw her cabinet-level appointment in June 2003 of Marcia Weinert as the newly created tourism liaison to facilitate state-industry cooperation and to draft performance measures for the HTA as indication that she too shared some of the concerns expressed by the authority's many critics.[107] Mike McCartney, chairman of the HTA's board and the chief executive of public television (PBS) in Hawaii, explained that the authority is still going through growing pains.[108] By late summer of 2004, the various controversies surrounding the HTA had largely subsided and HTA showed considerable professionalism and openness in its approach to carrying out its mandates. The public was informed on the execution of the new tourism marketing contracts, a new initiative was begun to develop health and wellness tourism, the $1.2 million sustainable tourism research project was completed, a new contract was negotiated with the National Football League to keep the annual Pro Bowl in Honolulu, and a new ten-year strategic tourism plan (2005–2015) was circulated for public comment and approved.

HTA's Mandate

Act 143 passed by the 2002 Legislature made several significant changes to the HTA board and stated more precisely its mandates. It increased the number of board members from thirteen to fifteen (thirteen voting), with two public voting members; the diversity of the board was increased to include retail, transportation, entertainment/visitor attractions; a minimum of one board member must have experience and expertise in Hawaiian cultural practices; and no more than three members can represent one sector of the industry. HTA was instructed to broaden its strategic marketing plan to include both leisure and business travel. All contracts of $25,000 and over must be referred to the Senate President and House Speaker. And a management and financial audit will be performed on all major contractors (defined as those with contracts valued at over $15 million).[109] Act 143 requires the HTA to create a vision and a long-range tourism plan for the state and develop, coordinate, and implement State policies and directions for tourism and related activities, taking into account the economic, social, and physical impacts of tourism on the state and its natural resource infrastructure, and to provide support to other State and county departments and agencies to manage, improve, and protect Hawaii's environment and areas frequented by visitors. HTA is also expected to coordinate the tourism work of all agencies and advise the private sector in the development of tourism-related activities and resources. It is charged to eliminate or reduce barriers to travel; market and promote sports-related activities and events; and coordinate the development of new product lines with the counties and other public and private sectors including sports, cultural, health, education, business, and ecotourism. Finally, HTA is asked to develop a public information and education program to inform residents about tourism, encourage the development of tourism education, training, and career counseling programs, and establish a program to monitor, investigate, and respond to complaints about problems stemming from tourism and take appropriate action as necessary.[110]

For decades, the visitor industry in Hawaii wanted to have more visibility in State government, including at times calls for the creation of a tourism czar. Perhaps the creation of the Hawaii Tourism Authority fulfills that wish. The board membership of the HTA, which is tilted in favor of the industry, clearly gives the industry much more visibility and influence in the state. It is also a source of disquiet among many residents because the authority is more than just about marketing; it is supposed to chart the future course of tourism in the entire state. There is valid concern that when push comes to shove the broader interests of the community will be sacrificed to the narrower interests of the various factions in the visitor industry. HTA chairman McCartney noted, "It's still public money. It is not visitor industry money. It's the taxpayer dollars. So we need to do a better job of integrating the two."[111] In theory, dedicating money from the room tax for the HTA was supposed to lessen legislative oversight. But greater visibility and responsibility will attract more outside scrutiny, not less. A review of the mandates of Act 143 indicates that the State government is likely to become *less* hands-off toward tourism than previously. However, it does not portend a tourism future that is dictated by a heavy-handed government. Judging by the way in which HTA carries out its mandate, it is more likely that the future model of tourism development in Hawaii is one of more cooperation with the private sector. Everything considered, the establishment of the HTA and its manner of financing were positive reforms carried out by the Cayetano administration.

Notes

1. Bonham and Mak (1996), p. 9. In 2003, the industry raised only $6.8 million. But the State did not keep its end of the agreement either; faced with a huge budget crisis, the California government trimmed its contribution in 2003 to $929,000. Governor Gray Davis had initially proposed to eliminate the Bureau of Tourism altogether. *Travel Weekly Daily Bulletin*, Article 39126.

2. Crampon (1976).

3. Rees (February 13, 1995), p. 5.

4. Rees (October 26, 2003), p. B1.

5. Bonham and Mak (1996), pp. 3–10.

6. For example, the nonrenewal rate in FY 1994 was greater than 22 percent according to the head of the HVCB Membership Department. Ibid., p. 6.

7. Mok (1986). A survey of tourism businesses conducted by the Legislative Reference Bureau found that 59 percent of the respondents did not spend any

private funds between January 1, 1997, and December 31, 2001, to advertise or promote Hawaii as a visitor destination. Pan (2002).

8. Bonham and Mak (1996), p. 8.

9. Ibid., p. 6.

10. Bonham and Mak (1996); also Mak and Miklius (1992), pp. 95–99.

11. Rees (October 26, 2003), p. B4.

12. See, for example, Rees (October 26, 2003), p. B1; and Whitney (April 2002), pp. 26–32.

13. Yamanouchi (2004a), p. C1.

14. Rees (October 26, 2003), p. B4.

15. Former managing director of the Hawaii Visitors Bureau Robert C. Allen opined that the relationship between the bureau and the State Legislature and its "watchdog" Department of Business, Economic Development and Tourism (DPED/DBEDT) was always an adversarial one. He noted that DBEDT had never been headed by someone with any background in tourism and characterized its relationship to the HVB as "a case of bureaucrats telling professionals how to run their business at the expense of taxpayers." Allen offered the (suspicious?) suggestion that "supervision and accountability . . . should be maintained through an intelligent program of cooperation between the HVB and the State." Allen (2004), p. 223. In his otherwise interesting, anecdotal book entitled *Creating Hawaii Tourism,* Allen did not have much good to say about the contribution of government in creating Hawaii tourism.

16. "Tourism Agency Signs Contracts" (January 3, 2004), p. C1.

17. Yamanouchi (2003b), pp. A1–A5.

18. Garvey and Gramann (July 29, 2003), p. A6.

19. Dentsu, however, announced that it planned to set up a not-for-profit subsidiary to handle the HTA contract.

20. See also Simpich (1971), chapter 3.

21. The 1973 Temporary Visitor Industry Council (1973), p. 47.

22. See the technical appendix in any of Hawaii's annual visitor research reports for definitions and methodology.

23. HVCB Tourism Industry Update, March 15, 2004, p. 2.

24. Ibid., June 1, 2004, p. 2.

25. Ibid., September 27, 2004, p. 2.

26. Hamilton (June 24, 1975).

27. See, for example, Craig (1963), pp. 63–71.

28. See, for example, Simon (1974), pp. 10–14. Economic theory posits that the amount of money spent on promotion is at the optimum when the last dollar spent on promotion generates (at least) a dollar of benefits to the destination.

29. Craig (1963), pp. 69–71.

30. Hawaii Tourism Authority (June 29, 1999).

31. Milligan (June 22, 2005).

32. Leu (2001), pp. 265–272.

33. Perhaps it would be asking too much to demand evidence that money spent on promotion yields the highest incremental benefit to the state relative to benefits from other potential uses.

34. State of Hawaii Legislative Auditor (1987).

35. Yamanouchi (2003c), pp. C1 and C4.

36. Ibid., p. C1. Similarly, the National Football League (NFL) prepared a study in 2004 that showed that national exposure due to the Pro Bowl held in Honolulu each year was worth $12.1 million in media advertising for the state compared to the $5.3 million that the State paid the NFL to hold the game in Honolulu. The study monitored live broadcasts of selected football games in 2003 and counted the number of references to Hawaii and the 2003 Pro Bowl during those live telecasts, estimating that the exposure was worth $4,719,167. Likewise, the study counted 855 articles in various publications that featured the 2003 Pro Bowl, generating 1,108 mentions of Hawaii that the NFL estimates were worth $3,690,856 in print advertising. The study also counted advertisements in all thirty-two NFL stadiums in 2003 for references to Hawaii and the Pro Bowl, including public address announcements and Jumbotron announcements, and estimated that those were worth $2,244,718 in media exposure. Masuoka (February 3, 2004), p. A1. A follow-up survey commissioned by the HTA found that twenty-two thousand out-of-state visitors came to Hawaii to attend the Pro Bowl in 2004 and spent $29.5 million in Hawaii, which generated $2.84 million in State taxes. HTA (March 12, 2004). The number of attendees in 2003 was eighteen thousand—four thousand fewer than in 2004.

37. For example, on the Japanese market, the October 1–3, 2003, presentation summarizes survey responses on the following: destinations considered; destinations in the past year/past three years; destinations planned for leisure within twenty-four months; satisfaction index; rating of Hawaii vs. competitive destinations; and ratings of Hawaii by important activity. It is not obvious how the responses relate specifically to marketing effectiveness.

38. See, for example, Whitney (2002) and Rees (October 26, 2003), pp. B1 and B4.

39. Hawaii Visitors Bureau (November 17, 1994).

40. DBEDT, 2002 *Visitor Satisfaction and Activity Report* (2002), p. 34.

41. DBEDT, *Annual Visitor Research Report* (2002), p. 9.

42. Crouch (1995).

43. "Tourism Liaison Ready for Task" (June 12, 2003), pp. C1 and C6.

44. Hawaii Tourism Authority (June 30, 1999), p. 1–9. Indeed, when a 1993 *New York Times*/CBS News poll on the U.S. mainland asked people where they wanted to go on their dream vacation, Hawaii was named more frequently than anyplace in the entire world. Tucker (1993), pp. 87–93.

45. First Hawaiian Bank (June 1972).

46. Pannel Kerr Forster Consulting (1985), p. VI–12.

47. Ibid.

48. A separate study prepared by Pannell Kerr Forster Consulting for the Department of Business and Economic Development estimated that the internal rate of return to a convention center would range from 17.89 percent to 53.59 percent, depending on the site. State of Hawaii Department of Business and Economic Development (February 1988).

49. State of Hawaii Convention Center Authority (1995); Mak (1993).

50. Convention Center Authority (1995), pp. 1–2.

51. Hawaiian Capital Securities (June 30, 1993). But Dr. Richard Kelley of Outrigger Hotels suggested at the 1984 Governor's Tourism Congress that perhaps the fairest way to finance the convention center would be to make all of Waikiki an improvement district and raise the property tax on all hotels and commercial properties.

52. State Auditor (2002), pp. 22–23.

53. "Convention Center Praised" (April 1, 2004), p. C1; also Hawaii Visitors and Convention Bureau (April 5, 2004), p. 2. The lowest ranking it received was twenty-second, for the amount of exhibit space. Starbulletin.com (April 2, 2004).

54. www.hawaiiconvention.com/center/space.html.

55. First Hawaiian Bank (June 1972); see also Yamanouchi (2004b), pp. F1–F2.

56. Arakawa (2005b), pp. C1 and C6.

57. Dingeman (2007a), pp. A1 and A9.

58. Perry (2003), p. 38.

59. HVCB Tourism Industry Update (February 18, 2005).

60. Darling and Beato (2004), p. 4.

61. Perry (2003), p. 38.

62. Tierney (June 11, 2005).

63. Bonham, Edmonds, and Mak (2006).

64. *State of Hawaii Data Book* (2000, 2001, and 2002 issues).

65. Convention Center Authority (July 1995), pp. 4–5.

66. Mak (May 10, 1995). At the draft stage, the average attendance per event was assumed to be seventy-five hundred.

67. DBEDT (July 1999), p. 18. HTA's *2003 Annual Report* (p. 14) reported seventeen bookings for FY 1998.

68. HTA, *2003 Annual Report to the State Legislature*, p. 14. The *2005 Annual Report* reported forty definite/final bookings and 132,697 delegates for 2003.

69. Ibid.

70. There are a few differences between the numbers in Table 5-1 as reported by the *Honolulu Advertiser* and the numbers reported in the HTA *2005 Annual Report to the Legislature*. The *Annual Report* shows fifteen and twenty-two final bookings for 1999 and 2001, respectively, and 132,696 delegate counts for 2003 and 162,515 for 2004.

71. In FY 2003, there were 213 events held at the convention center, including graduations, weddings, banquets, testing, festivals, public-gated shows, and so on, compared to thirty-eight bookings for offshore conventions/meetings.

72. Arakawa (November 8, 2004), p. C4.

73. Darling and Beato (2004), p. 17.

74. The total amount spent on MCI marketing was $6 million; if allocated on a per capita basis, the convention center's share should be around $2 million. Hawaii Tourism Authority (December 2003). However, HTA estimates annual marketing and sales expenses for the convention center at $6 million, which would increase the estimate of the operating expenditures from $6 million to $10 million. Arakawa (November 8, 2004), p. C4.

75. Refinanced in 2000 for a twenty-five-year term at 6 percent interest.

76. DBEDT (July 1999), p. 20.

77. Ibid.

78. DBEDT (July 1999), pp. 19–20.

79. See, for example, Mitchell (1970), pp. 1–21; Mak (2004), chapter 11.

80. Darling and Beato (2004), pp. 22–23.

81. See also Darling and Beato (2004).

82. Hawaii Tourism Authority, *2005 Annual Report to the State Legislature,* p. 14.

83. A phrase made famous by the former U.S. Federal Reserve Board chairman Alan Greenspan.

84. Dingeman (2007b), p. F1.

85. Garvey and Gramann (July 29, 2003), p. A6.

86. HTA (June 30, 1999).

87. Average party size of an MCI visitor in 2002 was 1.79.

88. Tarlow (2002), p. 49.

89. Sanders (January 2005).

90. *Travel Weekly Daily Bulletin,* Article 42113 and Article 44873.

91. *Travel Weekly Daily Bulletin,* Article 42029 and Article 41172.

92. Arakawa (November 8, 2004), p. C4; Sanders (January 2005), p. 1.

93. *Travel Weekly Daily Bulletin,* Article 42633.

94. *Pacific Business News,* March 26, 2004, and reported in *Japan Market Update,* April 2004 edition, at www.pacrimmarketing.com. But the deals had to be signed by January 31, 2005.

95. Arakawa (2005a), pp. C1 and C4.

96. Ibid.

97. Dingeman (2007b) reports that future bookings made as of May 16, 2007, are for fifteen events in 2008, sixteen in 2009, nine in 2010, and six in 2011.

98. Dingeman (2007b), p. F2.

99. Darling and Beato (2004), p. 24.

100. HTA, "History and Overview of the Hawaii Tourism Authority," at http://www.hawaii.gov/tourism/mandate.html.

101. Grandy (2002), pp. 115–116.

102. See, for example, Yamanouchi (2003a), pp. F1 and F3; Whitney (April 2002), pp. 26–32; Rees (October 16, 2003), pp. B1 and B4; and Jones (July 9, 2003), p. 8.

103. Waite (December 7, 2002), pp. A1 and A9. The Hawaii Supreme Court in a 3-2 decision on December 6, 2002, ruled that the Sierra Club did not have "standing" to challenge the HTA's decision not to perform such a study.

104. The Auditor of the State of Hawaii (2002), chapter 2.

105. Rees (September 9, 2002), p. A8.

106. Hooper (November 12, 2002), pp. A1 and A2. The board member just happened to be the CEO of Hawaii's largest hotel chain.

107. Yamanouchi (2003a), pp. F1 and F3.

108. Ibid.

109. Of course, only HVCB qualifies under the $15 million threshold.

110. HTA, "History and Overview of the Hawaii Tourism Authority," at http://www.hawaii.gov/tourism/mandate.html.

111. Yamanouchi (2003a), p. F3.

References

Allen, Robert C. 2004. *Creating Hawaii Tourism: A Memoir.* Honolulu: Bess Press.

Arakawa, Lynda. 2004. "Big Bookings Down Slightly." *Honolulu Advertiser,* November 8: C1 and C4.

———. 2005a. "Free Rent Attracts 11 Bookings." *Honolulu Advertiser,* February 1: C1 and C4.

———. 2005b. "Isles a Hard Sell to U.S. Taxpayers." *Honolulu Advertiser,* June 22: C1 and C6.

Bonham, Carl, Christopher Edmonds, and James Mak. 2006. "Impact of 9/11 and Other Terrible Global Events on Tourism in the U.S. and Hawaii." *Journal of Travel Research* (August): 99–110.

Bonham, Carl, and James Mak. 1996. "Private versus Public Financing of State Destination Promotion." *Journal of Travel Research* 35(2): 3–10.

"Convention Center praised." 2004. *Honolulu Advertiser,* April 1: C1.

Craig, Paul G. 1963. *The Future Growth of Hawaiian Tourism and Its Impact on the State and the Neighbor Islands.* Honolulu: University of Hawaii Economic Research Center (February).

Crampon, Jack. 1976. *Hawaii's Visitor Industry: Its Growth and Development.* Honolulu: University of Hawaii School of Travel Industry Management.

Crouch, Geoffrey I. 1995. "A Meta-Analysis of Tourism Demand." *Annals of Tourism Research* 22(1): 103–118.

Darling, Arthur H., and Paulina Beato. 2004. *Should Public Budgets Finance Convention Centers?* Economic and Social Study Series RE1-04-005. Washington, D.C.: Inter-American Development Bank (April).

Del Rosso, Laura. 2003. "California Division of Tourism Budget Takes a Hit." *Travel Weekly Daily Bulletin,* August 18, Article 39126.

Dingeman, Robbie. 2007a. "'Boondoggle Effect' Cancels Detroit Mayor's Island Trip." *Honolulu Advertiser,* May 18: A1 and A9.

———. 2007b. "Who Will Fill These Seats?" *Honolulu Advertiser,* May 27: F1–F2.

First Hawaiian Bank. 1972. "Hawaii Goes after the Convention Business." *Economic Indicators* (June).

Garvey, Gloria, and Brook Gramann. 2003. "Who Decides Hawaii's Brand?" *Honolulu Advertiser,* July 29: 6.

Grandy, Christopher. 2002. *Hawaii Becalmed: Economic Lessons of the 1990s.* Honolulu: University of Hawaii Press.

Hamilton, Thomas H. 1975. "Trip Procedure Encouraged Insight." *Honolulu Advertiser,* June 24.

Hawaii Tourism Authority (HTA). "History and Overview of the Hawaii Tourism Authority." At www.hawaii.gov/tourism/mandate.html.

———. 1999. *Competitive Strategic Assessment of Hawaii Tourism: Executive Summary.* Honolulu: HTA (June 29).

———. 2003. *Hawaii Marketing Effectiveness Study: Japan Market.* Honolulu: HTA (October 1–3).

———. 2003. *Report to the Twenty-Second Legislature, Regular Session of 2004, FY 02–03.* Honolulu: HTA (December 18).

———. 2003. *Report to the Twenty-Second Legislature, Regular Session of 2004: New Contract Provisions Designed to Significantly Increase MCI Marketing for the State of Hawaii.* Honolulu: HTA (December).

———. 2003. *2003 Annual Report to the State Legislature.* Honolulu: HTA.

———. 2004. "Visitor Research Study Reveals Positive Impact of 2004 Pro Bowl." News Release (March 12).

Hawaii Visitors and Convention Bureau. 2004–2005. *HVCB Tourism Industry Update.* Various dates (March 15, 2004, April 5, 2004, June 1, 2004, and February 18, 2005).

Hawaii Visitors Bureau. 1994. *FY 1995–1997: Hawaii Visitors Bureau Marketing Plan.* Honolulu: HVB (November 17).

Hooper, Susan. 2002. "Cayetano Explains $5M Cut from HTA." *Honolulu Advertiser,* November 12: A1 and A2.

Jones, Bob. 2003. "What's Really Wrong with Tourism." *MidWeek,* July 9: 8.

Leu, Walter. 2001. "National Tourist Offices." In A. Lockwood and S. Medlick, eds., *Tourism and Hospitality in the 21st Century* (Boston: Butterworth-Heinemann): 265–272.

Mak, James. 1993. *The Economics of the Convention Center.* Prepared for presentation at the Hawaii Association of Public Accountants Annual Conference, Honolulu (June 23).

———. 1995. *Hawaii Convention Center Draft Environmental Impact Statement: A Review.* Submitted to DBEDT, Honolulu (May 10).

———. 2004. *Tourism and the Economy.* Honolulu: University of Hawaii Press.

Mak, James, and Walter Miklius. 1992. "Why Can't the Tourist Industry Pay for Travel Promotion and a Convention Center?" In Randy W. Roth, ed., *The Price of Paradise* (Honolulu: Mutual Publishing): 95–99.

Masuoka, Brendan. 2004. "Study Puts $12.1M Value on Pro Bowl." *Honolulu Advertiser,* February 3: A1 and A8.

Milligan, Michael. 2005. "TIA Survey Finds State Tourism Budgets Grow 10 Percent in '04–'05FY." *Travel Weekly Daily Bulletin,* June 22, Article 47150.

Mitchell, Frank. 1970. "The Value of Tourism in East Africa." *Eastern Africa Economic Review* 2(1): 1–21.

Mok, Henry. 1986. "Effectiveness of Destinational Advertising: The Case of Hawaii's City Magazine Campaign." Ph.D. thesis in economics, University of Hawaii, Honolulu.

Pan, Peter G. 2002. *Private Sector Tourism Spending.* Report No. 5. Honolulu: Legislative Reference Bureau.

Pannel Kerr Forster Consulting. 1985. *Report on the Market Feasibility of a Proposed Convention Center.* Honolulu: DPED (March 22).

Perry, David C. 2003. "Urban Tourism and the Privatizing Discourses of Public Infrastructure." In Denis R. Judd, ed., *The Infrastructure of Play: Building the Tourist City* (Armonk, NY: M. E. Sharpe): 19–49.

Rees, Robert M. 1995. "The HVB: Private Gain vs. Public Good." *Pacific Business News,* February 13: 5.

———. 2002. "Travelin' on with the HTA." *Honolulu Advertiser,* September 9: A8.

———. 2003. "Tourism Mess Shows How Effort to Govern Ourselves Fails." *Honolulu Advertiser,* October 26: B1.

Sanders, Heywood. 2005. *Space Available: The Realities of Convention Centers as Economic Development Strategy.* Metropolitan Policy Program. Washington, D.C.: Brookings Institution (January).

Simon, Julian. 1974. "How Much Should an Airline Spend for Advertising: A Case Study Example." *Journal of Travel Research* (July): 10–14.

Simpich, Frederick, Jr. 1971. *Anatomy of Hawaii.* New York: Coward, McCann & Georghegan.

State of Hawaii Convention Center Authority (CCA). 1995. *Hawaii Convention Center, Honolulu, Hawaii: Final Environmental Impact Statement,* vol. 1. Honolulu: CCA (July).

State of Hawaii Department of Business and Economic Development. 1988. *Report on Projections of Economic and Fiscal Impact of Various Sites for the Proposed Convention Center.* Honolulu: Pannell Kerr Forster (February).

State of Hawaii Department of Business, Economic Development and Tourism (DBEDT). 1991–2005. *Annual Visitor Research Report.* Honolulu: DBEDT.

———. 1999. "Is the Convention Center Paying Its Way?" *Hawaii's Economy* (July).

———. 2000–2005. *State of Hawaii Data Book.* Honolulu: DBEDT.

———. 2001. "New Measures of Tourism." *Hawaii's Economy* (February).

———. 2002. *2002 Visitor Satisfaction and Activity Report.* Honolulu: DBEDT.

State of Hawaii Legislative Auditor. 1987. *Management Audit of the HVB and State's Tourism Program.* Report 87–14. Honolulu.

———. 2002. *Management Audit of the Hawaii Tourism Authority.* Report No. 02–04. Honolulu (February).

Tarlow, Peter E. 2002. "Tourism in the Twenty-First Century." *The Futurist* (September-October): 48–51.

The 1973 Temporary Visitor Industry Council. 1973. *The Report of the 1973 Temporary Visitor Industry Council.* Honolulu (November).

Tierney, John. 2005. "The Circus Maximum Syndrome." NYTimes.com, January 11.

"Tourism Agency Signs Contracts." 2004. *Honolulu Advertiser,* January 3: C1.

Travel Weekly Daily Bulletin. At www.twcrossroads.com/.

Tucker, Ken. 1993. "Is Hawaii Becoming Less Attractive as a Tourist Destination?" In Randy W. Roth, ed., *The Price of Paradise,* vol. 2 (Honolulu: Mutual Publishing): 87–93.

Waite, David. 2002. "High Court Won't Order Tourism Impact Study." *Honolulu Advertiser,* December 7: A1 and A9.

Whitney, Scott. 2002. "The Automatic Tourism Money Machine." *Honolulu* (April): 26–32.

Yamanouchi, Kelly. 2003a. "HTA Rebuts Critics' Concerns." *Honolulu Advertiser,* June 8: F1 and F3.

———. 2003b. "HVCB Deal Isn't Done." *Honolulu Advertiser,* July 29: A1 and A5.

———. 2003c. "Mission to Japan May Be Hard to Measure." *Honolulu Advertiser,* August 7: C1 and C4.

———. 2004a. "Visitors Bureau Returns Money to State." *Honolulu Advertiser,* January 6: C1.

———. 2004b. "Conventions Still Sluggish." *Honolulu Advertiser,* January 18: F1–F2.

Chapter Six

Protecting Hawaii's Natural Environment

What attracts tourists to Hawaii, first and foremost, is its natural environment. Hawaii Tourism Authority's *Hawaii Tourism Product Assessment* study (1999) noted that "Hawaii's unspoiled natural beauty is the foundation of Hawaii's tourism product."[1] This awareness provides both the industry and residents an economic incentive to protect its natural assets. Long before statehood, Hawaii's Territorial Legislature passed legislation (1927) to get rid of billboards. In 1957, the City and County of Honolulu passed the first sign ordinance restricting the size and placement of commercial signs.[2] The Outdoor Circle of Hawaii maintains a vigilant fight against efforts to reinstate billboards, aerial advertising, and illegal signs. Besides Hawaii, only three other states prohibit billboards today. The Outdoor Circle has fought against aerial advertising four times since 1947. In November 2004, a federal district court threw out a First Amendment free-speech lawsuit brought by a California antiabortion center to overturn Honolulu's thirty-three-year-old ordinance banning aerial advertising. U.S. District Court judge David Ezra ruled that Honolulu's airspace is not a traditional public forum and has not been declared a public forum by the government. Ezra wrote in his ruling that the ban "is designed to protect what is perhaps the state's most valuable and fragile economic asset—the natural beauty upon which Hawaii's tourism economy relies."[3] Visitors to Las Vegas and Hawaii cannot help but notice that the glitz of Las Vegas stands in sharp contrast to Hawaii's lack of it. The State's highly (some say overly) restrictive land use law (Act 187) was enacted in 1961, in part to prevent urban sprawl, save agriculture, and retain open space. At the end of 2005, only 4.8 percent of the state's 4.1 million acres of land had been designated for urban use; by contrast, 48 percent had been designated for conservation and another 47 percent had been designated for agricultural uses.[4] Former

State planning director Shelley Mark opined that Hawaii's unique land use law "did abet tourism growth, not only in preserving scenic vistas and assets, but in its early focus on comprehensive rather than scattered resort developments."[5]

After forty years, however, HTA's *Hawaii Tourism Product Assessment* study argues that land use (and other) restrictive laws need to be "revised to permit development of new niche tourism products."[6] A good example of such a niche tourism market is the fledgling agritourism business, which faces potential problems over State and county land use regulations.[7] During the 1960s and 1970s, public interest groups such as Life of the Land and the Outdoor Circle fought to keep commercial development from Diamond Head, Hawaii's signature tourism landmark.[8] In 1975, the Honolulu City Council enacted an ordinance making Diamond Head a historic, cultural, and scenic district.

Tom Coffman noted that during the 1970s, the State enacted environmental controls "that were possibly the most elaborate in the country. They included creation of an office of environmental quality control, strict air pollution standards, an open space plan, a shoreline setback on construction, new controls on water and sewage discharge into the ocean, and a natural area preserve system to protect endangered flora and fauna."[9]

There are some who believe that Hawaii is overly protective of its environment by enacting laws that duplicate federal statutes. When the *Hawaii Environmental Law Handbook* was written in 1992, it took 250 pages to summarize the State's environmental laws.[10] The editor of the *Handbook* opined that Hawaii's excessive number of environmental laws "hurt business and defy common sense."[11] Others disagree.[12]

The *Hawaii 2000* report notes that "Unfortunately, Hawaii's record on environmental protection and natural resource management is not very good in terms of the value of its resources and the level of funding for environmental protections and resource management."[13] The State's Environmental Council, a fifteen-member citizen committee appointed by the governor to be the watchdog of the state's environment, agrees. The council's annual report card on Hawaii's environment shows that between FY 1996 and FY 2005, State expenditures on environmental protection programs averaged $72 million (in current-year dollars) per year, representing 1.16 percent of total State spending, with no obvious trend; the nationwide average among the states (circa 2000) was 1.9 percent.[14]

Beginning in 1996, the State's Environmental Council began issuing an annual environmental report card to grade the status of Hawaii's environment. The 2004 Report Card gave the following grades:[15]

Energy use	D
Use & recycle of resources	C+
Biodiversity maintenance	C–
Air quality	A+
Water quality	B
Terrestrial quality	B
Public awareness & concern*	C–
OVERALL GRADE	C+

*This item includes the amount of money the State spends on environmental protection programs.

Hawaii gets high marks for its air quality and (usually) water quality. But an overall grade of C+ is barely above "Satisfactory." However, the council does not consider some of the environmental assets most highly valued by tourists. These include Hawaii's wonderful climate, its scenic beauty, and the quality of its beaches.

Kirk Smith, senior fellow in the environment program at the East-West Center (Honolulu), surmises that overall, "Hawaii's natural environment is in great shape (relative to all other places inhabited by human beings), even in and around Honolulu, our only big city. But we really can't take much credit for it. Hawaii's geographic isolation and natural processes have given the State a remarkably green environment despite post-statehood economic and population explosion. The biggest environmental threats are to its endemic species as evolution has produced over 10,000 species in Hawaii that don't exist anywhere else in the world. Hawaii is widely known as the 'endangered species capitol of the world.'"[16]

Tourism's Impacts on Hawaii's Natural Environment

Tourism and the environment are interdependent. While Hawaii's enormous popularity as a tourist destination can be attributed in no small part to the outstanding quality of its natural environment, that environment is also affected by tourism. In all destinations, tourism affects the natural environment in several ways. First, tourists and tourism suppliers consume natural resources such as water and energy; in Hawaii, most of the state's energy resources are imported.[17] Second, tourists and tourism suppliers pollute the environment by discharging waste and harmful substances onto the land and into the water and air. Third, tourists engage in activities—for example, walking on coral or trampling down native plants—that directly damage the natural environment. Tourists can also help to spread plant and fruit pests and bring in invasive species that can harm indigenous plants and animals.

In Hawaii, visitors consume more water and energy and discharge more solid waste, sewage, and air pollutants per person per day than residents (Table 6-1). This is because each tourist spends more money (i.e., buys more goods and services) per vacation day in Hawaii than each resident and hence consumes more resources and generates more residuals and discharges. But when we add up their total impact on an annual basis, Hawaii's resident population places far greater demands on the state's environmental resources than its visitors (Table 6-2).[18]

To reduce tourist and resident impacts on the natural environment requires that Hawaii's residents and tourists either (1) reduce their consumption of the state's natural resources, (2) reduce the amount of residuals generated from any given amount of goods consumed, or (3) encourage more recycling and reuse and thus reduce the amount of resources used and discharged into the environment.[19] The irony of this is that while the State's new 2005–2015 tourism strategic plan aims to attract more high-spending visitors per diem (see chapter 3), they are the very visitors who produce the largest environmental footprint in Hawaii.

Of course, most of the environmental impacts from tourism are not made by visitors personally. Visitors do not purchase water from the Board of Water Supply or energy from the local utility companies directly; they generally buy them indirectly when they buy goods and services while in Hawaii. It is the tourism suppliers who pay the water and utility bills that show up as visitor consumption of water and energy in Table 6-1. Most of these businesses also sell their products and services to local residents. Indeed, spending by visitors greatly exceeds spending by residents only in a handful of Hawaii's industries: hotels, sightseeing transportation, air transportation, car rentals, and the amusement industry.[20] Thus it would be difficult to develop a tourism-specific environmental policy for the state. In fact, the greater the impact on the environment by nontourism sources, the lower will be the likely success rate of environmental regulations that target solely the tourist industry.[21]

During the 1990s, Hawaii's State and county governments took actions

Table 6-1. Per person daily resource uses and waste discharges by Hawaii's visitors and residents: 1997 (Includes both direct and indirect uses and discharges)

	Visitors (per visitor day)	Residents (per resident day)
Resource Use		
Water (gals.)	206.7	138.9
Energy		
Electricity (kWh)	33.9	11.9
Propane (MMBtu)	0.027	0.003
Hwy gas & diesel (gals.)	0.91	0.80
Residuals/discharges		
Solid waste (lbs.)	7.3	5.5
Wastewater (sewage)	139.8	75.9
Air emissions		
Carbon dioxide (lbs.)	18.3	15.6
Methane (lbs.)	0.00050	0.00019
Nitrous oxide (lbs.)	0.00026	0.00016

Source: R. M. Towill Corp. Inc., et al. (2004), pp. 14 and 15. Per capita daily air emission figures were calculated from annual figures contained in the study. *Note:* "Direct use" is personal use by visitors or residents and "indirect use" is business use to produce goods and services that are ultimately consumed by visitors or residents.

to protect some of the state's most valuable recreational and touristic resources. On paper, government intervention is supposed to correct what the "market" is unable to accomplish. In practice, government intervention has often been a mixed bag. This chapter recounts the story of government regulation of tourism in three high-profile cases: Hanauma Bay Nature Preserve (Oahu), Hanalei River boating (Kauai), and waste dumping of cruise ships in the state's ocean waters. Hanauma Bay is a success story; regulation of Hanalei River boating, to date, has been a failure; and the verdict is still out on the regulation of cruise ship waste dumping in Hawaii.

Hanauma Bay Nature Preserve

Hanauma Bay Nature Preserve is one of Hawaii's most popular natural attractions. Located on the eastern end of Oahu about 12 miles from Waikiki, Hanauma Bay was created by an underwater volcanic eruption some thirty-five thousand years ago. Today it looks like a sunken crater with one side

Table 6-2. Total annual resource uses and waste discharges by Hawaii's visitors and residents: 1997 (Includes both direct and indirect uses and discharges)

	Visitors	Residents
Resource Use		
Water (millions of gals.)	11,856	61,429
Energy		
Electricity (Gwh)	1,944	5,253
Propane (mmBtu)	1,521,257	1,287,940
Hwy gas & diesel (millions of gals.)	52.1	353.7
Residuals/discharges		
Solid waste (millions of lbs.)	421.3	2,423.2
Wastewater (millions of gals.)	8,022	33,587
Air emissions		
Carbon dioxide (tons)	524,775	3,451,897
Methane (tons)	14.5	42.9
Nitrous oxide (tons)	7.5	35.2

Source: R. M. Towill Corp. Inc., et al. (2004), pp. 14 and 15.
Note: "Direct use" is personal use by visitors or residents and "indirect use" is business use to produce goods and services that are ultimately consumed by visitors or residents.

open to the sea, creating a bowl-shaped cove. Protected by fringing reefs, the placid waters of Hanauma Bay, combined with sunny and calm weather, make it an ideal place to sunbathe, swim, snorkel, and interact with marine life. The lands around the bay originally belonged to King Kamehameha I, and it was a favorite fishing place for Hawaiian royalty. In 1883, Hanauma Bay and the nearby lands became the property of Princess Bernice Pauahi Bishop and, later, her estate.[22] In 1928, the City and County of Honolulu purchased the property from the Bishop Estate for $1 and created the Koko Head Regional Park, which includes Koko Head, Koko Crater, and Hanauma Bay. The sale included a deed restriction that limits its use to public parks and rights of way. Once a private property, Hanauma Bay became an open-access resource and thus prone to be overused. Many residents fished in the bay, and by the 1960s few fish of any size remained. In 1967 Hanauma Bay was designated Hawaii's first Marine Life Conservation District and became a marine sanctuary and habitat for many species. This designation prohibits visitors from taking any marine life, shells, coral, rocks, or sand from the park. The preserve has two levels; currently the upper level consists of a picnic area, parking for three hundred cars and commercial vehicles, a snack bar, and an education center. The lower area consists of the beach, a grassy area, and the bay rim trails, accessible either on foot or by commercial trolley down a narrow and steep road; private vehicles are generally prohibited from going down to the beach.

Once word got around of its charms, Hanauma Bay became hugely popular with tourists. In 1975, about half a million visitors—residents and tourists—visited the park. In ten years that number grew to nearly 1.6 million visitors. By the late 1980s, attendance had risen to 2.8 million visitors per year, or about seventy-five hundred per day.[23] Tourists crowded out residents, and the number of residents visiting the park actually declined. In 1975, 68 percent of the park's visitors were Hawaii residents; by 1990, only 13 percent were locals.[24] The crush of visitors not only decreased the enjoyment of those who came to the park, there were also concerns that the marine environment was rapidly being degraded. Fish feeding had greatly increased the fish population—especially the aggressive varieties—and altered the biodiversity of marine life in the bay. At the end of the day, a film of suntan oil often floated on the surface of the water. Cigarette butts, food wrappers, and containers littered the beach and too frequently were blown into the water. Runoff from the open showers was another problem. There was also concern that people walking on the coral were damaging the reef. Visitors left their cars on the lawn, on roadways leading to the park, and along the highway. Commercial tours "monopolized" the picnic tables. It was getting out of hand, and something had to be done!

PROTECTING HANAUMA BAY

In 1989, the City Department of Parks and Recreation presented a management plan to the City Council to deal with crowding and related problems at the park. Commercial tour operators vigorously opposed the plan, because it would have banned them from bringing groups of visitors to the park other than for a brief sightseeing stop at the upper level parking area. Japanese tour operators were particularly incensed because most of the Japanese visitors to Hanauma Bay came on prepaid tours. In 1990, the Hanauma Bay Users Committee, comprised of both Hawaii and Japanese tour companies, offered a plan to regulate themselves by not bringing tours to the bay on Sundays and major holidays for a six-month period. Although the number of visitors did fall initially, the measure wasn't deemed enough. On June 12, 1990, the City implemented its own plan for Hanauma Bay.

The City had a three-pronged plan: (1) to restrict access to the park, (2) to educate visitors on the proper behavior at the park, and (3) to improve park facilities.

Access was restricted by hiring guards to turn away cars from the park when the three hundred parking stalls were filled and to prevent illegal parking along the highway leading to and away from the park. In addition, limousines, tour buses, and tour vans were prohibited from bringing visitors to the park other than for a brief fifteen-minute sightseeing stopover at the upper level of the park. Finally, the City closed the park each Wednesday morning to allow workers to perform maintenance work. The measures taken to restrict access clearly penalized tour groups and favored independent tourists and residents.

In August 1990, the Friends of Hanauma Bay, a public interest group of volunteers, joined with the City and the University of Hawaii Sea Grant Program and established the Hanauma Bay Education Program (HBEP) to educate the public on the proper use of the park. Friends of Hanauma Bay set up a table on the beach and provided information about the bay, conducted tours, picked up trash, and offered alternative fish food to visitors—who were feeding inappropriate foods such as frozen peas, bread, and picnic leftovers to the fish—until fish feeding was finally banned. Volunteers from HBEP also gave lectures at schools and to community groups. The preserve recently began to open some evenings to attract local families to visit the preserve and participate in HBEP activities and programs on local marine life. In October 1994, a smoking ban was put into effect at the park.

The City's Master Plan for Hanauma Bay included significant improvements to the park infrastructure, including fixing the toilet facilities to prevent runoffs, moving the snack bar to the upper level of the park, and building an education center.

The City's management plan for Hanauma Bay did encounter start-up problems, as the access restrictions were not seamless. For example, tour operators would bus their customers to a nearby shopping center and transport them to the park via taxis. The City implemented new rules allowing taxis to make one drop per day, but they were allowed to wait for fifteen minutes to pick up a fare leaving the park. Visitors arriving in vehicles that were turned away by the guards would park their cars at a scenic lookout a half mile away or in nearby neighborhoods (causing a lot of complaints from residents) and walk into the park. The park manager estimated that as many as five hundred people were walking into Hanauma Bay each day.

Many tourists decided to ride the City bus instead, which was not banned from the park; park officials had to negotiate with the bus company not to add more buses on the route. Despite the many ways that people employed to circumvent these restrictions, the new management plan did reduce the number of visits to the park. The problem was that the management plan increased the cost of operating the park (by around $210,000 a year), yet it generated no revenues to pay for it.

IMPLEMENTING AN ADMISSION FEE

In 1993, a bill was introduced in the City Council proposing a parking fee as well as a $5 admission fee (or a $15 annual pass) for all visitors going down to the beach, with the revenues earmarked for park improvements. The mayor opposed the bill because it would also have charged residents for visiting the park. Indeed, a survey of Hanauma Bay visitors conducted by University of Hawaii students during the 1994 Veterans Day holiday found that tourists were willing to pay the $5 charge, but not residents. Residents strongly preferred the first-come-first-served rationing system.[25]

Nonetheless, in May 1995, the City Council passed an ordinance (No. 95-36) by a 6-3 vote to impose an entry fee at Hanauma Bay. Out-of-state visitors aged thirteen and over were charged $5 each to go down to the beach; Hawaii residents who could produce an ID were exempt. Fees were also assessed on commercial vehicles and taxis entering the park for sightseeing purposes.

The City administration did not oppose the fee in 1995 partly because elections brought in a new mayor, and a looming $50 million budget deficit compelled the administration to look for new sources of revenue. Existing user charges at municipal golf courses, the zoo, and the botanical garden were raised, and new charges were levied on school summer fun programs and at Hanauma Bay. In sum, the Hanauma Bay admission fee was never intended to discourage visits; it was strictly a budgetary decision. On July 1, 1995, the City began collecting admissions at the nature preserve.

The entry fee turned out to be a prolific revenue generator. For the first six months, the admission fee and commercial vehicle fees generated over $2.3 million; 568,673 visitors went through the gate. Among them, 82.7 percent were out-of-state tourists, and the remaining 17.2 percent were locals.[26]

The admission fee generated very few complaints from visitors—only one in the first three months. The story was different at the City Council. As soon as the ordinance was implemented, some council members tried to change it. The tourist industry first lobbied for a uniform fee for residents and tourists, arguing that it was unfair to charge tourists but not residents. The mayor countered that residents already paid their fair share through their property taxes. Having failed to achieve their objective, one council member led an all-out effort to rescind the ordinance altogether. Some sympathetic council members feared that a discriminatory fee would give Hawaii a bad image and ultimately hurt the tourist industry. Some were concerned that revenues from the fees were being diverted into the General Fund rather than into a special fund for exclusive use at Hanauma Bay. Moreover, since the fees were expected to generate about $4 million per year, while it cost the City about $1.2 million (including capital costs) to maintain the park, the fee could be construed to be a new tax, which the City is not permitted to levy without prior authorization from the State government. One council member simply objected to using Hanauma Bay as a "cash cow." Another noted that the City must live up to its agreement to keep the lands and bay in noncommercial, public, and conservation use. By charging an admission fee, the City was in effect operating the park as a commercial attraction and hence in violation of the original deed agreement.

On December 8, 1995, seven months after Ordinance No. 95-36 was passed, the same council members voted 8 to 1 to rescind it. Columnist Robert Rees noted that the repeal was the result of "industrial strength lobbying by Trans Hawaiian and other tour operators."[27] The repeal did not discourage the mayor, as he ordered signs to be posted to solicit voluntary contributions until an agreement on a new fee structure could be worked out with council members. In January 1996, he introduced a new bill (Bill 1) that eliminated fees on commercial vehicles and lowered the admission fee on tourists from $5 per person to $3. Bill 1 did not include an entry fee for residents; instead, a $1 parking fee was levied on all cars (including those driven by residents) staying thirty minutes or longer. The revenues collected would go into a special fund—the Hanauma Bay Preserve Fund—to be used for the operation, maintenance, and improvement of Koko Head District Park as well as neighboring parks. By a vote of 7 to 2, the council passed the bill in April 1996.

It was clear that the passage of Bill 1 was a compromise to appease diverse stakeholders in order to achieve political equilibrium. While not everyone got what they wanted, each stakeholder group got something. The $3 admission fee was clearly less than what visitors were willing to pay, but had it not been reduced there might not have been a fee at all. So, the City and the residents of Oahu did get a benefit. Moreover, residents were still not required to pay the admission fee. Tourists and tour operators generally were also winners since the admission fee was reduced and the commercial vehicle fees were rescinded. Environmentalists should have been happy as well, because money became available for a carrying capacity study and for educational and informational programs. The only people who might have been worse off were the Japanese tour operators (and many Japanese tourists) because they were still prohibited from bringing groups to the nature preserve other than for a brief sightseeing stop at the upper bay area. At $3 per tourist, the fee wasn't high enough to discourage a lot of visits, so the nonprice rationing measures (such as putting up road blocks, banning most commercial groups, and closing the nature preserve one day each week) had to be left in place. In the end, it was the visitors who were willing to expend the most effort that got to visit Hanauma Bay and not those who were willing to pay the most. The new revenue source financed a massive capital improvement program, including new offices, a gift shop, a snack shop, and an award-winning education center, where first-time visitors must view a short video before they are permitted to go down to the beach.

LEGALITY OF THE ADMISSION FEE

There were still questions about whether it was legal for the City to levy any admission fee at the nature preserve—especially a fee that exempted local residents. In July 2001, a tourist from San Diego sued the City in federal court for charging her and other tourists the $3 admission fee at Hanauma Bay.[28] The suit alleged, first, that the City was violating State law by charging for beach access, a right that she believed was protected under the Hawaii Constitution, and by restricting freedom of movement along a public right-of-way. Second, she argued that charging her but not residents also violated the U.S. Constitution because it discriminated against visitors on the basis of their residency. The suit further alleged that the City can only impose fees that the State government had authorized by statute, and the State had not authorized the City to charge an admission fee at Hanauma Bay.

Beach access in Hawaii has always been considered a fundamental right. Hence, a representative of the American Civil Liberties Union of Hawaii (which was not a party to the suit) sided with the tourist, opining that "Clearly the city cannot charge Hawaii's residents to go to the beach. If they can't charge state residents, I don't see how they can charge out-of-state residents, either."[29] The City countered with the argument that the main goal of the fee "is to preserve Hanauma Bay's fragile and unique ecosystem. . . . Giving preference to kama'aina is a long-standing practice in Hawaii. We believe charging non-residents is legal, and we will stick by it."[30] U.S. Federal District Court judge Alan Kay ruled in favor of the City. He ruled that the admission policy did not violate Hawaii's law granting free access to beaches because the admission fee was "only an incidental impediment to her enjoyment of the park."[31] Judge Kay further ruled that because residents already pay taxes that "underwrite" upkeep at the preserve, "it is appropriate to exempt or to preclude them from being charged an admission fee. . . . It is a permissible fee for a specific purpose, not an unauthorized tax."[32] However, the judge stipulated that the money collected must be set aside to be spent only on Hanauma Bay, and revenues previously diverted to other parks must be returned.[33] Judge Kay's ruling was upheld by the Ninth Circuit Court of Appeals in October 2004.[34] Levying an admission fee at Hanauma Bay paved the way for similar fees at other parks. Diamond Head was next in line to levy an admission fee. The Hawaii Community Development Authority is considering user charges on commercial users (e.g., fitness classes, filming, etc.) at the Kakaako Waterfront Park.[35] User charges make a lot of sense when most or all of the benefits go to identifiable users and nonpayers can be excluded at a reasonable cost.[36]

The number of visits to Hanauma Bay has declined since the entry fee was implemented in July 1995 (Fig. 6-1). For the same six months in 2005, total attendance was 456,398 compared to 568,673 in 1995, a decline of 19.7 percent. During the month of August 2005,[37] the average daily attendance was 3,725 compared to 4,213 in August 1995.[38] The decline in the number of visitors actually forced the City to raise the entry fee back up to $5 beginning July 1, 2003. Current revenues from admissions and the $1 parking fee average around $3.5 million per year, compared to the $2.3 million collected in just six months in 1995 when the City began levying an entry fee and commercial vehicle fee. By imposing a fee on tourists but not on residents, the City had hoped to encourage more locals to visit the preserve, but the number and percentage of local visitors actually declined.

Was the decline in visits (residents and tourists) to Hanauma Bay due to the entrance fee or to other factors? The sharp decline in the number of Japanese visitors to Hawaii (Oahu) since 1997 could have contributed to the decline in the number of nonresident visitors to Hanauma Bay. But that cannot explain the decline in the number of resident visitors who didn't have to pay an entry fee. The nonprice rationing measures were no doubt a significant reason for the decrease in demand by both tourists and residents for visits to Hanauma Bay. Under the plan, it became more of a hassle to visit the nature preserve. Visitors can arrive late and be turned away at

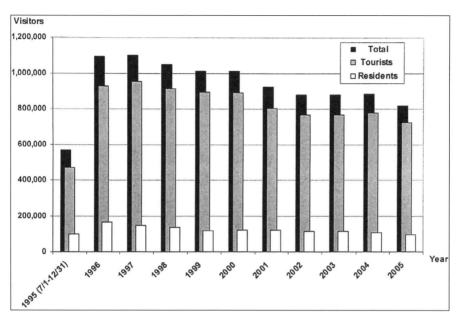

Fig. 6-1. Annual visitors to Hanauma Bay: 1995–2005.
Source: Hanauma Bay Nature Preserve; data kindly provided by Alan Hong (manager).

the entrance; once in, they would have to stand in line at the ticket booth to pay, to verify state of residence, and then have to watch a film on how to conduct themselves properly at the preserve (unless they had registered with the park on an earlier visit) before being allowed to go down to the beach. For people who are interested only in sunbathing or swimming and not snorkeling, it was simpler to go to one of the many other beaches on Oahu. Indeed, that's precisely the message that the City has tried to send out to potential visitors: Hanauma Bay is a nature preserve, not just another beach park. Anecdotal evidence indicates that conditions at the park have greatly improved following the implementation of the City's management plan. By most accounts, Hanauma Bay has been a success story in government intervention. Hanauma Bay, described by Dr. Beach as "a perfect little jewel," was named the best beach in America in 2004.[39]

Hanalei River Boating

The majestic Na Pali Coast on the North Shore of Kauai is a place of stunning beauty. Its remoteness and inaccessibility make a sightseeing trip along the coast even more desirable. For most tourists, the only way to see this nature's bounty is by boat. A number of entrepreneurs began operating commercial boats along the Na Pali Coast in the mid-1970s, ferrying small groups of campers who wanted to avoid the arduous 11-mile trek by land to the Kalalau Valley. The best known among the boat operators was Clancy Greff (famously known as Captain Zodiac), who started his Na Pali Coast tours using small, motorized rubber boats in 1976; for a time, he became the biggest operator.[40]

Running commercial boating tours of the Na Pali Coast requires government permission. Regulations governing boating in Hawaii are quite complex as they involve both the counties and the State government. Under the State's Coastal Management Act (HRS Chapter 205A), the counties were given the responsibility for regulating coastal development on lands above the high-water mark via their authority to issue special management area (SMA) permits. Special controls were placed on development in these SMAs to protect the state's natural resources and to ensure adequate access to beaches, recreation areas, and preserves. The State Department of Land and Natural Reources (DLNR)—or simply the "Land Board"—regulates commercial activities in the conservation district and on State land (beaches fall under both areas). People who apply for permission from the DLNR to conduct commercial activities along the Na Pali Coast must also get Kauai County SMA permits or a waiver from the County before the DLNR will process their applications.

The rapid growth of boating tours during the 1980s triggered alarms among residents of Hanalei who felt that too many boats and too many passengers would overcrowd the river mouth and harm its ecology, and they wanted the government to place limits on the growth of the industry. Boat operators saw any government-imposed restriction as a threat to their survival. Some operators maintained that the County had no authority to regulate boating on the Hanalei River since parts of it are a navigable waterway and thus open to the public under U.S. law. One operator (Ralph Young) contended that his business predated the 1975 SMA law and petitioned the Planning Commission to exempt him from SMA regulations.[41] In response to concerns expressed by residents, the State House of Representatives passed a resolution in 1985 directing the Department of Transportation (DOT) to examine the numerous conflicts over the use of coastal waters and beaches on Kauai and suggest a plan to resolve the conflicts.[42] The DOT plan, presented to the 1986 Legislature, essentially recommended keeping the level of boating activity at the 1985 level. The Land Board rejected the recommendation.

In 1985, there were an estimated twenty-two boating companies operating on the North Shore, most of them from the mouth of the Hanalei River at the Black Pot Beach Park. A careful study by the State Department of Business, Economic Development and Tourism found that in 1990, the tour boat business on Kauai generated direct revenues of $12.5 million per year and employed 340 persons, of which 57 percent of the revenues and 54 percent of the employees were derived from boat tours based in Hanalei. In that year about eighty-five thousand tour boat passengers took boating trips out of Hanalei, or an average of three to five hundred people per day, depending on the season.[43]

The mouth of the Hanalei River lies within the SMA; hence it lies within County jurisdiction. In 1987 the Kauai Planning Commission approved a request for a permit from Michael and Patricia Sheehan to open a boatyard along the Hanalei River to serve as a launching base. The County had encouraged them to build the yard across from Black Pot Beach Park so it could make the boatyard the key to the regulation of the North Shore boating industry.[44] Among the conditions of approval, the Sheehans could allow only operators with valid State permits to use their facilities.[45] In the meantime, the DOT also took over DLNR's umbrella SMA permit issued by the County. The umbrella permit allowed the DOT to issue permits to boat operators to conduct business from Sheehan's boatyard.[46] The DOT also instituted new rules that allowed no future growth of the industry and restricted boats to certain landing times.

In October 1988, frustrated by the hassles of applying for a renewal of its umbrella SMA permit from the County, the DOT withdrew its application, leaving thirty-one boat operators without permits. At issue was whether the DOT had to prepare an environmental impact statement as one of the conditions for extending its permit; the environmental group Wai Ola had previously sued the County for issuing permits to boat operators without an environmental impact statement. The DOT then decided that it didn't need a permit because the DOT's new rules aimed to limit and reduce the number of boats operating out of Hanalei and not to encourage new development. A flurry of lawsuits ensued involving the State, the County, environmentalists, and boat operators. The most important outcome from these lawsuits was a ruling and injunction issued by Fifth Circuit Court judge George Masuoka (April 5, 1989) that boating under Chapter 205A can be construed as development, thus requiring boat operators to obtain county SMA permits to operate within the SMA of the Hanalei River mouth.[47] The fifteen tour boat operators named in the County suit were enjoined "from ordering, initiating, conducting, performing or executing any tour boat activity within the Special Management Area that includes the Hanalei River mouth area."[48] Violators would be subject to a civil fine of up to $10,000 and up to $500 per day.

In 1989, Mayor JoAnn Yukimura tried to resolve the conflict between boat operators and residents via mediation. That quickly fell apart when boat operators walked out of the meeting with County and environmental representatives.[49] In mid-1991, the DOT announced that it would begin to enforce its Ocean Recreation Management rules.[50] That lasted only eight days, as an order from higher-ups in the DOT halted all enforcement activities, much to the dismay of Mayor Yukimura. The County realized that it did not have the ability to control boating on the Hanalei River and was counting on the State to enforce both State and County boating regulations.[51]

With State enforcement dead in the water, Mayor Yukimura then directed the County Planning Department to organize a community planning effort to craft a plan for a boating industry that would not have significant negative impacts on the Hanalei River Estuary. In September 1992, the day before Hurricane Iniki struck Kauai, the Hanalei Estuary Management Plan (HEMP), which came out of a series of town meetings, was put into effect. HEMP's intent was not to make commercial boating a "growth industry." HEMP recommended allowing up to six commercial boat operators to operate from the Hanalei River, each running a maximum of two trips per day with no more than seventeen passengers per boat. In the end, permits were issued to seven operators from among twenty-six applicants.[52] The seven permitted operators included two kayak companies, three sailing companies, and two motorized tour operators, carrying a maximum of 180 persons per day. Among the many conditions, the sailing and powerboats were required to moor their boats in Hanalei Bay and not in the river, and passengers had to be shuttled to the boats in crafts using electric motors or human power. HEMP put some operators out of business and spawned lawsuits, but it did not eliminate the illegal boat operators because, as one resident put it, "Our fine government didn't enforce the rules."[53]

Hurricane Iniki devastated Kauai in late 1992. By 1994, only four of the seven permitted operators were still in business. The four who had County permits found it difficult to compete against the illegal boaters. Indeed, "dozens" of boats were cruising up and down Hanalei River illegally in 1994, and their operators made no attempt to hide their activities. The four permitted companies were restricted by their size and hours of operation, while the illegal companies were working out of the Hanalei River without restrictions. The permitted companies had to pay 2 percent of their gross receipts to the State, while the unlicensed companies did not. The unlicensed operators were estimated to serve up to a thousand customers per day, compared to the 120 allowed the four permitted companies.[54] Ralph Young, owner of Hanalei Sport Fishing and Tours (one of the permittees), complained that the two trips per day he was legally allowed to operate were not enough to keep him competitive with the illegal boaters; the illegal operators had more business and thus deeper pockets. Young further noted that the controversy over Hanalei boating was not even an environmental issue: "The fish aren't dying, the limu's still alive. What you've got is a traffic problem."

In 1993, Mayor Yukimura wrote to Governor John Waihee, asking him to vigorously enforce State boating regulations, which included requiring boat operators to obtain County SMA permits as a condition of obtaining State permits. About a year later, the State issued one hundred citations, but they were quickly withdrawn because the State found it difficult to prosecute violators.[55] Shortly thereafter, a new mayor—Maryanne Kusaka—came into office, and she initially asked the State to withhold enforcement of its boating regulations. But by mid-1996, she too became frustrated by the lack of State enforcement. In an interview with the *Honolulu Advertiser* (July 1996), she said, "We had a commitment from [Land Board chairman] Mike Wilson and the governor to enforce county regulations. With the [State's] Kauai office of the Marine Patrol having been shut down, there was no enforcement at all."[56] At a meeting held at Kauai Community College on June 10, 1997, chairman Wilson announced that there would be no State enforcement until at least 1998 and until new regulations were drafted. He told the audience, "We will let the boaters know when we're coming to enforce."[57] He opined that ultimately, "This is a county issue."[58]

In 1996, three of the permitted boaters took matters into their own hands by suing more than thirty boat companies and hotel activity desks for "unfair competition" by illegally promoting and selling Na Pali Coast tours operating from the Hanalei River. Their lawyer explained, "The legal boat operators just got tired of waiting for the government to put a stop to this blatant disregard of the law." [59] But the suit was unsuccessful; it never went to trial. Then in June 1996, the State Supreme Court denied a petition filed by lawyers for the four legal boat operators asking the court to order the County Prosecuting Attorney's Office to prosecute the illegal boaters.[60]

Without vigorous enforcement, HEMP was doomed to fail. Finally, in late 1997, the State heeded the County's plea for help.[61] In December Governor Cayetano told the County to "Get out of the way, and we'll take care of it."[62] Kauai Mayor Maryanne Kusaka said gladly, "It is to Kauai's advantage that Cayetano has finally realized this as a state issue."[63] The State's first step was to try to amend HEMP. DLNR (the Boating Division had been transferred back to DLNR from the DOT) recommended the number of permits be increased to fifteen for an interim three-year period, during which a carrying capacity study would be conducted. There would be no limits on the number of boats, but there would be a maximum of 750 passengers permitted per day. The limit applied only to Hanalei River and not to Anini Beach or the Tunnels, which would be allocated additional permits.[64] Many North Shore residents opposed the DLNR's proposed plan and demanded to know why the existing HEMP rules that permitted only two tour boat companies operating out of the estuary with a maximum of eighty-four passengers were never enforced.[65] Land Board chairman Mike Wilson subsequently announced that the State would scrap its proposed rules and adopt the County rules.[66]

In January 1998, Kauai Mayor Maryanne Kusaka, who had earlier indicated that the County was going to step back from the controversy and let the State handle the hot issue, announced that the County and DLNR would begin prosecuting boaters who violated County boating rules.[67] In the same month, Michael Sheehan announced that the family would close its Hanalei boatyard, from which some of the nonpermitted boaters launched their boats, forcing them to look for new launching sites. The yard, which was built to handle fourteen hundred people per day, was seeing only a fraction of that number, and it wasn't profitable to keep it open.[68] By the summer of 1998, all the illegal boat operators had left Hanalei, most of them relocating to Port Allen on the southern coast of Kauai. The run from Port Allen to the Na Pali Coast, however, is close to 70 miles round-trip versus less than half that distance from Hanalei, and it is also less scenic.[69] If all of this is not confusing enough, there is more!

During the election campaign of 1998, Governor Ben Cayetano visited Hanalei and was "appalled" by the commercialism that he saw there. He subsequently ordered a ban on all commercial boating on the Hanalei River, a decision that prompted yet another round of lawsuits.[70] First, three boaters with County permits took the State to Kauai Circuit Court and won a suit against DLNR, holding that it was acting in violation of the State

Administrative Procedures Act. Then in 2000, the DLNR adopted new rules to outlaw all commercial boating on the Hanalei River. The three boaters sued the State in federal court. In August 2001, U.S. District judge Helen Gilmore issued a permanent injunction prohibiting the Department of Land and Natural Resources from closing down the three remaining boaters operating regularly out of Hanalei Bay. She ruled, "No state has the right to prohibit commercial vessels properly licensed by the U.S. Coast Guard from operating in navigable waters of the United States—including Hanalei Bay."[71] Her ruling applied to any federally licensed boating company. Judge Gilmore's ruling, however, did not address the question of whether boaters had a right to load and unload passengers and launch and retrieve their boats from lands adjoining Hanalei Bay. The County may still be able to limit the number of boaters and boats by its authority over land use. County planning director Bee Crowell observed, "Tour boats may be able to sail in Hanalei Bay, but if they want to use the land, they're going to need permits for a launch site, parking areas, restroom facilities. We can still limit the number of boats able to use the land."[72] The bizarre story has come full circle.

No issue has taken so long to resolve or spawned more lawsuits on Kauai than the fight over the regulation of boating on the Hanalei River.[73] Why did government intervention succeed at Hanauma Bay but fail in Hanalei? To be sure, Hanalei's problems were more complex. In Hanalei, there was bitter conflict between residents and tourist businesses that was not present at Hanauma Bay. There were also two governments involved in the dispute in Hanalei, not one as at Hanauma Bay. In Hanalei, emotions ran high and positions became hardened; as time went on, legal remedy became the remedy of choice rather than hard bargaining and compromise. Early and more Solomon-like leadership on the part of the State and County governments might have defused the dispute and produced a political equilibrium. That did not happen. It is obvious that in this case, the State and County governments dropped the ball. Hanalei River boating is not an example of market failure but of government failure. There was little cooperation between the State and the County to address problems arising from overlapping jurisdiction. Indeed, at times one level of government seemed to be working against the other. There was also never any clear statement of the objectives of regulation. Nor was there any systematic, well thought out plan to enforce regulations. An editorial in the *Honolulu Star-Bulletin* was right on the mark when it said, "The state, in conjunction with the county, should discuss the problems with the boat businesses and the public, lay out its plans and move ahead systematically. Otherwise, it can look forward to sailing in rough waters."[74]

Cruise Ship Waste Dumping

Cruising is growing spectacularly in Hawaii. So is concern about its potential negative environmental consequences. That is because a lot of the waste produced on cruise ships is dumped at sea.[75] Dumping becomes a particularly controversial issue when it occurs near shore.

In July 2001, the State of Alaska enacted a new law regulating cruise ship dumping in its state waters.[76] The new law applies to all cruise ships carrying fifty or more overnight passengers, as well as ferries in the Alaska Marine Highway System.[77] Florida opted to take another route, signing a Memorandum of Understanding (MOU) in March 2000 with the Florida-Caribbean Cruise Association on cruise ship waste dumping. Critics note that an MOU has no force of law, nor is there any penalty for breach of trust. To cite an example, the City of Monterey, California, had signed an agreement with Crystal Cruises not to discharge waste into the Monterey Bay Marine Sanctuary, yet in October 2002, one of its ships did just that. The company allegedly claimed that they "didn't violate the law, only their word."[78] In 2003, Governor Gray Davis signed into law two bills that banned cruise ship discharges of sewage sludge, hazardous waste, and oily bilge water into waters along California's coast and in marine sanctuaries. In 2004, California enacted tougher legislation that would bar cruise ship blackwater and graywater discharges and waste incineration in waters along California's coastline.[79] In 2004, Maine also enacted legislation that regulates cruise ship dumping of graywater off the Maine coast; but in contrast, in the same year, the State of Washington, the Port of Seattle, and the NorthWest CruiseShip Association (NWCA) signed an MOU regarding waste dumping.[80]

Hawaii opted to follow the approach of Florida and Washington. In October 2002, Governor Ben Cayetano signed an MOU with the NWCA that prohibited most wastewater discharges into state waters within 4 nautical miles from shore.[81] While the MOU had no sunset date, it had a provision to allow the parties to cancel the agreement. Proponents of this voluntary agreement argued that an MOU is more flexible than legislation and thus more easily changed if needed. Indeed, the agreement stipulates that the

MOU will be reviewed each year. Another advantage of the MOU is that, if it works, it also eliminates the need for costly enforcement. One harsh critic who helped to write Alaska's cruise ship legislation observed that Hawaii's MOU with the NWCA was a "worthless piece of paper" because it relies on self-policing by an industry that has "literally run amok since the 1970s."[82] Cruise ship owners responded that violations of the MOU would attract media attention and the ensuing negative publicity would be a strong deterrent to irresponsible behavior.[83] If the State's record in enforcing regulations on Na Pali Coast boating tours provides any indication of its likely effectiveness in enforcing cruise ship waste dumping, perhaps it is just as well that industry self-regulation be given a trial first.

But within a year of signing the MOU, the association reported that the agreement was violated about fifteen times, and some ships committed several violations.[84] The association noted that not a single gallon of raw sewage was spilled; it was mostly graywater. Two of the cruise ship companies pointed out that they were in compliance with the wastewater discharge standard over 99 percent of the time.[85] The Health Department agreed that the cruise ship reports "show substantial compliance."[86] The chairman of the Senate Transportation Committee, Cal Kawamoto, saw no need to regulate the cruise ship industry in Hawaii, explaining that "Environmentalists haven't come up with anything that's not covered in the MOU."[87]

During the 2004 legislative session, bills were introduced to regulate cruise ship wastewater discharges in Hawaii state waters, with fines for noncompliance. In testimony before Senate committees on February 14, 2004, industry officials cautioned that outright prohibition of dumping would provide a disincentive to owners to invest in advanced wastewater treatment systems onboard ships.[88] They pointed out that Alaska allows continuous discharges even in port as long as the ship has an advanced wastewater treatment system approved by the Coast Guard. For the Norwegian Cruise Line, which would begin interisland cruises during the summer of 2004, an outright ban even on treated wastewater would be "problematic." Unlike its ships that travel to Fanning Island in the Republic of Kiribati, which spend little time in state waters and can dump their waste in international waters, interisland cruises in Hawaii require cruise ships to spend extensive time within the state's coastal waters. An outright ban on dumping would likely force the cruise line to alter its ships' itineraries. One cruise industry expert argued that even treated wastewater presents a problem in Hawaii because "they don't deal with nutrient loading, which becomes problematic for reefs. No one is talking about this issue."[89] Nutrient loading refers to excess amounts of nitrogen generated from human fecal and food wastes. That could pose a threat to the state's coral reefs, which were recently valued at $10 billion and generate annual revenues of $360 million.[90]

Following several violations of the MOU, environmentalists renewed their lobbying efforts at the Legislature to impose penalties on unauthorized dumping. Finally, in 2005, the State Legislature passed Act 217, commonly referred to as the "cruise ship control law." Act 217 became law without Governor Linda Lingle's signature. In a letter to the Senate, she wrote, "The State of Hawaii presently regulates cruise ship discharges through a Memorandum of Understanding (MOU), which is more comprehensive than this legislation, protects a wider area, does not conflict with federal law, and allows for greater flexibility to adjust to changing environmental and industry conditions."[91] Critics of the new law agreed that it does provide for less area coverage than the MOU. While the MOU limited wastewater and ash dumping to 4 miles beyond the 100-fathom (600-foot) markers on depth charts of waters surrounding the Hawaiian Islands, the new law prohibits dumping within 3 miles. State jurisdiction over the ocean goes out only to 3 miles; beyond that is federal jurisdiction. Environmentalists became alarmed when the NorthWest CruiseShip Association president John Hansen subsequently announced that the cruise ship industry would be "transitioning out of the MOU as of December, 2005."[92] Apparently, the environmentalists wanted both the law and the MOU. Later, NWCA Hawaii lobbyist Charles Toguchi reassured the public by announcing that the industry intends to "honor the spirit" of the MOU.[93]

Act 217 still allows self-reporting of violations by the cruise ship companies. The executive director of the environmental group KAHEA noted that under the new law, "There is zero monitoring. The industry reports their own numbers. There's no mechanism for the state to do onboard inspections. At the [Department of Health] director's discretion, they can request the reporting documents, but there's no regular reporting schedule."[94] As Alaska's residents have found out, enforcing cruise ship regulations is not an easy thing to do. In 2006, Alaskans voted to pass a citizen initiative, Ballot Measure 2, which among other things would levy a $4 tax on each cruise ship berth to pay for onboard ocean rangers on every voyage to monitor ship pollution.[95] A bill (House Bill 164) has since been introduced to scuttle that requirement.[96]

In the U.S. Congress, legislation has been introduced to enact federal law (H.R. 1636, the Clean Cruise Ship Act of 2005) to set national standards for discharges from cruise ships.[97] In 2007, the environmental group Friends of the Earth filed a lawsuit against the federal Environmental Protection Agency, alleging that the agency has failed to respond to petitions filed seven years ago asking it to assess and regulate cruise ship pollution.[98] To date, there have been no benefit-cost analyses performed on cruise ship pollution legislation.[99] The issue of cruise ship regulation will not be resolved soon.

Concluding Observations

In this chapter, we have seen that (1) government intervention in environmental disputes does not always make things better; indeed, it can make things worse; (2) as conflicts often spill across jurisdictional boundaries, cooperation among the stakeholders and regulators is essential to resolve them; (3) regulations without enforcement are useless, and they also undermine people's trust in their government; and (4) as tourism continues to grow in Hawaii, competition between residents and tourists/tourism suppliers over use of the state's natural resources is bound to increase, and strategies must be developed to deal with them if Hawaii does not want to see local resentment rise against the tourism industry. An interesting approach that the State government is using is to bring together focus groups on each island to search for solutions to conflicting usage (e.g., commercial vs. recreational) of the beaches in Hawaii. Any solution must involve both the counties and the State government because the counties control the land and the State controls the sandy beaches and the ocean.[100] Of course, rules and regulations that come out of these meetings must be enforced.

Notes

1. Hawaii Tourism Authority (June 30, 1999), pp. 1–10.

2. www.outdoorcircle.org.

3. Bernardo (November 10, 2004). The Center for Bio-Ethical Reform planned to use a 50-by-100-foot sign to show pictures of aborted fetuses.

4. *State of Hawaii 2005 Data Book,* at http://www.hawaii.gov/dbedt/.

5. Personal communication. The latter part of the statement is contradicted by a 1972 State tourism study, which noted that "scattered development has been considered a widespread feature of tourism in Hawaii." State of Hawaii DPED, vol. 1 (1972), p. 123.

6. Hawaii Tourism Authority (June 30, 1999), pp. 1–15.

7. Arakawa (November 15, 2004), pp. F1–F2.

8. www.outdoorcircle.org; Wang (1982), pp. 206–207; Johnson (1991), pp. 260 and 373.

9. Coffman (2003), p. 203.

10. Munger (March 3, 1996), p. B2.

11. Ibid. David Callies argues that while State and county efforts at protecting coastal areas, wetlands, air, and water are worthwhile efforts, environmental regulations that prevent use of the land by private owners that "protect less than the human environment for health and safety" constitute a "regulatory taking" that needs to be fully compensated. Callies (1994), p. 80.

12. Achitoff (March 3, 1996), p. B2; Tobin and Higuchi (1992), p. 126; Dator et al. (December 1999), p. 17.

13. Dator et al. (December 1999), p. 17.

14. State of Hawaii, *Environmental Report Card* (Annual).

15. Accessible at http://www.state.hi.us/health/oeqc/annualrpts/index.html.

16. Dator et al. (December 1999), p. 17.

17. Hawaii is more oil dependent than any of the other forty-nine states. The state relies on petroleum imports for about 89 percent of its primary energy needs. State of Hawaii Environmental Council, *2006 Annual Report*, p. 2, at http://www.state.hi.us/health/oeqc/annual/reports/index.html.

18. Except for the consumption of propane gas.

19. Mak (2004), pp. 166–168.

20. R. M. Towill Corporation et al. (2004), p. 6. The ratio of visitor spending to resident household spending in 1997 was 22 to 1 in hotels, 19 to 1 in sightseeing transportation, 5 to 1 in air transportation, 10 to 1 in car rentals, and 3 to 1 in the amusement industry.

21. Caribbean Group for Co-operation in Economic Development (2000), p. viii.

22. For a more detailed history of Hanauma Bay, see www.co.honolulu.hi.us/parks/facility/hanaumabay/history/htm.

23. Those early numbers were based on estimates and not actual counts.

24. Mak and Moncur (May 1998), p. 217.

25. Mak and Moncur (1995).

26. Mak and Moncur (1998), p. 220.

27. Rees (January 3, 1996), p. 5.

28. Webster (July 11, 2001), pp. A1 and A6.

29. Nakaso (July 12, 2001), pp. A1 and A6. Interestingly, in a 1978 decision, the U.S. Supreme Court ruled in *Baldwin v. the Montana Fish and Game Commission* that tourists can be charged higher fees than Montana residents for elk-hunting licenses because elk hunting is not a "fundamental right."

30. Webster (July 11, 2001), p. A6.

31. Waite (October 18, 2002), p. A2.

32. Ibid. It should be noted that residents of the Neighbor Island counties who do not pay property taxes to the City and County of Honolulu are also admitted free as "residents."

33. The ruling did not apply to the disposition and use of concession revenues. Until 2000, concession revenues went into the County's general fund; in 2000, the County Council enacted an ordinance assigning the concession revenues to the Hanauma Bay Nature Preserve Fund. In 2004, the mayor tried unsuccessfully to get the council to reassign the concession revenues back to the General Fund. He failed to divert about $1.1 million of the $1.4 surplus in the Preserve Fund to balance the County's budget. Roig (2004a), pp. A1–A2.

34. Roig (2004b), p. B1.

35. Vorsino (April 23, 2007).

36. Mak (2004), p. 153.

37. July and August are usually the two peak months, and Wednesday is typically the peak day of the week. The preserve is closed on Tuesdays.

38. Recall that in the late 1980s, average daily attendance had soared to around seventy-five hundred. What we don't know is if tourists stay longer once admitted into the preserve after paying the entry fee.

39. http://www.drbeach.org/drbeach/ and HVCB *Industry Update* (June 1, 2004). This was the fourteenth annual ranking; once a beach earns the top spot, it is removed from future surveys. In 2003, the best U.S. beach was Kaanapali Beach on Maui. Since 1991, ten Hawaii beaches have received the top spot on Dr. Beach's "America's Best Beaches" list.

40. For an excellent interview with Greff, see Dixon-Stong (April 20, 1991), pp. A1 and A6.

41. He was unsuccessful. Nitta (November 13, 1992), pp. 1 and 3; Nitta (April 24, 1996), p. 2.

42. "Foot-Dragging Agencies No Match for Runaway Boats" (September 1991), p. 11.

43. MacDonald and Markrich (1992).

44. Nitta (1997b), pp. 1–2.

45. "Foot-Dragging Agencies No Match for Runaway Boats" (September 1991), p. 11.

46. Ibid.; also, "Owners of Hanalei Boatyard Allege Former Mayor Promised Them Profits" (January 1994), pp. 2–3.

47. "Development" is defined in the law as the change in the intensity of use of the water or land.

48. "Foot-Dragging Agencies No Match for Runaway Boats" (September 1991), p. 12. Judge Masuoka's ruling was reaffirmed by federal judge David Ezra in 1996 when he dismissed a $36 million SLAPP suit filed by the Sheehans in 1993 against Kauai County and several private citizens alleging that they were denied constitutionally protected due process when the County implemented a boating plan for Hanalei that impaired their ability to make a living. SLAPP suits are

frequently brought against environmental groups by developers to intimidate them from speaking out against controversial developments. "County Has Right to Regulate Hanalei Boaters, Federal Judge Finds" (October 1996), p. 6; see also Dixon-Stong (1993b), pp. A1 and A3, and Nitta (December 7, 1993), pp. 1 and 3.

49. "A Brief History of Tour Boats on the North Shore of Kauai" (December 1997), pp. 6–8.

50. Spring (June 11, 1991), p. 3A.

51. "A Brief History of Tour Boats on the North Shore of Kauai" (December 1997), p. 7.

52. Dixon-Stong (1993a), pp. A1 and A6.

53. Dixon (1997b), p. 1.

54. Conrow (September 6, 1994), p. A8.

55. "A Brief History of Tour Boats on the North Shore of Kauai" (December 1997), p. 7.

56. Ibid. Before that, DLNR had assigned two "marine patrol officers" to Kauai to oversee State boating regulations.

57. TenBruggencate (June 11, 1997), p. B4.

58. Beaudoin (June 12, 1997), p. 1.

59. Conrow (May 13, 1997), p. A5.

60. "Supreme Court Denied Petition to Force Boater Prosecution" (June 14, 1995), p. A1.

61. Nitta (1997a), pp. 1–2.

62. Cook (December 8, 1997), p. 1.

63. Moore (December 12, 1997), p. A4.

64. Sommer (December 14, 1997), p. 1.

65. Dixon and Sommer (December 17, 1997), pp. 1–2.

66. TenBruggencate (January 20, 1998), p. B1.

67. Ibid.

68. Ibid.

69. DLNR required boats operating from the commercial pier at Port Allen to pay a fee equal to 2 percent of their gross revenues. Subsequently, the U.S. District Court, Hawaii (2001), ruled in *Captain Andy's Sailing, Inc. v. Timothy E. Johns* that the fee was in violation of the constitutional ban against tonnage duties.

70. TenBruggencate (May 15, 2002), p. B6. On October 30, 1998, President Bill Clinton named Hanalei River an American Heritage River.

71. Sommer (February 4, 2002), p. A1.

72. Ibid., p. A7.

73. Dixon (1997a), p. A4.

74. *Honolulu Star-Bulletin* (February 6, 2002), p. A12.

75. Dixon et al. (2001).

76. www.state.ak.us/dec/water/cruise_ships/index.htm.

77. For additional facts on Alaska's law, see "Cruise Ship Fact Sheet" (February 12, 2004), at www.state.ak.us/dec/water/cruise_ships/pdfs/cruisefaqs.pdf.

78. Griffith (October 8–13, 2003), p. 5.

79. *Travel Weekly Daily Bulletin,* August 26, 2004.

80. State Environmental Resource Center (2005).

81. While the MOU addressed several forms of waste disposal, the most contentious issue has been wastewater dumping. For details of Hawaii's MOU, see http://www.hawaii.gov/doh/publichealth/nwcruiship-mou.pdf.

82. Dawson (December 11–17, 2002), p. 5.

83. Hansen (November 8, 2002), p. A20.

84. Yamanouchi (September 12, 2003), p. C1. By comparison, in 2002 the Alaska Department of Environmental Conservation sent one Notice of Violation to Holland America Line for fecal coliform violations by two of its vessels. In 2003, seven compliance letters were sent for sampling problems but no Notice of Violation. (In 2003, fifty-two vessels were registered under Alaska's law, compared with forty-four vessels in 2002.)

85. Ibid.

86. Ibid., p. C3.

87. Griffith (October 8–13, 2003), p. 5.

88. This is a weak argument, since cruise ships move from route to route depending on the time of the year.

89. Griffith (October 8–13, 2003), p. 5.

90. Cesar et al. (2002).

91. McNarie, *Hawaii Island Journal* (2005a).

92. McNarie, *Honolulu Weekly* (2005b).

93. Ibid.

94. Ibid.

95. Alaska Division of Elections (2006). The citizens of Alaska took the matter into their own hands after the Alaska Legislature failed to pass legislation containing the same package of provisions on cruise tourism. The law applies only to large cruise ships.

96. Jainchill (2007). Alaska law allows citizen initiatives to be amended but not repealed if the amendment does not change their core intentions.

97. The bill is accessible at http://www.theorator.com/bills109/hr1636.html.

98. Bolt (2007).

99. Godwin, *Travel Weekly Daily Bulletin* (May 21, 2007).

100. Aguiar (December 31, 2006), pp. A33 and A37.

References

Achitoff, Paul H. 1996. "Environmental Laws: Do They Hurt the Islands? No: Such Laws Are a Last Defense against Pollution." *Honolulu Advertiser,* March 3: B2.

Aguiar, Eloise. 2006. "Focus Groups Launched to Lessen Beach-Activity Conflicts." *Honolulu Advertiser,* December 31: A33 and A37.

Alaska Division of Elections. 2006. *For an Act Proving for Taxation of Certain Commercial Ship Vessels, Pertaining to Certain Vessel Activities and Related to Ship Vessel Operations Taking Place in the Marine Waters of the State of Alaska.* Posted 7/13/06, Petition ID: 03 CTAX, at http://www.elections.state .ak.us/petitions/03ctax.htm.

Arakawa, Lynda. 2004. "Farmers Embrace Agritourism." *Honolulu Advertiser,* November 14: F1–F2.

Beaudoin, Chris. 1997. "Governor Wants Mayors to Lead." *Garden Island,* June 12: 1–2.

Bernardo, Rosemary. 2004. "Judge Clip Sky Signs in Waikiki." Starbulletin.com, November 10.

Bolt, Kristen Millares. 2007. "Environmental Group Sues EPA over Cruise Ship Pollution." Seattlepi.com, May 9, at http://seattlepi.nwsource.com/ local/315059_cruise10.html.

"A Brief History of Tour Boats on the North Shore of Kauai." 1997. *Environment Hawaii* 8(6): 6–8.

Callies, David L. 1994. *Preserving Paradise: Why Regulation Won't Work.* Honolulu: University of Hawaii Press.

Caribbean Group for Co-operation in Economic Development. 2000. *Tourism and the Environment: An Economic Framework.* Report No. 20453–LAC. Washington, D.C.: Environment Department, World Bank (June).

Cesar, Herman, Pieter van Beukering, Sam Pintz, and Jan Dierking. 2002. *Economic Valuation of the Coral Reefs of Hawaii.* Arnhem, the Netherlands: Cesar Environmental Economics Consulting.

Coffman, Tom. 2003. *The Island Edge of America: A Political History of Hawaii.* Honolulu: University of Hawaii Press.

Conrow, Joan. 1994. "Hanalei a Haven for 'Pirate Tours'." *Honolulu Star-Bulletin,* September 6: A1 and A8.

———. 1997. "Legal Tour Owners to Kauai Court: Back Us Up." *Honolulu Star-Bulletin,* May 13: A5.

Cook, Chris. 1997. "State Vows to End Tour Boat Conflict." *Garden Island,* December 8: 1–2.

"County Has Right to Regulate Hanalei Boaters, Federal Judge Finds." 1996. *Environment Hawaii* 7(4): 6–7.

Dator, James, Michael Hamnet, Devin Nordberg, and William S. Pintz. 1999. *Excerpts from Hawaii 2000: Past, Present and Future.* Report prepared for the Office of Planning, Department of Business, Economic Development and Tourism. Honolulu: Social Science Research Institute, University of Hawaii (December).

Dawson, Teresa. 2002. "They're Heeere!" *Honolulu Weekly,* December 11–17: 5.

Dingeman, Robbie. 2007. "Farmers Sold on Ag-Tourism." *Honolulu Advertiser,* May 23: C1 and C3.

Dixon, John, Kirk Hamilton, Stefano Pagiola, and Lisa Segnestam. 2001. *Tourism and the Environment in the Caribbean.* Environment Department Paper No. 80. Washington, D.C.: World Bank.

Dixon, Susan. 1997a. "Will the A Team Listen to the B Team?" *Kauai Times,* October 4: A4.

———. 1997b. "Hanalei Boating: Positions Entrenched." *Garden Island,* November 4: 1–2.

Dixon, Susan, and Anthony Sommer. 1997. "Community Denounces Boating Plan." *Garden Island,* December 17: 1–2.

Dixon-Stong, Sue. 1991. "Small Boats, Big Stakes." *Weekend Kauai Times,* April 20: A1 and A6.

———. 1993a. "NS Boaters Expect Half-Dozen Permits." *Weekend Kauai Times,* April 18: A1 and A6.

———. 1993b. "Boatyard Owners Sue County." *Weekend Kauai Times,* December 5: A1 and A3.

"Foot-Dragging Agencies No Match for Runaway Boats." 1991. *Environment Hawaii* 2(3): 2–12.

Godwin, Nadine. 2001. "Environmental Group Seeks Tougher Regulations by Cruise Ships." *Travel Weekly Daily Bulletin,* May 21: article 156469.

Griffith, Lesa. 2003. "Crap of Luxury." *Honolulu Weekly,* October 8–13: 5.

Hansen, John. 2002. "Cruise Industry Stands by Its Word." *Honolulu Advertiser,* November 8: A20.

Hawaii Tourism Authority. 1999. *Hawaii Tourism Product Assessment,* vol. 1: *Executive Summary.* Honolulu: HTA (June 30).

Honolulu Star-Bulletin. 2002. Editorial. February 6: A12.

Jainchill, Johanna. 2007. "Changes Proposed for New Alaska Cruise Legislation." *Travel Weekly Daily Bulletin,* April 24: article 55985.

Johnson, Donald D. 1991. *The City and County of Honolulu: A Governmental Chronicle.* Honolulu: University of Hawaii Press and City and County of Honolulu.

MacDonald, Craig, and Mark Markrich. 1992. *Hawaii's Ocean Recreation Industry: Economic Growth, 1981–1995, and Management Considerations.* Honolulu: DBEDT.

Mak, James, and James Moncur. 1995. "Sustainable Tourism Development: Managing Hawaii's 'Unique' Touristic Resource, Hanauma Bay." *Journal of Travel Research* (Spring): 51–57.

———. 1998. "Political Economy of Protecting Unique Recreational Resources: Hanauma Bay, Hawaii." *Ambio* 27(3): 217–223.

McNarie, Alan D. 2005a. "A Lack of Cruise Control." *Hawaii Island Journal,* at http://www.hawaiiIslandjournal.com/2005/2a05a.hml.

———. 2005b. "A Shipload of Trouble." *Honolulu Weekly,* December 7, at http://honoluluweekly.com/cover/2005/12/a-shipload-of-trouble/.

Moore, Trish. 1997. "State Takes Over Kauai Boating Dispute." *Honolulu Star-Bulletin,* December 12: A4.

Munger, Lisa. 1996. "Environmental Laws: Do They Hurt The Islands? Yes: They Burden Business; Defy Common Sense." *Honolulu Advertiser,* March 3: B2.

Nakaso, Dan. 2001. "Challenge to Bay Fee Foreseen in 1995." *Honolulu Advertiser,* July 12: A1 and A6.

Nitta, Greg. 1992. "Planners Postpone Vote on Young Petition." *Garden Island,* November 13: 1 and 3.

———. 1993. "Sheehan Files Suit against Mayor, County." *Garden Island,* December 7: 1 and 3.

———. 1996. "Young Sues Over Boat Business." *Garden Island,* April 24: 2.

———. 1997a. "State Prepares to Dive into N.S. Tour Boat Stalemate." *Garden Island,* January 22: 1–2.

———. 1997b. "Sheehan Ties Resolution of His Lawsuit to New Boat Plan." *Garden Island,* March 9: 1–2.

"Owners of Hanalei Boatyard Allege Former Mayor Promised Them Profits." 1994. *Environment Hawaii* 4(7): 2–3.

Rees, Robert. 1996. "Punchout on Punchbowl." *Honolulu Weekly* 6(1): 5.

R. M. Towill Corporation, Progressive Analytics, University of Hawaii at Manoa Department of Urban and Regional Planning, and the University of Hawaii Economic Research Organization. 2004. *Planning for Sustainable Tourism in Hawaii,* part 2: *Economic and Environmental Assessment Modeling Study.* Prepared for the State of Hawaii Department of Business, Economic Development and Tourism. Honolulu: DBEDT (July 1).

Roig, Suzanne. 2004a. "Critics Ask Where Hanauma Money Goes." *Honolulu Advertiser,* September 6: A1–A2.

———. 2004b. "Hanauma Tourist Fee Stands." *Honolulu Advertiser,* October 27: B1.

Smith, Kirk R. 1993. "Are We Adequately Protecting Our Environment?" In Randall W. Roth, ed., *The Price of Paradise,* vol. 2 (Honolulu: Mutual Publishing): 259–263.

Sommer, Anthony. 1997. "Q & A about Boating Plan." *Garden Island,* December 14: 1.

———. 2002. "Hanalei Boating Debate Flares Up." *Honolulu Star-Bulletin,* February 4: A1 and A7.

Spring, Sarah. 1991. "County, State Crack Down." *Garden Island,* June 11: 3.

State Environmental Resource Center. 2005. *Cruise Ship Pollution,* at http://www.serconline.org/cruiseShipPollution.html. As of October 1, 2004, the center ceased operations.

State of Hawaii Department of Planning and Economic Development (DPED). 1972. *Tourism in Hawaii: Hawaii Tourism Impact Plan,* vol. 1. Honolulu: DPED.

"Supreme Court Denied Petition to Force Boater Prosecution." 1995. *Kauai Times,* June 14: A1.

TenBruggencate, Jan. 1997. "State Promises Not to Enforce Hanalei Boating until Mid-'98." *Honolulu Advertiser,* June 11: B4.

———. 1998. "County Boating Rules to Be Enforced." *Honolulu Advertiser,* January 20: B1.

———. 2002. "Hanalei Braces for Boats." *Honolulu Advertiser,* May 5: A1 and A6.

Tobin, Richard J., and Dean Higuchi. 1992. "Environmental Quality in America's Tropical Paradise." In Zachary A. Smith and Richard C. Pratt, eds., *Politics and Public Policy in Hawaii* (Albany: State University of New York Press): 113–129.

Towill Corporation. See R. M. Towill Corporation.

United States District Court, Hawaii. 2001. *Captain Andy's Sailing, Inc. v. Timothy E. Johns,* Civ. No. 00–00051 SOM–LEK (December 28).

Vorsino, Mary. 2007. "Kakaako Park Fees Considered." *Honolulu Advertiser,* April 23: B1 and B6.

Waite, David. 2002. "Hanauma Bay Fee Policy Rules Valid by Judge." *Honolulu Advertiser,* October 18: A1–A2.

Wang, James. 1982. *Hawaii State and Local Politics.* Hilo: University of Hawaii at Hilo.

Webster, Jessica. 2001. "Visitor Sues City Over Bay Access Fee." *Honolulu Advertiser,* July 11: A1 and A6.

Yamanouchi, Kelly. 2003. "Cruise Lines Admit Pollution Violations." *Honolulu Advertiser,* September 12: C1.

Chapter Seven

Improving Waikiki

Waikiki is a paradox. Visitors generally give Waikiki the lowest satisfaction ratings among Hawaii's resort destinations, yet it remains the state's most important visitor destination. For millions of visitors to Hawaii, Waikiki has been the window through which Hawaii is viewed. Until direct flights to the Neighbor Islands became possible (see chapter 8), Waikiki was the sole gateway to Hawaii. Waikiki accommodated 80 percent of the visitors to the state in 1960; this declined to 60 percent a decade later.[1] On Oahu, tourism was synonymous with Waikiki.[2] Waikiki has remained the flagship of Hawaii's tourist industry, even as tourism has grown faster on the Neighbor Islands since the 1970s. In 2002, 6.4 million tourists came to Hawaii and 3.7 million of them stayed (for at least some time) in Waikiki. On a typical day, Waikiki's 31,717 visitor accommodation units housed nearly 72,000 visitors per day, or about 44 percent of the state's daily visitor census. Waikiki accounted for over $5 billion (45.5 percent) of total visitor spending in Hawaii, 8 percent of the state's gross domestic product, 10 percent of its civilian jobs, and 12 percent of total State and county tax revenues in Hawaii.[3] Not surprisingly, keeping Waikiki attractive to tourists is a matter of statewide concern.

As important as this tiny 0.92-square-mile piece of real estate is to the tourist industry today, Waikiki is more than just a tourist enclave. It is also home to tens of thousands of Oahu residents (Table 7-1). Indeed, despite the rapid increase in land values and housing rents, the number of Waikiki residents actually increased since statehood (1959).

The 2000 U.S. census counted more than thirty-two thousand jobs in the Waikiki zip code area (96815), which includes a large part of Kapahulu (Census Tracts 15, 16, and parts of 17), and 40 percent of these jobs were in the lodging sector. Waikiki is also a popular playground and gathering place for social and business functions among local residents.

Table 7-1. Waikiki's daily population

	1960	1970	1980	1990	2002
Residents	11,075	13,124	17,384	19,768	19,720*
Visitors	7,717	21,926	46,500	71,600**	71,756

Source: Waikiki Improvement Association (1989), p. 3; *State of Hawaii Data Book 2003*, Tables 1.15 and 7.30.
Notes: * Year 2000 resident population; ** 1989 (estimated).

Prestatehood History

Waikiki was not always such a valuable piece of real estate. In 1906, Lucius E. Pinkham, president of the Territorial Board of Health, declared the area now known as Waikiki a public nuisance and health hazard. At that time, Waikiki was comprised mostly of duck ponds, rice paddies, and swampland. Pinkham offered a reclamation plan that called for Waikiki to be drained, dredged, and filled. He envisioned that the filling of Waikiki would enable the area to become an "absolutely sanitary, beautiful and unique district; one that would add immensely to the reputation of Honolulu at home and abroad."[4] Pinkham's reclamation project began in 1922 and was completed seven years later. A canal was also dredged to divert streams flowing into Waikiki; the project began in 1921 and was completed in 1924. The Ala Wai Canal became the geographic marker that separated Waikiki from the rest of Oahu.[5] With the completion of the canal, Waikiki was totally changed, as the ancient irrigation systems, the farms, the ponds, and the mosquitoes disappeared. The construction of the canal also created new lands that became the site of the current Ala Wai Golf Course.

Between 1930 and 1945, residential construction boomed in Waikiki, and the number of residents living there increased rapidly. While Waikiki had a distinctive local residential atmosphere, tourism development there was not at a standstill. Following a sharp reversal after the stock market crash of 1929, the number of visitors began to rise again after 1935. Glen Grant recounts the decade of the 1930s as perhaps Waikiki's most famous era.[6] Steamships arrived regularly at Honolulu Harbor on Boat Days to the strains of Hawaiian music played by the Royal Hawaiian Band, and tourists mingled with residents in Waikiki in what was quickly becoming a world-renowned tropical tourist destination.

Pre–World War II tourism development in Waikiki catered to the wealthy from America who had the money and could spare the time it took to travel nearly five days each way on a Matson steamship from the West Coast to Honolulu, plus another three or more weeks in the Islands. Many brought their own servants and luxury automobiles. These well-heeled visitors were all individual travelers who required a lot of personal attention. According to Chuck Gee, dean emeritus of the University of Hawaii at Manoa School of Travel Industry Management, "elegance, meticulous service, impeccable quality and a sense of permanence were the hallmarks of Waikiki tourism in the early 20th century."[7] When the Royal Hawaiian Hotel was opened in Waikiki on February 1, 1927, the *Honolulu Star-Bulletin* published a special eighty-page edition to celebrate the occasion, and the paper called the hotel the "finest resort hostelry in America," predicting that Hawaii would become the "playground of the Pacific."[8]

During World War II, Hawaii's tourist industry was suspended, as the U.S. military took over most of the hotels for its use. When tourism resumed after the war, debate surfaced over how best to develop Waikiki. Around 1952, the Board of Supervisors, with the support of a group of prominent citizens, wanted to revise the Waikiki beach master plan to allow hotels to be built on Kuhio Beach. Mayor John Wilson argued that cluttering the beach with hotels would serve to drive tourists away. He expressed his desire that the shoreline be reserved for public parks and beaches and that hotels should be built *mauka* (i.e., mountainside) of Kalakaua Avenue. The Board of Supervisors went ahead and approved the building of the Surfrider Hotel on the beach, right next to the Moana Hotel.[9] *Honolulu Advertiser* writer Bob Krauss surmises that it could have been worse and credited Mayor Wilson's "determined opposition" to development on Waikiki Beach as "a major factor in preserving the open space that now exists there."[10]

In 1955, Mayor Neal Blaisdell, in his inaugural address, proclaimed "orderly development" of Waikiki as a top priority of his administration. Unfortunately, no one could agree on what "orderly development" was. Property owners made it known that they did not want the government to tell them what they could do with their properties. In 1957, the Territorial Legislature briefly entertained an idea of creating a Waikiki beach development authority that would be independent of the control of the City's supervisors and the planning commission. There was even a proposal to make Waikiki a separate city.[11]

Rising Concerns

Statehood in 1959 gave Hawaii tourism a big boost. In 1963, Mayor Neal Blaisdell formed the Citizen Advisory Committee on Waikiki (1963–1966) to assess the conditions there. The committee reported that public services could not keep pace with the growth in Waikiki and recommended that it be downzoned.[12] More studies and reports followed. Between 1906 and 1969, twenty-six studies and plans were completed on how to improve Waikiki.[13] By 1976, the number had risen to twenty-eight.[14] Another advisory committee appointed by Mayor Frank Fasi in 1969 to study Waikiki concluded in its final report (1971) that "from 1906 to the present, it appears that the most significant factor in the development of Waikiki has been a similar inability, or failure, to act on plans and proposals to guide such development in an orderly and pleasing manner."[15] The committee put the blame not on the lack of studies and planning but on the lack of action.[16] It was politically less risky to authorize another study than commit to concrete action.

The 1970 State Legislature was also keenly interested in the situation in Waikiki and asked Tom Hamilton to prepare a document to be used as a basis for legislative discussion on Waikiki. In his *Memorandum* (dated December 28, 1970), Hamilton wrote, "Waikiki has deteriorated in almost every way. The important thing, however, is that it is not deteriorated to the point beyond redemption. If we act, and act now, we can not only save this asset from further deterioration, restore it to something of its former self, and, indeed, make of it an example of what a concerned community can do to preserve such an asset."[17] Hamilton did not offer his own recommendations to improve Waikiki; instead he pointed out that two plans completed by the Oahu Development Conference in 1968 and the Waikiki Improvement Association in 1969 were available, and that Mayor Fasi's Advisory Committee on Waikiki and Diamond Head still had to submit its plan.[18] A separate State study in 1972 concluded that "the extent of public improvements in the Waikiki area has been lower proportionately than for other resort regions in the State, and an acute need for public improvements such as parks, sewer lines, etc. has been demonstrated."[19] In 1972, the State Senate and House of Representatives issued concurrent resolutions requesting the City and County of Honolulu to rezone Waikiki to reduce allowable densities, establish new land use regulations, and fix an optimal size for the area.[20] The age of the jumbo jet and mass tourism in Hawaii had only just begun.

Waikiki's Problems

Waikiki's problems were not unlike those seen in other big cities plagued by rapid growth and too much density. In 1954, the Bennett-Maier Report, commissioned by the City's Planning Commission, warned of impending infrastructure problems in Waikiki due to uncontrolled growth and offered thirteen recommendations.[21] Ten years later, another report prepared for the City called for a planned development of Waikiki and Diamond Head.[22] Among its recommendations, the report proposed a limit of 23,650 permanent residents and from 18,500 to 27,000 visitors for Waikiki. In the same year, the City Council adopted its first General Plan for Oahu, which set forth the "Council's policy for the long-range comprehensive physical development of the City and County of Honolulu."[23] The plan recommended that "if Waikiki is to continue to attract an increasingly greater number of visitors each year that more emphasis be placed upon planted open space, underground utilities, building height limitations, bulk and density controls, improved vehicular and pedestrian circulation and widened and improved beaches."[24]

In 1969, Mayor Frank Fasi appointed a Planning Advisory Committee for Waikiki–Diamond Head (1969–1970) comprised of representatives from twenty-five organizations, one council member, and six of his department heads. The task assigned to the committee was exhaustive: to recommend goals for population, land use, economy, housing, transportation and traffic, recreation and open space, community facilities and services, social conditions, and the environment.[25] The committee's final report did not find much that was not already known about Waikiki. It noted that Waikiki suffered from inadequate public facilities and services such as streets, transportation, social services, overcrowding, lack of open space, poor aesthetics, and so on.[26] It cited "two general deficiencies": (1) inappropriate zoning (Waikiki was "over zoned") and political inaction or mistakes; and (2) rapid growth and the inability of public facilities to keep pace with growth. To remedy the problems, the committee offered over seventy recommendations, among them a key recommendation suggested earlier (1969) by the Waikiki Improvement Association (WIA)—a private interest group of tourism industry and property owners in Waikiki—to cap Waikiki's maximum daily census at approximately 65,000 people, consisting of 42,000 visitors and 23,000 residents by 1980 or 1985. That implied a ceiling of roughly 26,000 hotel rooms and 11,500 residential dwelling units. By comparison, existing zoning would have allowed 68,000 hotel rooms and about 9,000 dwelling units.[27] In 1970, Waikiki had a daily census of about 35,000 people, comprising 13,000 residents and 22,000 visitors, and about 17,000 hotel rooms (see Table 7-1); hence, there was still plenty of room to grow under the proposed caps.

The proposed unit ceilings became widely accepted as the optimum level of development for Waikiki. For example, in 1970, Governor John Burns' Travel Industry Congress adopted a resolution calling for a limit of 26,000 hotel room units in Waikiki.[28] The 1973 State Temporary Visitor Industry Council recommended a maximum of 26,000 hotel rooms and 11,500 dwelling units for Waikiki. In 1974, the City Council hired University of Missouri professor Robert H. Freilich to develop a growth control and density reduction plan for Waikiki, and he too recommended a hotel room cap of 26,000 units. In the same year, the State Department of Planning and Economic Development recommended 26,000 hotel rooms and 10,000 dwelling units for Waikiki.[29]

In February 1970, while the mayor's committee was doing its work, the administration asked the council to put a stop on all new construction in Waikiki for one year while the required analyses to determine the appropriate public policy were performed.[30] But the City Council did not impose a building moratorium on Waikiki until September 1974, four and a half years later. City planning director Robert Way speculated that "if the moratorium and the analyses that we suggested had been approved, much of the other ill-conceived construction in Waikiki would not now be in existence."[31] The building moratorium expired in 1976.

Waikiki Special Design District

University of Hawaii law professor David Callies observed that "there are few matters of public policy in Hawaii that do not include planning for the use of land."[32] That would be especially true for the improvement of Waikiki. In December 1975, the City Council enacted Ordinance No. 4541, enabling the establishment of Special Design Districts as part of the Comprehensive Zoning Code (CZC) for lands located within the State's urban district designation. The Waikiki Improvement Association played a crucial role in convincing the City Council and the mayor to establish the Waikiki Special Design District (WSDD). Many small Waikiki landowners were opposed to the proposed WSDD in hearings before the City Council, arguing that new setback requirements would reduce the value of their properties. Out of 800 private land parcels in Waikiki, 570 were less than 10,000 square feet. One property owner testified that, under the new setback requirements, he could develop only 400 square feet of his 3,600-square-foot property.[33] Proponents of the ordinance responded that small lots would no doubt have to be consolidated anyway since it was not economical to develop them. Indeed, since the mid-1960s, there was a trend toward the consolidation of small lots in Waikiki. The 1969 Comprehensive Zoning Code also encouraged lot consolidation; for example, the CZC required a minimum of 15,000 square feet of land for hotel development in H-1 and H-2 (hotel) zoned districts and a minimum of 5,000 square feet for hotel sites in B-4 and B-5 (business) zoned districts.[34]

In April 1976, the City Council designated the area bounded by the Ala Wai Canal, Kapahulu Avenue, and the Pacific Ocean—an area that encompasses U.S. census tracks 18, 19, and 20—the Waikiki Special Design District, and in 1986 it shortened the name to Waikiki Special District, or WSD (Fig. 7-1). As the zoning ordinance for Waikiki, the WSD imposed guidelines—which pretty much followed the earlier recommendations offered by the Waikiki Improvement Association—for new developments.[35] It aimed to (1) guide the orderly growth and development of Waikiki; (2) preserve, protect, and enhance the area; and (3) ensure that development in Waikiki would complement the new Diamond Head Historic, Cultural, and Scenic District ordinance that prohibits structures that would further obstruct the view of Diamond Head from Waikiki and Punchbowl.[36]

Prior to the establishment of the WSD, development in Waikiki was guided by the County's 1964 General Plan. Developers would send their building applications to the City's Building Department for approval, and they would get permits to build as long as their buildings conformed to code. In contrast, under the new ordinance, all "significant" projects in the district must first obtain the approval of the City Council. Thus, major developments in Waikiki came under the direct control of politicians rather than bureaucrats.

The new ordinance divided Waikiki into separate districts for residential (apartment precinct), commercial (resort-commercial precinct), and visitor accommodations (resort-hotel precinct). It also established urban design guidelines, a circulation plan, height, bulk, setback, sign, and off-street parking regulations and for the first time considered visual and physical impacts of proposed developments.[37] While building heights were earlier

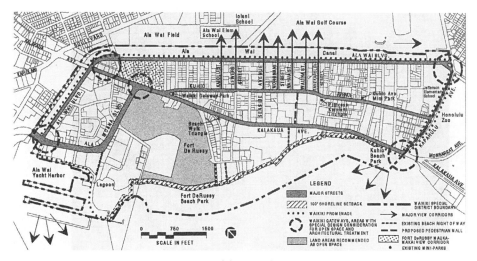

Fig. 7-1. Waikiki Special District.
Source: City and County of Honolulu, Department of Land Utilization,
Waikiki Special District Design Guidelines (1997), p. 24.

set at 350 feet, now building heights were reduced to as low as 25 feet, with most areas restricted to 220 to 300 feet.[38] Significant view corridors were also preserved.

The WSD ordinance did not specifically establish a ceiling on the number of hotel or residential dwelling units permitted in Waikiki, but it did establish a "floor area ratio" guideline to control density in new developments.[39] The maximum floor area ratio for new apartment/condominium buildings was reduced from 4.0 to 1.5 and for new hotels from 4.5 to 2.8.[40] Summarizing the effect of the WSD on development in Waikiki, a Waikiki Tomorrow Conference task force report (1989) observed that the effect of WSD "has been to create a sort of frozen situation or equilibrium."[41] The observation was incorrect, as a liberal grandfather clause allowed more than forty projects to be constructed under the previous, less restrictive zoning regulations. Thus, the new zoning ordinance actually accelerated development in Waikiki—at least initially. The number of hotel rooms in Waikiki increased from 22,117 units in 1976 to over 30,000 units in 1980 (Fig. 7-2). In 1981, the City Council adopted a new Development Plan for the Primary Urban Center whereby the optimum number of visitor units in Waikiki was increased from 26,000 units to "about 30,000 units" to accommodate the additional units that were built under the grandfather provision.[42] Finally,

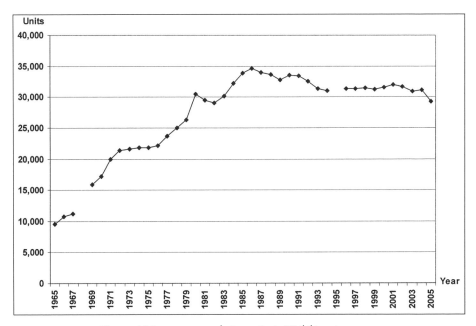

Fig. 7-2. Visitor accommodation units in Waikiki: 1965–2005.
Source: State of Hawaii DBEDT records, kindly supplied by Cy Feng; 2004
and 2005 from DBEDT, *Visitor Plant Inventory.*

in 1992, the City Council imposed an "absolute cap" of 32,800 visitor units in Waikiki, roughly corresponding to the actual number of visitor lodging units. The room cap was supposed to be in place for five years until 1997, and thereafter it would be reviewed every five years.[43] As of 2004, the original cap has not been readjusted because there was no demand for additional rooms during the 1990s and after 9/11.

Looking back twenty years, Patrick Onishi, director of the City's Department of Land Utilization, declared that the WSD ordinance lived "to slow down the growth that had been rampant prior to 1976—and it did do that."[44] Following the initial burst of construction activity, the records show that during the 1980s less than four thousand new visitor and residential units were constructed under WSD, compared to seventeen thousand units during the 1970s.[45] The growth *rate* of hotel rooms also fell, and many of the added visitor units during the 1980s were not newly constructed units but converted condominium units.[46] The WSD also discouraged the construction of massive, dense structures and improved the appearance of new buildings. Speaking before the Waikiki Tomorrow Conference (October 1989), city managing director (and future Honolulu mayor) Jeremy Harris proclaimed the WSD "the most important piece of legislation involving Waikiki since Statehood. It moved Waikiki planning from an emphasis on quantity to an emphasis on quality."[47]

But as it turned out, the 1976 WSD ordinance was found to contain major flaws. It was believed to discourage building owners from renovating and replacing their old buildings, and thus it worked against the City's effort to rejuvenate Waikiki.[48] Over 90 percent of the buildings in Waikiki were built before 1976.[49] The Department of Land Utilization found that 52 percent of the parcels in Waikiki exceeded mandated densities and 24 percent contained nonconforming uses.[50] Major renovations of nonconforming buildings would have been uneconomic because the original ordinance would have required building owners to comply with the more stringent density restrictions. In some cases, it would have meant tearing down entire buildings. The WSD was amended in 1996 to allow for more flexibility in approving developments in Waikiki, thereby reducing the economic disincentive to renovate or to rebuild.[51] However, not everyone favored the amendments. Donald Bremner, a former chief executive officer of the Waikiki Improvement Association, opined that the 1996 amendments posed a threat to "the attractive environment of Waikiki with over-crowding by fostering population densities like those found in New York City and Tokyo."[52] It is still too early to tell if Bremner's concern will become reality until tourist travel to Waikiki picks up again, following the shocks of 9/11, the Iraq War, and SARS.

The 1996 amendments also added a new provision requiring new buildings to "promote an Hawaiian sense of place at every opportunity."[53] Exactly what is "an Hawaiian sense of place" remained unclear: "Just as there is no universally accepted definition of 'aloha,' there is no universally accepted definition of an Hawaiian sense of place. Certainly, it can be seen and experienced within the physical form of Waikiki's historical, architectural and environmental elements. However, it is only through a combination of physical improvements, ongoing social and cultural programs and activities, as well as our people's attitude that [we can] truly create this experience."[54] Thus, "an Hawaiian sense of place" is more than just about building designs and densities, although both are elements in creating such an experience. To make the concept operational in determining which new building and renovation projects would be approved, the City published a guideline for developers—the *Waikiki Special District Design*

Guidelines—which details "the various physical elements that contribute to an Hawaiian sense of place."[55] The Hawaii Convention Center is widely complimented for evoking "an Hawaiian sense of place."[56]

Obstacles to Improving Waikiki

The road to an improved Waikiki in the post-statehood era has been a lengthy and arduous one, beginning with the development of Oahu's first General Plan in 1964. A number of reasons have been offered to explain the delays.[57]

Money, or the lack of it, has been a big obstacle to public investment in Waikiki. In his 1970 *Memorandum* to the State Legislature, Tom Hamilton estimated that it would take about $90 million over six years to pay for the "very needed" public capital improvements in Waikiki.[58] Honolulu City planning director Robert Way estimated that between 1969 and 1975, the City spent $11.5 million in capital improvements in Waikiki in the areas of transportation, public works, and parks but figured that it would require upwards of $100 million to "do it right."[59] Even in good economic times, Waikiki has not been high on the State and County governments' priority lists for capital improvement projects.[60] Good times tend to limit interest in policy changes.

Second, the residents of Waikiki and the coalition of landowners and the tourist industry have not always seen eye-to-eye on how Waikiki should be improved. A task force report issued by the 1989 Waikiki Tomorrow Conference noted that "The basic difference between residents and the industry is that residents are more cautious about change, while hotels and landowners are more willing to invest in private or public improvements, which will upgrade Waikiki's visitor market and its land values."[61]

At the center of the difference is the question, Improvements for whom? Residents have reason to be wary that expensive improvements they will probably be required to help fund but that largely benefit the tourist industry will hurt them or price them out of Waikiki. Indeed, the expansion of tourism has changed the economics of Waikiki. As old housing stock was demolished and replaced by hotels and condominiums, rising rents drove many middle- and lower-income residents out of Waikiki. In 1970 the annual median income of Waikiki households was $10,398, versus $12,035 for all Oahu households; by 1990, the annual median income of Waikiki households was $4,000 higher than the island median—$42,000 versus $38,000. In 1990, the median monthly rent in Waikiki was $754, compared to the islandwide median of $615, and the effective price difference was larger because Waikiki renters also had to settle for smaller units.[62]

There exists a strong consensus in the community—and that includes the tourist industry—that there should be a permanent place for residents in Waikiki because they provide diversity and stability to the area.[63] The residents, in turn, constitute an influential political interest group that neither the mayor nor the City Council can easily ignore.[64] Residents have actively opposed developments and improvements that they perceived might work against their interests. In response to growing concerns that tourists were occupying housing stock intended for residents, the State Legislature passed legislation in 1980 regulating the conversion of residential units to time-share use. In 1989 the City enacted tighter regulations on the conversion of condominium units to "transient vacation units" in areas not zoned for hotels.[65]

Overlapping jurisdiction between the City, the State, and the federal governments at times has also made it more difficult to bring about change in Waikiki. Although the State's 1961 Land Use Law assigned control of all lands in the urban district to the counties, the State and the federal government also have important jurisdictional responsibilities in Waikiki.[66] For example, the U.S. Army controls Fort DeRussy, which is currently the largest open space in Waikiki. The army's development plans for Fort DeRussy have run into conflict with goals in the City's Waikiki Master Plan. The State has jurisdiction over the ocean and Waikiki Beach as well the Ala Wai Canal, the Ala Wai Yacht Harbor, the Thomas Jefferson Elementary School, and the nearby Hawaii Convention Center. It also controls the major roadways/highways (Ala Moana Boulevard and the H-1 Freeway) entering and leaving Waikiki.[67] A developer planning a project in Waikiki may have to obtain environmental permits from all three levels of government before he can proceed with construction.[68] One mainland observer was surprised to find that despite Hawaii's relatively simple government structure, intergovernmental disputes over land use in urban areas are just as prevalent in Hawaii as they are on the U.S. mainland; in Hawaii, controversy arises most often over where the State's role ends and the counties' begins.[69] Turf battles between the City and the State have been known to tie up public improvement projects for years.

The issue of home rule has been an extremely sensitive issue for Hawaii's counties in dealings with the State over land use and development. There are divergent views on whether the City or the State ought to manage the development of Waikiki.[70] In October 1972, Governor John Burns asked Dr. Fujio Matsuda, director of transportation (and future University of Hawaii president) to review the impasse between the State and the City over the release of funds appropriated by the Legislature for Waikiki improvements (Act 204/72) and to propose a recommendation on which level of government should have the final say on when and under what conditions the appropriated funds should be released—in essence, to ascertain who controls Waikiki! In his *Report to the Governor* (dated October 1973), Matsuda stated his views as follows: "To bring to order the somewhat chaotic conditions which now prevail in Waikiki, the following recommendations are submitted for your consideration. In making these recommendations, we are guided by the philosophy that the development of the plans for Waikiki and the implementation thereof are basically the responsibility of the County. The State should not interject itself into the process without compelling reasons, and only if there are no alternatives."[71]

Matsuda pointed out that the State did have recourse to remedies if the City failed to perform, but it should not include a takeover of the City's responsibility for Waikiki:

> The first is to compel the City to discharge its obligations through appropriate sanctions and inducements available to the State Executive and the Legislature. One obvious way is to withhold all further State financial aid on all or selected County projects and programs. . . . On the inducement side, it would be desirable to remove the restrictions on the Act 204/72 funds. . . .
>
> The second approach is for the State to intervene and implement the improvements. . . . The inherent difficulty of proceeding in this manner is obvious since the actual accomplishment of the improvement district will involve and depend upon appropriate legislative and administrative actions by the County. . . . This second approach . . . is fraught with frustrations and delay if the County assumes a less than cooperative attitude. It is quite possible that the entire matter may end in court action, which may turn out to be the only way to accomplish the desired end of meeting Waikiki's needs, but it is hardly the most expeditious way. Even more important in the long run than the difficulty involved is the inevitable weakening of the principle of home-rule. . . . The State's intervention may even lead ultimately to the revision of existing law in order to permit the State to

proceed in Waikiki without County cooperation and approval. The situation must be critical indeed to warrant such extreme measures, and is not recommended unless a crisis situation affecting public safely and public health is obtained.[72]

Given that both the State and the City and County of Honolulu have huge economic stakes in Waikiki, the home rule issue has not been an easy one to resolve. There were occasions when the State has been only too willing to steamroll over the counties when it wanted its high-priority projects or programs implemented. In 1988, the State was set to override Honolulu's zoning regulations in order to build a massive, State-owned convention center in the middle of Waikiki, until it decided to build the convention center elsewhere.[73]

During Frank Fasi's twenty-two years (between 1969 and 1994) as mayor of Honolulu, contentious relations between him and the State governors further complicated the task of improving Waikiki. This was dramatically illustrated in 1971 after the Legislature passed Act 197 (later amended to become Act 204/72), appropriating $9 million for Waikiki improvements. In June 1971, Mayor Fasi asked Governor John Burns to release $1 million to initiate a planning study. Governor Burns refused and instead asked for more detailed information.[74] In his response, the governor pointed out that the legislative mandate covering appropriations states that "The governor shall determine when and the manner in which authorized projects shall be initiated."[75] Over the next four years, the mayor made ten requests to Governor Burns and Acting Governor Ariyoshi to release the money, but without success. A letter from Ariyoshi to Mayor Fasi, dated July 8, 1974, staked out the State's position:

> It is very clear to us that the original intent of the $1 million ear-marked for planning was and continues to be to fund project design and engineering activities. That is, they are to get the top priority improvement projects ready for early construction. They are not intended for such conceptual general planning studies as you now begin to indicate.
>
> It is indeed difficult to understand why for an area as important as Waikiki its general plan would not be current, and that we would now need to spend $1 million or even $300,000 in such a deliberately general manner as you outline. We would be led to believe that to recognize and undertake such an effort only now would be a serious

indictment of your failure over the years to recognize the importance
of this part of our community and economy. . . .

   To get on with the work, a plan of action for immediate implementation of priority public improvement projects and systems, as determined by your appropriate public works agencies, including your
transportation, traffic, parks, and water and sewerage departments
will be very much appreciated. When such a plan is presented, funds
authorized for general improvement planning under Item I-K-67 of
Act 197, SLH 1971, will be released expeditiously for engineering design and plans of specific priority projects in Waikiki.[76]

The Mayor's response to Acting Governor Ariyoshi, dated July 16, 1974,
reads in part as follows:

Your response to my request for the release of funds to lay the
groundwork for Waikiki improvement is appalling. You have delib-
erately sought to distort my request by stating that "it does not seem
that a $1 million planning effort is needed." Your statement implies
that all the planning has been done. Yet you ask me to submit a "plan
of action."

   I can only conclude that either you are toying with me, which is
inexcusable, or you really do not have any understanding of the task
to be undertaken. . . . I cannot comprehend what you are proposing.
You want "a plan of action" but no planning. Are you proposing that
we simply solicit a list of projects from each department and then put
them all together as the basis for proceeding with improvements to
Waikiki? This is the uninformed engineer's approach to planning.

   This approach results not in a plan, but a hodgepodge of individual
projects which may lead to further deterioration of Waikiki, not its
"enhancement." . . .

   Furthermore, your attack on my administration's planning efforts
is insulting to me and to the City's professional staff who have been
diligently working to improve planning for Oahu. The fact that your
statements were not a necessary part of your reply makes them all
the more offensive. It is incredible that an Administration which has
failed to produce any viable State plan can have the courage to attack
the City's planning efforts.

   Your statements demonstrate a total lack of comprehension of
our efforts to revise the General Plan, the nature of current plans

for Waikiki, and the planning required to resolve the current and emerging problems in Waikiki. The issues in this area do not simply concern digging new sewers and widening streets but the issues of growth and densities in Waikiki. Physical improvements must be a part of the resolution of these issues rather than ends in themselves.

Finally, at the conclusion of a meeting attended by both Governor Ariyoshi and Mayor Fasi in February 1975, the governor acknowledged that there had been too much politics involved and asked the mayor to submit another request for the money. By 1977, only $3,689,981 of the initial $9 million appropriation had been released to the City.[77] City planning director Robert Way charitably attributed the delay to both parties having different interpretations of the word "planning."

Obviously, one solution to avoid such State-City disputes is for the two sides to merge their responsibilities in Waikiki, but no effort was put forth to do so because neither party wanted to cede jurisdiction over what each considers its political turf.[78] The City's 1992 Waikiki Master Plan rejected a plan to coordinate State and County planning for Waikiki under a separate authority.[79] Getting the State and the County to work together to revitalize Waikiki took on more urgency in the late 1990s when Hawaii's economy was in the "doldrums" and tourism from Japan was in decline. One of the recommendations put forth by Governor Cayetano's Economic Revitalization Task Force in 1998 was to "establish a joint city/state analysis group to revitalize Waikiki."[80] Bills (H.B. 2556 and S.B. 2203) were introduced at the Legislature but did not pass. Instead, a joint State and County working group—the Joint Waikiki Task Force—was established in 1998 pursuant to a Senate and House concurrent resolution. Its membership includes representatives from the Waikiki visitor industry serving as "citizen members." The purpose of the Joint Waikiki Task Force is to "be a forum for both public and private investment and action needed to encourage revitalization" of Waikiki and, more specifically, to make sure that "state and city officials are fully aware of each other's plans."[81]

It is still too early to conclude how well this new cooperative relationship between the State and the County will improve planning for Waikiki over the long run. Waikiki certainly has not lacked for planning, task forces, or public discussions over its future. One review of the City's 1992, twenty-year Waikiki Master Plan pointed out that what it lacked was an implementation strategy and a menu of "carrot and sticks" to encourage private investment.[82] As an aging destination, Waikiki needed both new private and public investment. However, the City has few tools, other than zoning, to direct private investment. Through its power of zoning, the City can restrict private investment, but it can't make investment happen. Thus, it is more likely to be reactive rather than proactive when it comes to private development plans. Even the State, with its much larger arsenal of fiscal weapons, has limited leverage over private investment (see chapter 4).

Successful Private-Public Cooperation in Waikiki

Unlike the master-planned destination resorts on the Neighbor Islands, Waikiki faces complex cooperation problems. At Maui's Kaanapali, for example, a single developer is able to capture all the benefits of money spent on improving the resort, so he is not reluctant to make the necessary expenditures to keep the resort in attractive shape. This is not so in Waikiki, where ownership and interests are diversely spread. As we have seen in the case of generic destination promotion, businesses that don't contribute also benefit from the monies spent to attract tourists to the destination (chapter 5). Thus, the overwhelming incentive facing a single business owner is to free ride on someone else's contribution. Not surprisingly, private efforts to organize cooperative action amongst all who might benefit from destination tourism promotion typically fail to generate a sufficient amount of contributions. The same is true when it comes to private initiatives to make public improvements in Waikiki.

Since its founding in 1967 as a nonprofit Hawaii corporation by businesses and individuals committed to improving Waikiki, the Waikiki Improvement Association has spearheaded many initiatives to upgrade Waikiki. For instance, it led the successful effort to have Waikiki designated as a special district. But as a voluntary membership association, it faces the same cooperation problem faced by all such organizations. How do you get people to contribute money to a cause even when everyone recognizes that cooperation may not produce outcomes that will benefit them all? Not easily!

If private action was not sufficient, WIA found another way. It spearheaded an effort to persuade State and County lawmakers to designate Waikiki a business improvement district. A State law (HRS 46-80) was enacted in 1999 to authorize the establishment of business improvement districts; the corresponding Honolulu County ordinance (Ordinance No. 00-03) was passed in April 2000. Finally, in June 2000, Ordinance No.

00-40 authorized the establishment of the Waikiki Business Improvement District No. 1—Hawaii's first improvement district.[83] Once designated an improvement district, all the businesses in Waikiki are required by law to pay an annual assessment set by a private, nonprofit corporation—the Waikiki Business Improvement District Association (WBIDA). There are no free riders! The association's mandate is to work "in partnership with business and government to develop and implement programs that will strengthen the physical and economic vitality of Waikiki and help maintain its position as a world class resort destination."[84] Although the WBIDA is a separate corporate entity from the Waikiki Improvement Association, their closeness is evident by their sharing of office and administrative expenses.

So far, WBIDA has focused its attention on two programs launched in March 2001: a "Streetscape" maintenance program, which uses Malama Waikiki crews to provide supplementary street cleaning, landscape maintenance, and other beautification and maintenance services along the main Kalakaua-Kuhio Corridor, and a "Security" program, which uses Aloha Patrol officers to provide additional security patrols along the Kalakaua-Kuhio Corridor to discourage crime in Waikiki. In FY 2006, a total of $1.675 million was raised from the mandatory assessments levied on all commercial and nonresidential properties located in Waikiki, and an amount of $1.483 million was spent on program services.[85] Those businesses that benefit directly from the program services—that is, businesses located along the main Kalakaua-Kuhio Corridor—pay the highest rate ($.43/$1,000 assessed value in FY 2007) and those that benefit "indirectly" pay lower rates ($0.1433/$1000 assessed value for properties located in Kalakaua Makai and $0.1075/$1000 assessed value for properties in Greater Waikiki). The Waikiki Business Improvement District is a highly successful private-public cooperative effort to achieve a common goal that the government had been unwilling to undertake and private effort alone could not accomplish.

Action, Finally

During Mayor Jeremy Harris' administration (1994–2004), the City spent over $70 million between 1997 and 2004 to improve and beautify Kalakaua Avenue, Kuhio Avenue, and along the Ala Wai Canal.[86] Perhaps shaken by the decline of tourism beginning in the late 1990s, the industry has announced more than a billion dollars of new private investment in Waikiki.[87] In one massive redevelopment project, Outrigger Enterprises Inc.

transformed what was a narrow street, described as a "dark canyon," into a $585 million retail, hotel, and entertainment complex: the Waikiki Beach Walk.[88] Market forces appear to be working!

The *National Geographic Traveler* magazine notes that "As little as a decade ago, Honolulu was a decaying capital of kitsch, known for Don Ho and dashboard hula baubles. Savvy travelers hastily bypassed the city on the way to Hawaii's more glamorous outer islands. Today, the Hawaiian capital is paradise for culture vultures and food fanatics. . . . Waikiki may still have tchotchke shops teeming with tourists who sport bright red sunburns, but today they're over-shadowed by clean, wide walkways that meander past soothing cascades, gardens of ruby-colored ginger, and palmy hillocks. The only thing that hasn't changed are the crystal-lapis waters."[89]

Giving credit where it is due, State tourism liaison Marsha Wienert recently observed, "The whole revitalization of Waikiki has been a phenomenal development process. From just the overall appeal to what they are doing now in Kuhio; widening the sidewalks, putting [in] those trees. The City and County of Honolulu [are] the people that came up with the plan for that redevelopment effort and revitalization of Waikiki. They are the ones who have been implementing the infrastructure improvement. Along with the infrastructure improvement, of course, is the private sector who are realizing that they need to change their products as well."[90]

To be sure, not everyone is happy with the current improvements being made in Waikiki. Many residents have complained about the potential loss of public parking spaces and increased traffic congestion because the size and number of traffic lanes were reduced as a result of the City's new pedestrian-first policy for Waikiki.[91] Concerns over potential safety hazards caused by overhanging tree branches that could block the view of traffic signals convinced new mayor Mufi Hanneman to remove many of the newly planted trees. Honolulu architect Charles Palumbo argues that current changes are barely scratching the surface of what could be done with Waikiki, and a bolder and grander makeover should be considered.[92] But at least for now, no one is asking if anything is being done about Waikiki. For the future, the challenge facing Waikiki is to maintain a steady pace of renewal.

In reviewing the history of more than forty years of efforts to improve Waikiki, one cannot escape the observation that the issues have remained pretty much the same. To borrow shamelessly from Shakespeare, Waikiki is like a set stage; over the years, the same play is staged over and over again—only the actors have changed. This chapter has highlighted several fundamental themes that emanate from that play: State versus County jurisdiction; development versus open space and shoreline protection; private property prerogatives versus public goals; quality versus quantity in development; and residents' welfare versus tourist industry profits. These themes, no doubt, will be played around for years to come.

Notes

1. State of Hawaii Department of Planning and Economic Development (DPED), vol. 1 (1972), p. 51.

2. In 1965, Waikiki had 95 percent of Oahu's hotel inventory and 75 percent of the state's. In 2002, the corresponding numbers were 87 percent and 45 percent, respectively.

3. *State of Hawaii Data Book, 2003*, Table 7.30, at www2.hawaii.gov/dbedt/ from DBEDT, e–reports, *The Economic Contribution of Waikiki.*

4. Mayor's Planning Advisory Committee for Waikiki–Diamond Head Report (1971), Section 3, p. 1; hereafter referred to as the Mayor's 1971 Report.

5. An excellent early history of Waikiki, with pictures, can be found in Grant (1996).

6. Ibid.

7. Gee (1989), p. 15.

8. Cohen (2001), p. 42.

9. Krauss (1994), pp. 331–336; Johnson (1991), pp. 361–362.

10. Krauss (1994), p. 334.

11. Johnson (1991), pp. 362–363.

12. Arakawa et al., p. 59. Mayor Blaisdell's Citizen Advisory Committee came up with detailed physical plans for Waikiki and called for a limit of fifty thousand people in Waikiki, including tourists. Its recommendations generally conformed to the 1964 Oahu General Plan. Waikiki Improvement Association (1969), p. 2.

13. Mayor's 1971 Report, pp. 4–5.

14. Farrell (1982), p. 37.

15. Ibid., p. 2. The committee was charged with looking at Diamond Head as well. Wary of overdevelopment of Diamond Head, on August 5, 1969, the City Council passed Bill No. 102, enacted as Ordinance No. 3443, to amend the Oahu General Plan in the Diamond Head area to park and recreational uses. In February 1971, the mayor submitted a proposed ordinance to the City Council to establish the Diamond Head Historic, Cultural, and Scenic District. The purpose of the designation was "to preserve and protect Diamond Head's appearance; and to preserve and protect prominent views of Diamond Head." In June, the Planning Commission recommended the approval of this proposed ordinance. However, the ordinance was not enacted by the council until October 1975, four and a half

years later. The Save Diamond Head Association played a huge role in getting the Diamond Head HCS passed. City planning director Robert Way observed that if the ordinance had been adopted as requested, the Kaimana Beach Hotel could not have been built. Despite the delay, passage of these ordinances went a long way toward the ultimate resolution of the "Diamond Head issue." The establishment of the Diamond Head HCS contained the eastward expansion of Waikiki; thereafter, the center of development in Waikiki moved westward toward downtown. In addition to the Diamond Head Historic, Cultural, and Scenic District, there were other historic, cultural, and scenic districts enacted as well, including the Hawaii Capital District (enacted June 1972) and the Punchbowl District (enacted August 1975).

16. Farrell (1982), p. 3.

17. Hamilton (December 28, 1970), p. 1.

18. Ibid. The two plans are attached to Hamilton's *Memorandum.*

19. State of Hawaii DPED (1972), p. 59.

20. Freilich and Leitner (1974), p. 13.

21. Waikiki Improvement Association, "Position Paper of the Land Use Committee" (1969), p. 1, in Hamilton (1970).

22. Ibid.

23. City and County of Honolulu (1964), p. 2.

24. Ibid., p. 4.

25. Mayor's 1971 Report.

26. Ibid., p. 8.

27. Waikiki Improvement Association (1969), p. 3.

28. Arakawa et al., p. 60.

29. Letter from Robert R. Way, City planning director, to the City Council dated February 26, 1970, in Way (1975).

30. Ibid.

31. Ibid., p. 3.

32. Callies (1992), p. 131.

33. Arakawa et al. (1976), p. 53.

34. State of Hawaii DPED, vol. 1 (1972), p. 58.

35. City and County of Honolulu Department of General Planning (1992), p. 11; hereafter referred to as the Waikiki Master Plan (1992).

36. Ibid. (1976), p. 54.

37. City and County of Honolulu Planning Department (February 1996), pp. 3–5.

38. See City and County of Honolulu Department of Land Utilization (1997), p. 31.

39. The floor-area ratio is the total floor area of all buildings on a land parcel related to the area of the parcel on which the buildings are situated.

40. State of Hawaii DPED, *Physical Resources* (1978), p. 336.

41. Waikiki Improvement Association, *Report of the Physical Environment Task Force* (1989b), p. 11.

42. Waikiki Master Plan (1992), p. 12.

43. City and County of Honolulu Planning Department (February 1996), pp. 3–4.

44. Pang (1996a).

45. Waikiki Master Plan (1992), p. 12.

46. Ibid., p. 11.

47. Harris (1989).

48. Rosen (1998), p. 53.

49. City and County of Honolulu Planning Department (February 1996), p. 2-2.

50. Ibid., p. 3-5.

51. Ibid., pp. 3-5 to 3-7; Rosen (1998), pp. 52–56; City and County of Honolulu Department of Land Utilization (1997). Another reason for amending the 1976 WSD was to bring it to conformance with the 1992 changes to the City's urban center development plan.

52. Quote from Mr. Donald Bremner in Rosen (1998), p. 13.

53. Ibid.; also City and County of Honolulu Department of Land Utilization (1997), p. 1.

54. City and County of Honolulu Department of Land Utilization (1997), p. 3.

55. Ibid.; also Rosen (1998), pp. 15–16.

56. Although the Hawaii Convention Center is not located in the Waikiki Special District.

57. Wylde and Goodgold (1992). See also chapter 5.

58. Hamilton (1970), pp. 3–4.

59. Way (November 18, 1975), p. 2.

60. Wylde and Goodgold (1992), p. I-2.

61. Waikiki Improvement Association, *Report of the Physical Environment Task Force* (1989b), p. 6.

62. Ibid.

63. During his administration, Mayor Jeremy Harris even initiated programs such as Sunset on the Beach (which offers free movies on Waikiki Beach) and Brunch on the Beach to entice residents to visit Waikiki. Started after the 9/11 terrorist attacks, Sunset on the Beach has been enormously popular with tourists and residents—by Harris's own estimate, over a million people had attended the showings through June 2004—but there has been controversy over the cost of both programs to the City treasury. Between FY 2001 and December 2004, the free movies and brunch events cost the City treasury over $4.5 million. A 2005 City audit showed that resources were diverted from road maintenance projects to fund the brunch and free movie events on the beach. Newly elected mayor Mufi Hannemann vowed to end direct City subsidy of the events by 2006. *Honolulu*

Advertiser (January 14, 2005), p. B1; Gonser (June 12, 2005), pp. A1–A2; Leidemann (June 22, 2005), pp. A1 and A6; Dingeman (June 25, 2005), pp. A1 and A2.

64. Waikiki Improvement Association, *Report of the Economic Trends Task Force* (1989a), p. 13.

65. Wylde and Goodgold (1992), p. II-2.

66. Rosen (1998), pp.14–15.

67. Ibid., p. 15.

68. Ibid.

69. Rosen (1998), p. 31, footnote 52.

70. Ibid.

71. Matsuda (1975).

72. Ibid., pp. 4–5.

73. Wylde and Goodgold (1992), II-10.

74. In May 1974, the City provided a scope of work for the $1 million whereby $300,000 would be used to update the Waikiki General Plan and the remaining $700,000 would be used for detailed engineering and architectural planning. Way (November 18, 1975), p. 7.

75. Letter from Governor John A. Burns to Mayor Frank Fasi dated October 4, 1972. Subject: General Improvement Planning in Waikiki, reproduced in Way (November 18, 1975).

76. Ibid.

77. State of Hawaii DPED, *Physical Resources* (1978), p. 332. Of that amount, $2,629,117 was for land acquisition, $1,044,364 for construction of drains, and $16,500 for planning.

78. Rosen (1998), p. 15.

79. Ibid.

80. Grandy (2002), p. 116.

81. Joint Waikiki Task Force (1999), p. 14.

82. Wylde and Goodgold (1992).

83. A chronological history of the Waikiki Business Improvement District can be found on its Web site at http://www.waikikibid.org/.

84. Ibid. Its motto is "Malama Waikiki," meaning "Caring for Waikiki."

85. WBIDA, *Financial Statement for the Year Ended June 30, 2006,* at http://www.waikikibid.org/news.annualrpt.htm.

86. Gonser (December 15, 2004), pp. B1 and B10.

87. Shapiro and Brannon (January 30, 2003), pp. A1 and A12.

88. Sunderland (February 14, 2007), pp. 34 and 41

89. Kayal (2005), p. 40; see also Seidan (2006) and Dingeman (May 13, 2007), pp. F1–F2.

90. Alcantara (July 15, 2004).

91. See, for example, Fox (September 6, 2004), p. A11; Leidemann (October 26, 2004), pp. B1 and B6; Wu (January 21, 2005), pp. 1 and 28.

92. Wang (May 5–11, 2004).

References

Alcantara, Nelson. 2004. "The Future of Hawaii Tourism." *Travelvideo.TV* (July 15).

Arakawa, Milton M., Jr., Christina B. Ariola, Sylvia T. Hirahara, Rosella W. Sussman, and Ken T. Takahashi. 1976. *Special Design Districts for Honolulu.* Honolulu: Pacific Urban Studies and Planning Program, University of Hawaii at Manoa (June).

Callies, David. 1992. "Dealing with Scarcity: Land Use and Planning." In Zachary A. Smith and Richard C. Pratt, eds., *Politics and Public Policy in Hawaii* (Albany: State University of New York Press): 131–145.

City and County of Honolulu Department of General Planning. 1992. *Waikiki Master Plan.* Honolulu (May 15).

City and County of Honolulu Department of Land Utilization. 1997. *Waikiki Special District Design Guidelines.* Honolulu.

City and County of Honolulu Planning Department. 1964. *General Plan Oahu.* Honolulu.

———. 1996. *Waikiki Planning and Program Guide.* Honolulu (February).

Cohen, Stan. 2001. *The Pink Palace.* Missoula, MT: Pictorial Histories Publishing Company (June).

Dingeman, Robbie. 2005. "True Cost Double on Beach Events." *Honolulu Advertiser,* June 25: A1–A2.

———. 2007. "Outrigger Turns 60." *Honolulu Advertiser,* May 13: F1–F2.

Farrell, Bryan H. 1982. *Hawaii: The Legend That Sells.* Honolulu: University Press of Hawaii.

Fox, Galen. 2004. "Kuhio Ave., Ala Wai Projects a Mistake." *Honolulu Advertiser,* September 6: A11.

Freilich, Robert H., and Martin L. Leitner. 1974. *Establishing a Sound Future for Waikiki through Density and Planning Controls.* Submitted to the City Council of the City and County of Honolulu (July 25).

Gee, Chuck Y. 1989. "Resort Life Cycles: The Impact of Development." Presented at the Waikiki Tomorrow Conference (October 12): 15.

Gonser, James. 2004. "Waikiki Beautification Complete." *Honolulu Advertiser,* December 15: B1 and B10.

———. 2005. "Beach Festival Future Cloudy." *Honolulu Advertiser,* June 12: A1–A2.

Grandy, Christopher. 2002. *Hawaii Becalmed.* Honolulu: University of Hawaii Press.

Grant, Glen. 1996. *Waikiki Yesteryear.* Honolulu: Mutual Publishing.

Hamilton, Thomas H. 1970. *Memorandum addressed to the Honorable David C. McClung, President of the Senate and the Honorable Tadao Beppu, Speaker of the House* (December 28).

Harris, Jeremy. 1989. "Address to the Waikiki Tomorrow Conference." Honolulu: Waikiki Improvement Association (October 12).

Johnson, Donald D. 1991. *The City and County of Honolulu: A Government Chronicle.* Honolulu: University of Hawaii Press and the City Council of the City and County of Honolulu.

Joint Waikiki Task Force. 1999. *Recapturing the Magic of Waikiki: Report of the Joint Waikiki Task Force.* Honolulu (December).

Kayal, Michele. 2005. "Aloha, Again." *National Geographic Traveler* (January/ February): 40–44.

Leidemann, Mike. 2004. "Ala Wai Work Nearly Complete." *Honolulu Advertiser,* October 26: B1 and B6.

———. 2005. "Audit Slams Harris Team for Poor Roads." *Honolulu Advertiser,* June 22: A1 and A6.

Matsuda, Fujio. 1975. *Report to the Governor on Waikiki Improvement.* Reproduced in Robert Way, *Waikiki Presentation* (Honolulu: City and County of Honolulu).

Mayor's Planning Advisory Committee for Waikiki–Diamond Head. 1971. *Report.* Honolulu.

Pang, Gordon. 1996a. "People Taking Sides Early on the Proposal." At http:// starbulletin.com/96/04/02/news/story3.html, April 2.

———. 1996b. "Waikiki: Is Bigger Better?" Starbulletin.com, April 3.

Rosen, Mark J. 1998. *Waikiki Developments: Streamlining the Regulatory Process.* Report No. 4, State of Hawaii Legislative Reference Bureau. Honolulu: (December).

Seidan, Alan. 2006. "Hawaii Renovates: Waikiki Special Report." *Travel Weekly* (November), at http://travelweekly.com/multyimedia/waikiki2006113/p03 .html.

Shapiro, Treena, and Johnny Brannon. 2004. "Mayor Won't Rule Out Tax Hike." *Honolulu Advertiser,* January 30: A1 and A12.

Sokei, Debbie. 2003. "Renaissance Continues for Waikiki." Pacific.bizjournals .com, September 12.

State of Hawaii Department of Business, Economic Development and Tourism (DBEDT). 1998. *Waikiki: Hawaii's Premium Visitor Attraction.* Report of the Waikiki Planning Working Group. Honolulu: DBEDT.

———. 2003. *The Economic Contribution of Waikiki,* at www2.hawaii.gov/ dbedt/ (May).

———. 2005. *2004 Visitor Plant Inventory,* at http://www.hawaii.gov/dbedt/ info/visitor_stats/visitor_plant/. See also *2005 Visitor Plant Inventory.*

State of Hawaii Department of Planning and Economic Development (DPED). 1972. *Tourism in Hawaii: Tourism Impact Plan,* vol. 1. Honolulu: DPED.

———. 1978. *State Tourism Study: Physical Resources.* Honolulu: DPED.

Sunderland, Susan K. 2007. "The Making of New Waikiki." *Midweek,* February 14: 34 and 41.

"Sunset Events to Be Cut Back." 2005. *Honolulu Advertiser,* January 14: B1 and B4.

Waikiki Improvement Association (WIA). 1969. *Position Paper of WIA.* Repro-
    duced in Thomas Hamilton, *Memorandum* (1970).
———. 1989a. "Report of the Economic Trends Task Force." Presented at Wai-
    kiki Tomorrow: A Conference on the Future (October 12). Honolulu: WIA.
———. 1989b. "Report of the Physical Environment Task Force." Presented at
    Waikiki Tomorrow: A Conference on the Future (October 12). Honolulu:
    WIA.
Waikiki Master Plan. See City and County of Honolulu Department of Plan-
    ning (1992).
Wang, Li. 2004. "Healing Waikiki." *Honolulu Weekly,* May 5–11: 8–11.
Way, Robert. 1975. *Waikiki Presentation.* Honolulu: City and County of Hono-
    lulu (November 18).
Wu, Nina. 2005. "The New Kuhio Avenue: So Was It Worth It?" *Pacific Busi-
    ness News,* January 21: 1 and 28.
Wylde, Kathryn, and Sally Goodgold. 1992. *A Public-Private Partnership for
    Waikiki.* Honolulu: Vision for Hawaii 2020 (December).

Chapter Eight

The Neighbor Islands

Tourist travel to the Neighbor Islands before the arrival of mass tourism used to comprise side trips from a primary destination base in Waikiki (Oahu). The Neighbor Islands were somewhat out of the way, as the only way to get there was via connecting interisland flights at Honolulu after a strenuous flight of at least five hours to Hawaii. There was also much less to do on these outer isles, as they were "more rural, less urbanized, and far less sophisticated" than Honolulu.[1] Life on these isles has always been lived at a much easier pace. Indeed, stressed out and overworked Oahu residents would flee to the Neighbor Islands to spend long weekends in order to unwind, just as the Neighbor Island residents would travel to Honolulu to shop, dine, and enjoy its urban amenities. Hawaii's interisland airlines depended on these *kamaaina* (local) tourists to help boost their bottom line. Scholars who study tourism development would call Hawaii's Neighbor Islands the "peripheral regions" or, simply, the "peripheries."[2]

Hawaii's experience is not atypical of tourism development in other island destinations. Mass tourism tends to first cluster around major urban centers, although high-end specialized facilities may be located in peripheral areas.[3] Several factors help to explain this. First, the location of airports and harbors in major cities tends to make them gateways or entry points to the destination. Second, support services are more readily available to tourism suppliers in the central cities; so is the supply of qualified manpower. Third, pleasure travel is often a complement to business travel, and business travel is more likely to be concentrated in cities.

Tourism on the Neighbor Islands came alive beginning in the mid-1960s, although the statistics needed to show this are not very precise. Statistics on westbound visitor arrivals (i.e., mostly visitors from North America) have always been pretty reliable, but not so of data on eastbound arrivals

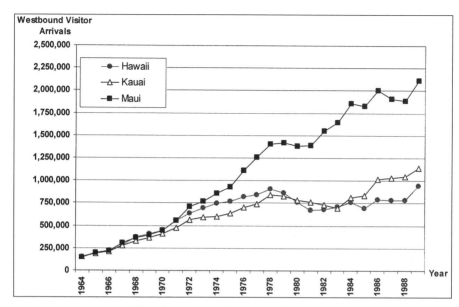

Fig. 8-1. Westbound visitor arrivals: Hawaii, Kauai, and Maui Counties.
Source: State of Hawaii Data Book, 1977–2005 issues.

(i.e., mostly visitors from Japan and Australia). Before 1990, the only reliable statistics on visitor arrivals to the Neighbor Islands comprised westbound visitor data. Fortunately, in the early days Hawaii's tourists were overwhelmingly westbound visitors.

Figure 8-1 displays the growth of *westbound* visitor arrivals in the Neighbor Island *counties* of Maui, Hawaii, and Kauai between 1964 and 1989. Maui County saw the greatest increase in visitor arrivals between the early 1970s and 1989.[4]

Figures 8-2 and 8-3 display the growth of *total* (including westbound and eastbound) visitor arrivals and visitor days on the *islands* (not counties) of Maui, Kauai, and the Big Island since 1990. Maui has seen virtually no growth in visitor arrivals; Kauai is still recovering from the devastation caused by Hurricane Iniki in 1992; and only the Big Island has seen modest growth in visitor numbers (Fig. 8-2). This does not mean that tourism has been in hibernation on the Neighbor Islands, as visitors have been staying longer and both Maui and the Big Island have seen some increases in visitor days (Fig. 8-3).

Another measure to track the growth of Neighbor Island tourism is the increase in the number of visitor accommodation units.[5] While the number

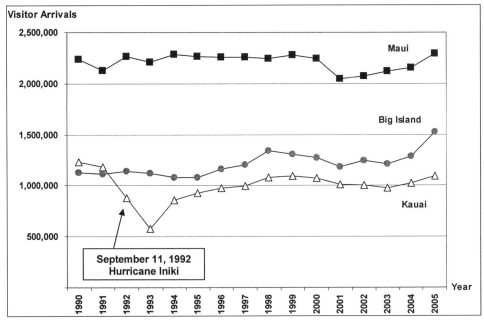

Fig. 8-2. Visitor arrivals on Maui, Big Island, and Kauai.
Source: Data kindly supplied by Cy Feng, State of Hawaii DBEDT.

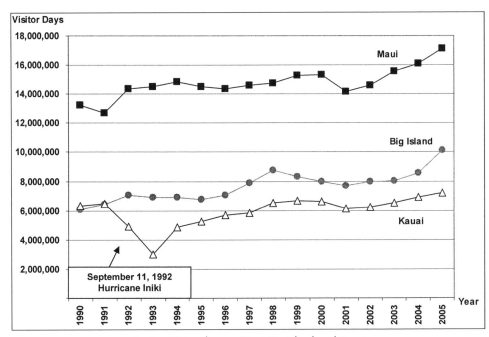

Fig. 8-3. Visitor days on Maui, Big Island, and Kauai.
Source: Data kindly supplied by Cy Feng, State of Hawaii DBEDT.

of tourist accommodations on Oahu increased from 10,031 to 36,851 units between 1965 and 1992 (the year statewide visitor plant inventory reached its peak), the number of units on the Neighbor Islands increased from 2,872 to 36,238 units.[6] Thus, by the early 1990s, half of Hawaii's visitor accommodations units were on the Neighbor Islands. Again, Maui County saw the fastest growth, followed by the Big Island and Kauai. The development of hotels and tourist arrivals progressed in tandem. (Unless otherwise noted, subsequent mention of Maui, Kauai, and the Big Island refers to islands and not counties. See chapter 1 for clarification.)

The Dynamics of Interisland Competition

Hotels on the Neighbor Islands were initially single properties built at points of interest, such as the Big Island's Volcano House, located on the rim of the Kilauea Crater; Hotel Hana Maui, located in "the last Hawaiian place"; and Kauai's romantic Coco Palms, known famously for its coconut groves and later also for its daily evening torchlight ceremony.[7] In the early 1950s, Inter-Island Resorts became the first Neighbor Island hotel chain, with properties on the Big Island, Maui, and Kauai. Island Holidays soon followed as the Neighbor Islands' "other" local hotel chain. Longtime Hawaii tourism executive Robert Allen recalled that "the two companies went head-to-head for a number of years, pioneering neighbor island hotel development well before the mega-resorts of Sheraton and Hilton."[8] The Kauai Surf Hotel, completed in 1960, was the first high-rise outside of Honolulu, and it didn't sit too well with some people who thought that Neighbor Island hotels should be low-rise structures with shake roofs.[9] Early island hotels were simple affairs; common features of the guest rooms included rattan furniture, tiki lamps, and tapa wall hangings.

In the early 1960s, Amfac Inc. began to build its now renowned Kaanapali Beach Resort in West Maui.[10] The master-planned destination resort was designed to provide just about everything a tourist wanted for a prolonged stay: hotels, restaurants, shopping, golfing, equestrian riding trails, tennis, and so on.[11] Amfac really had no choice but to include the full complement of amenities on the property; other than the nearby historic whaling town of Lahaina, the resort was located quite a distance from the island's population centers in Kahului and Wailuku. For years, the most common complaint of tourists about the Neighbor Islands was that there wasn't enough to do there.[12] The difficulty of getting around (i.e., mobility, or the lack of it) other than by rental cars was also a frequent complaint.[13] Tourists became bored in their hotel, as there were no other hotels, restaurants, and attractions nearby! Not surprisingly, the typical length of stay on the Neighbor Islands was brief—an average of about three days in the early 1970s. The development of Kaanapali was the beginning of a real change in Neighbor Island tourism. In 1971, Kaanapali had four hotels with 1,086 rooms and 262 condominiums.[14] By the late 1970s, it had about 4,500 units.[15] It would become the model for much of the future destination resort development on the Neighbor Islands.[16] Kapalua, another luxury destination resort also located in West Maui, came on line in the late '70s. Bryan Farrell writes, "Kapalua is the product of the personal creativity of one [majority owner Colin Cameron] who would not let go the concept of excellence while being yet willing to acknowledge changing public attitudes."[17] Alexander & Baldwin's Wailea resort in the Maalaea-Makena region of Maui counted two hotels with 950 rooms and three condominiums with 694 units in 1979.[18] The three luxury resorts on Maui would present a serious challenge to Waikiki for tourist visits to Hawaii.

University of Hawaii ethnic studies professor Noel Kent has argued that destination resorts are bad for Hawaii for several reasons. First, destination resort tourism "requires increased government subsidies" because the resorts are typically located away from existing infrastructure facilities and "built on a monumental scale."[19] There is, however, no evidence to indicate that destination resorts *require* government subsidies. Whether an individual destination resort generates more public revenues than costs depends on a number of factors; among the most important of these is how many in-migrants it will attract to the area.[20] While it is true that allowing resort development to sprawl may increase the (per capita) cost of providing public services to tourists, it does not follow that the added cost must be borne by local taxpayers.

Kent further observed that "Land speculation periodically grips the destination resorts, driving land prices to a level far beyond the means of even well-off locals."[21] However, housing and land price appreciation and speculation have not been confined only to destination resorts. The entire state has experienced episodes of sharp real property appreciation and speculation.[22] The causes of housing and land price inflation can be traced to several factors, among the most important being restrictive government land use regulations.[23]

Another one of Kent's complaints about the destination resort experience is that it is "over-seas dominated in the extreme."[24] He further claimed—but provided no quantitative evidence—that the tourist industry "repatriates huge sums of capital back to the metropole."[25] Data on capital flows are unavailable, but as long as the industry was expanding, it was unlikely that capital was flowing back to the metropole; the reverse was more likely the situation. All things being equal, Hawaii residents would be better off if its tourism enterprises were owned and operated by locals. But all things are not equal. Hawaii needed overseas investment dollars to develop its tourist industry.[26] The inflow of outside capital has raised overall income in Hawaii, although more consideration might have been given to how the benefits from tourism growth are shared among the residents.

Finally, Kent noted that "the destination resort literally engulfs the area where it is located."[27] That has been true on the Neighbor Islands. Indeed, a large destination resort development built within or near a small rural community can bring massive changes to the local lifestyle and split the community over the wisdom of permitting such a development. On the plus side, developers of these master-planned resorts on the Neighbor Islands have built and then maintained their properties in attractive condition. Planned resort development has avoided many of the negative spillovers associated with fragmented, "hodge-podge" development as seen in Waikiki and Kihei (Maui). Author and noted Hawaii photographer Robert Wenkam wrote the following about land development on the Big Island (1975):

> Citizen activists have played an important role in protecting Hawaii's scenic resources. But the natural beauty that is coveted so highly by tourist industry and conservationist alike has been saved not so much by courageous politicians and active conservationists as through an unusual combination of obstacles thrown up by nature . . . in concert with remnants of feudalistic land ownership. Three-quarters of Hawaii Island is owned by Kamehameha Schools Bishop Estate, corporate sugar plantations, large ranches, and the state of Hawaii. Land monopolies of this magnitude can afford to wait for the opportune time to develop. They are able to invest large sums in elaborate and carefully considered master plans and, perhaps most important, are able to undertake major investments in quality land improvements without demanding immediate payoffs.[28]

Public investment went hand in hand with private investment in tourism on the Neighbor Islands. Over on the island of Hawaii, a new jet runway was completed in Hilo in 1965, and two years later the Civil Aeronautics

Board (CAB) approved direct commercial passenger air service between the U.S. mainland and Hilo.[29] Hilo's expanded airport (General Lyman Field, renamed Hilo International Airport in 1989) opened another gateway to Hawaii.[30] In addition to bringing more tourists to the Neighbor Islands, it relieved congestion at Honolulu International Airport, made it easier for Neighbor Island residents to travel to the U.S. mainland, and provided direct shipment of Big Island produce—especially papaya and cut flowers—to mainland markets. It was a win-win situation for both tourists and residents. Unfortunately, direct air service between the mainland and Hilo was short lived, as rainy Hilo proved not to be as popular among tourists as many had hoped. Kona—on the west side—became the preferred destination on the Big Island.[31] In the 1970s, the airlines began cutting back overseas service to Hilo, and finally all direct service was terminated in 1987.[32] As direct overseas service at the General Lyman Field was decreasing, the Big Island's other major airport, the new Keahole (now Kona International) Airport was dedicated in 1970, and its runway was extended to facilitate direct overseas flights in 1994.

Throughout the 1960s and '70s, the State's official stance was to direct tourism development to the Neighbor Islands, and it did channel money there for tourism infrastructure development (see chapter 3). Improving and expanding airport facilities and highways on the Neighbor Islands were priority public investments. However, the real reason for the expansion of tourism to the Neighbor Islands was the desire of the industry to develop new markets.[33] The profit motive—not public investment or new transportation technology—was the primary driver of Neighbor Island tourism development. The dynamics of tourist travel in Hawaii had begun to change in a dramatic way.

Tourism on the Neighbor Islands grew faster than on Oahu for two reasons. First, among westbound visitors who came to Hawaii, about the same percentage continued to visit the Neighbor Islands. But increasingly, many who used to split their time in Hawaii between Oahu and one or more of the Neighbor Islands now chose to skip Oahu. In the early 1970s, nearly 95 percent of the westbound visitors to the state spent some time on Oahu; over 60 percent traveled to at least one Neighbor Island.[34] For example, in 1970, 358,000 visitors visited Oahu only, 387,000 visited Oahu and Maui, 383,000 visited Oahu and Hawaii, and 356,000 visited Oahu and Kauai.[35] By 1992, the proportion of westbound tourists to Oahu had fallen to 64 percent; nearly 36 percent of the westbound tourists visited only the Neighbor Islands, compared to less than 4 percent during the early 1970s.

This increase was aided by the inauguration of direct flights to Maui, Kona, and Kauai from the U.S. West Coast. Direct U.S. mainland to Maui flights began in January 1983, to Kona in the same year, and to Kauai in August 1984.[36] Only Kona has been able to attract direct flights from Japan to the Neighbor Islands.

Second, over time, visitors also preferred to do less island-hopping. Among all visitors, foreign and U.S., nearly 70 percent visited only one island during their stay in 1992. Oahu was still the most popular island, especially among Japanese visitors. Among westbound visitors, 63 percent visited only one island.[37] With fewer island stops per trip, westbound visitors spent more days on each island, although the total number of days spent in Hawaii (per trip) actually declined slightly, from 11.0 days during the early 1970s to 10.5 days in 1992. Curiously, the jump in the average length of stay on each of the islands occurred in 1983, about the same time that direct flights from the U.S. mainland to Kona, Maui, and Kauai began.[38] No one has yet figured out whether it was merely a coincidence or whether one (i.e., direct flights) caused the other. Westbound visitors to Oahu used to spend twice as many days on Oahu (about six days) as they did on the Neighbor Islands; by the early 1990s, the average length of stay (about seven days) was almost the same on all the major islands.[39] Among all visitors, foreign and domestic, the present average length of stay is around 7.0 days on Oahu, 7.5 days on Maui, and 6.6 days on the Big Island and Kauai.[40] Some 77 percent of all the visitors to Hawaii in 2005 stayed only on a single island. Thus, Hawaii has witnessed the fragmentation of what was once a single travel destination based in Waikiki into multiple destinations, with each island trying to develop its own distinct market brand. The Neighbor Islands are no longer the "peripheries."

On Maui and Kauai, tourism development took on a different character than on Oahu and, to some extent, the Big Island.[41] The traditional short-term visitor comes and leaves and stays at a full-service hotel—a transient rental. On Maui and Kauai, visitors are more likely to be part-time or "interval residents." They own a condo or—the current rave—a time-share.[42] Together, condos and time-shares now make up half the visitor accommodation units on Maui and Kauai. By contrast, on the Big Island and Oahu the figures are 27 percent and 15 percent, respectively. In the Lahaina/Kaanapali/Kapalua corridor, condo units and time-shares make up 53 percent of all accommodation units; in the Poipu/Kukuiula (Kauai) area, there are 1.6 visitor condo and time-share units for every traditional hotel room. At Princeville on Kauai, there are five times as many condo and time-share units as there are hotel rooms.[43] On Kauai, large numbers of time-shares were converted from former condominium and hotel units damaged by Hurricane Iniki in 1992.[44]

The visitor today is increasingly a stakeholder, a homeowner, and a member of a homeowners association. Visitors' representatives testify at public hearings. It makes a difference to the visitor's balance sheet whether the island's airport is upgraded, the highway to the resort is widened, or whether property tax rates are raised or lowered. These living units are not cloistered behind gated communities, but partly for economic reasons (i.e., most locals can't afford to live there), they are de facto physical and cultural enclaves. In a provocative article, John Knox suggested that separation between tourists and locals may contribute to the formation of negative stereotypes.[45] It is the very thing that concerns the industry the most about the growth of tourism: the erosion of Hawaii's famous hospitality—the Aloha Spirit. Among the 68 percent of the respondents to the Hawaii Tourism Authority's 2001 *Resident Sentiments Survey on Tourism in Hawaii* who believed that there is not as much Aloha Spirit toward visitors as there was "ten or twenty years ago," 37 percent cited "cultural differences" as the main reason for the change.[46] "Economic issues" (19 percent) and "competing for resources" (18 percent) were a distant second and third. Unfortunately, responses were not cross-tabulated by island of residence. Nonetheless, viewed from Knox's perspective, it is not surprising why both the industry and policy makers on Oahu have long insisted on reserving both living and recreational spaces in Waikiki for residents so tourists and residents (and not just tourism employees) can interact. On the other hand, the ongoing controversy over the proliferation of (illegal) vacation home and bed-and-breakfast establishments in residential neighborhoods suggests that interaction between tourists and residents may be good, but only in the right situations and settings.

Tourism's Impacts

One can hardly blame State and County officials for their enthusiastic support of tourism development on the Neighbor Islands in the 1950s and '60s. For at least three decades beginning in 1930, population on the Neighbor Islands declined as employment opportunities tied to plantation agriculture dwindled (Table 8-1).[47]

Keeping the Islands' young people at home and families together, instead of forcing them to move to Oahu or to the U.S. mainland to seek

Table 8-1. Resident population on Oahu and the Neighbor Islands: 1930–2000

Year	Oahu	Maui	Big Island	Kauai	State
1930	202,887	48,756	73,325	35,806	368,300
1940	257,696	46,919	73,276	35,636	422,770
1950	353,006	40,103	68,350	29,683	499,794
1960	500,394	35,717	61,332	27,922	632,772
1970	630,497	38,691	63,468	29,524	769,913
1980	762,534	62,825	92,053	38,856	964,691
1990	836,231	91,361	120,317	50,947	1,108,229
2000	876,151	117,644	148,677	58,303	1,211,537

Source: DBEDT, *2005 State Data Book* (2006); *State of Hawaii Data Book* (1976), p. 5.

employment, were laudable social goals that appealed to both politicians and plain, ordinary citizens. Citing "the disproportionate distribution of population and economic activity on Oahu," Governor John Burns placed the development of tourism on the Neighbor Islands as one of his top priorities.[48] Tourism was seen as the catalyst that would bring jobs and people back to the Neighbor Islands. Governor Burns' goal has been achieved. Tourism development has added a new economic and employment base to the Neighbor Island economies and helped to reverse the population decline, but it has increased the Neighbor Islands' vulnerability to external economic conditions and instability.[49]

On the negative side, the tidal wave of affluent tourists who descended on the Neighbor Islands put huge strains on the existing public infrastructure designed for small communities with modest demands. It has also taxed the tolerance of residents for more tourism development. By 2000, the average daily census of tourists on Oahu was 85,000; it was 44,000 on Maui, nearly 22,000 on the Big Island, and 18,000 on Kauai.[50] The ratio of tourists to residents was highest on Maui, where for every 2.5 residents on average there was one tourist. By comparison, on Oahu the ratio was ten residents for every tourist. During the peak month of the year (July), you can add another 20 percent to the average visitor count. In their now-classic 1976 book, *The Golden Hordes*, Louis Turner and John Ash surmised that "'Waikikification' of the outer islands seems inevitable."[51] The reference to Waikiki wasn't meant to be complimentary. "Waikikification" of the Neighbor Islands has not happened, nor is it likely to be acceptable to Neighbor Island residents anytime soon.

Political historian Tom Coffman argues that tourism growth brought political and social dividends to Hawaii, in that "More than any other single factor, the rise of mass tourism paid the bills of Hawaii's political liberalism . . . rapid economic growth was a powerful companion to the Democratic Party's goal of developing a politically progressive, multiracial society."[52]

University of Hawaii sociologist Andrew Lind had another take on this. Lind feared that the sheer number of tourists would pose a mounting threat to Hawaii's harmonious race relations.[53] In Hawaii, everyone is a member of an ethnic minority. Native Hawaiians have become more vocal in recent years about being marginalized by tourism.[54]

Newly arrived permanent residents to the Islands, drawn by the rapid growth of employment opportunities created by tourism, pose an even greater challenge to the state's social harmony. At a conference on Alternative Economic Futures for Hawaii held in March 1973, State Statistician Robert Schmitt presented statistics that compared the demographics of Hawaii's newcomers *(malihini)*—those who were living elsewhere a year earlier—for 1971 versus longtime residents *(kamaaina).* He noted that the newcomers were much younger than the *kamaaina* (median age of 21 vs. 27); disproportionately Caucasian (70 percent vs. 25 percent); better educated (38.5 percent of those 25 and over among the newscomers had at least thirteen years of schooling vs. 24.6 percent among the *kamaaina*); and held higher status jobs (35.2 percent among newcomers were professional or managerial workers vs. 28.6 percent for the *kamaaina*).[55] The current resident populations of the Neighbor Islands are significantly more "white" than Oahu's.[56] If the post–World War II political history of Hawaii is about the mixing of peoples from different ethnicity and backgrounds, as Coffman suggests, how the recent changes in Hawaii's demographics affect the future concentration of political and economic power and race relations in the Islands remains somewhat cloudy. Even less clear is whether the coming changes are likely to make Hawaii a better or worse place for tourists and residents.

Visitor and Resident Sentiments on Tourism

Post-trip visitor satisfaction surveys find that tourists—especially those from North America and Europe—like their visits to the Neighbor Islands a lot (Table 8-2).

The percentages reported in Table 8-2 have remained relatively stable in recent years. Visitors to Maui are more likely to report an excellent trip experience than visitors to the other major islands. Kauai is not far behind.

Table 8-2. Island experience rated as excellent: 2005 (percent)

Visitors from	Oahu	Maui	Big Island	Kauai
U.S.	55.1	73.3	59.3	70.6
Japan	53.7	57.8	50.9	47.9
Canada	54.6	68.0	56.9	65.3
Europe	57.5	68.2	56.8	69.9

Source: DBEDT, *2005 Visitor Satisfaction and Activity Report* (2006), pp. 14–16.

In 2006, readers of *Travel + Leisure* magazine voted Kauai the second-best island in the world (after Bali); Maui came in third and the Big Island seventh, based on natural attractions, activities and sights, restaurants and food, people, and value.[57] Year after year, readers of the competing travel magazine *Conde Nast Traveler* have rated Maui as their best island in the world.[58]

Island residents, by comparison, harbor mixed sentiments on tourism. The Hawaii Tourism Authority's *2006 Survey of Resident Sentiments on Tourism in Hawaii* tallied the following percentages in responses to several general statements about tourism on their island:

Statement: This island is being run for tourists at the expense of local people.

	Oahu	Maui	Big Island	Kauai
Strongly agree	33	46	31	44
Somewhat agree	27	31	26	25
Somewhat disagree	23	8	13	12
Strongly disagree	12	9	25	11
Don't know/refused	5	5	4	6

Statement: Overall, tourism has brought more benefits than problems to this island.

	Oahu	Maui	Big Island	Kauai
Strongly agree	46	34	43	44
Somewhat agree	30	34	29	19
Somewhat disagree	12	14	10	15
Strongly disagree	7	12	14	12
Don't know/refused	5	6	4	8

Statement: My island's economy is too dependent on tourism.

	Oahu	Maui	Big Island	Kauai
Strongly agree	53	64	44	58
Somewhat agree	26	22	27	23
Somewhat disagree	12	6	8	12
Strongly disagree	7	5	12	4
Don't know/refused	4	2	1	2

Statement: Even if more visitors come, I don't want to see any more hotels on this island.

	Oahu	Maui	Big Island	Kauai
Strongly agree	45	50	38	58
Somewhat agree	21	21	14	18
Somewhat disagree	15	8	9	10
Strongly disagree	14	19	17	32
Don't know/refused	5	3	3	1

Statement: We need more tourism jobs on this island.

	Oahu	Maui	Big Island	Kauai
Strongly agree	30	18	32	21
Somewhat agree	22	25	22	23
Somewhat disagree	21	17	11	17
Strongly disagree	19	34	31	34
Don't know/refused	8	6	5	4

Several observations can be made about these responses. First, responses vary among residents from the different islands. Oahu and Big Island residents appear to be more positive on tourism than residents of Maui and Kauai. Maui County is the most tourism dependent county in the state; 39 percent of its economy (the "gross county product") is attributable to tourism, compared to 19 to 29 percent for the other counties.[59] With so much of their income derived from tourism, one might think that Maui residents would be the most receptive toward tourism. This is not so! Second, most respondents see tourism as bringing more "benefits" than "problems" to their island, even though the majority of them believe that tourism interests are given preferential treatment over their interests. This is arguably the most important revelation about residents' overall positive or negative attitude toward tourism. Third, responses to some of the statements don't necessarily reflect either negative or positive feelings toward tourism. For example, many people who believe that the state is too dependent on tourism do not necessarily harbor ill feelings toward tourism. They prefer a more diversified economy. Responses to the statement about the need for more tourism jobs may be influenced by the respondents' views on the economy's dependence on tourism. Thus, for most Hawaii residents, tourism's net balance sheet is positive rather than negative.

Extant literature suggests that resident sentiments toward tourism depend on the stage of tourism development at a destination. G. V. Doxey, for instance, suggests that reactions of residents toward tourists/tourism go through four stages: *euphoria, apathy, annoyance,* and *antagonism.*[60] At first, residents are excited by the prospects of tourism development in their community. More jobs! More money! They welcome tourists with open arms. In time, euphoria gives way to apathy and then to irritation, as tourists increasingly compete with residents for access to resources and threaten the residents' way of life. Conflict soon follows. Finally, irritation leads to something more serious: antagonism. Tom Hamilton offered a similar progression of resident reactions toward tourism (see chapter 2). John Ap and John Crompton, however, suggest that residents make adjustments to adapt to the presence of tourists.[61]

The evidence from Hawaii suggests a somewhat different path of resident reactions toward tourism. For that we compare two separate surveys of Hawaii residents conducted thirty-one years apart: 1975 and 2006. In 1975, Hawaii hosted 2.8 million tourists, compared to 7.5 million in 2006. While the wording of the survey instruments in the two studies are not exactly the same, they are reasonably close. For example, in the 1975 survey, respondents were asked to respond to the following statement: "In general I believe tourism is: (1) good for Hawaii, (2) bad for Hawaii, (3) of uncertain value to Hawaii, and (4) no reply to this question." In the 2006 study, respondents were asked to respond to the following statement: "Overall, tourism has brought more benefits than problems to this island: (1) strongly agree, (2) somewhat agree, (3) somewhat disagree, (4) strongly disagree, and (5) don't know/refused." If it is permitted to accept the sum of the responses

to "strongly agree" and "somewhat agree" (2006) as "good" (1975), the sum
of "somewhat disagree" and "strongly disagree" (2006) as "bad" (1975), and
the sum of "uncertain value" and "no reply to this question" (1975) as "don't
know/refused" (2006), we have the following changes in the distribution of
resident attitudes toward tourism by county between the two years:[62]

	Oahu	Maui	Big Island	Kauai
	1975/2006	1975/2006	1975/2006	1975/2006
Good	73.1 / 76.0	71.5 / 69.0	80.6 / 72.0	71.5 / 63.0
Bad	5.6 / 19.0	5.9 / 26.0	4.4 / 24.0	2.7 / 27.0
Don't know/refused	21.3 / 5.0	22.6 / 6.0	15.0 / 4.0	25.8 / 8.0

Given that the two survey instruments are worded somewhat differently,
we accept only large changes in the response rates as suggestive of substantive opinion changes over time. The distribution of the responses suggests
that after thirty-one years and more than a doubling of tourist arrivals,
most (and by a substantial margin) of Hawaii's residents still think that
tourism is more beneficial than harmful to their county/island. The erosion, if any, in the positive attitude has been slight, and then only detectible
on the Neighbor Islands. Where the responses have changed is the sharp
increase in the percentage of the respondents who believe that tourism is
bad for their county/island and the corresponding sharp decrease in the
percentage of the respondents who don't know (or refused to answer). Thus,
if people's attitudes on the whole have become more negative on tourism
in the past three decades, it has largely been due to the shift of attitudes
from among those people who were uncertain about the value of tourism
to those who have a more negative perception. Tourism growth appears
to have helped to change the views of people who were balancing on the
proverbial (uncommitted) fence.

The history of tourism development in Hawaii since statehood definitely
has not been conflict free. Maui is a good example. Mansel Blackford recounts in detail how various groups formed to oppose proposed tourism
development projects on Maui and have successfully forced developers to
make compromises in order to gain regulatory approval.[63] Citizen activism
—and a weak economy (there wasn't enough money)—finally convinced the
State government in March 2000 to give up its plan to extend the Kahului
Airport runway to accommodate jumbo jets.[64] It was a controversial ending

to what many Maui residents consider to be the most divisive political issue on Maui during the 1990s.[65]

Maui is a good place to study the impact of tourism because of the rapid growth of tourism on the island in the past and because it has the highest ratio of visitors to residents in the state. Maui residents like to tell the world that *Maui no ka oi*—"Maui is the best." But in community meetings leading to the development of the *Maui County Tourism Strategic Plan (2006–2015)*, participants raised numerous problem issues. Many of them, such as over-crowding, traffic congestion, lack of affordable housing, and the diminution in the quality of life, were—rightly or wrongly—attributed to tourists and tourism.[66] Maui residents are concerned about Internet Web sites and guidebooks guiding tourists to dangerous places or onto private property. They are also concerned about inadequate infrastructure at beaches and parks and the County's ability to manage and protect its natural resources. The growth of cruise tourism on Maui has residents concerned about congestion at the Kahului and Lahaina harbors, as well as the potential impact of cruise ships on the quality of the ocean water and the destruction of coral reefs. During the whale-watching season, residents report seeing too many boats crowding the whales and not obeying regulations. Most of these have been perennial concerns of Valley Isle residents. What has the County done to address these concerns, as it is the level of government that is closest to the people?

Maui County Tourism Policy Planning

Until the completion of the HTA–initiated county tourism strategic plans in late 2006, Hawaii's Neighbor Island counties did not have stand-alone, strategic tourism plans. That does not mean that the counties did not have official tourism policies. They did, but they were embedded in their general plans. Maui County's General Plan was adopted by Ordinance No. 1052 and became effective on June 24, 1980. The General Plan was updated in 1990 as required by the County Charter. But even before the 1980 General Plan was drafted, Maui's charismatic and undisputed boss, Mayor Elmer F. Cravalho, was the central figure in guiding much of the County's political and economic affairs until he resigned in June 1979.[67] During his administration, Maui County was regarded by many as the best-run county in Hawaii. He was named "Man of the Year" by *Hawaii Business* magazine in 1978. Bryan Farrell considered Mayor Cravalho to have been "the single most important person in Maui tourism development."[68] According to Farrell, "cautious developmental growth and stringent controls [were] always part of Cravalho's stated policy."[69] By withholding land use approvals and the delivery of County services, Cravalho could make it very difficult for development projects that he didn't like to go forward. Thus, one wonders whether he fully approved of the astonishing pace of tourism growth that occurred in Maui County during the 1970s (see Fig. 8-1). Transparently, the desire for economic growth pulled by the new tourism engine trumped other County goals. Of course, a strong economy was imperative for Maui County to escape from under the tight fiscal control of the State Legislature and enable it to exercise "home rule."[70] In 1980, the newly elected mayor of Maui, Hannibal Tavares, reflected that "Maui has grown too fast. What we need now is quality growth."[71]

Inclusiveness has been a trademark of community planning in Hawaii. The crafting of the 1980 Maui General Plan involved a large number of people (246) from various backgrounds who were appointed to accomplish the task. A draft plan was completed and distributed in December 1977. It contained two objectives and ten policies for tourism.

Objectives
  1. Resort development which enhances the social, economic, manmade and natural environments of the County and its people.
  2. Orderly and quality growth of the visitor industry limited by the resources of the County in a manner which would not detract from stated agricultural goals and social lifestyles.

Policies
  1. Reaffirm the resort destination areas to be Wailea-Makena, Kaanapali-Kapalua, and Kaluakoi.
  2. Encourage and support quality and harmonious development by the visitor industry.
  3. Ensure that the social, economic and physical environment of Maui County's people are maintained in the development of resort areas.
  4. Require that new developments bear their fair share of the cost of public services and utilities through assessments, commitments or other means necessary to meet the needs of such development.

5. Cooperate with the State Department of Education, the University of Hawaii system and other levels of government and organizations in providing educational and training programs enabling residents to acquire all of the skills needed in the visitor industry.
6. Support a program of public awareness of the role of the visitor industry to the economy and of the perpetuation of the Aloha spirit.
7. Prohibit direct-scheduled mainland and international passenger flights to the County of Maui.
8. Enforce the provision prohibiting the use of condominium projects for hotel use in non-hotel zoned districts.
9. Encourage a programmed rate of visitor industry development to maintain stable employment activity.
10. Relate visitor industry development to employment needs and housing opportunities.

It took the County Council two and a half years to review and approve the twenty-seven-page plan (including the introduction and the preface). The tourism component of the final plan comprised less than two pages. It deleted mention of specific areas such as Kapalua and Makena to be designated for resort development but did call for limitation in the number of hotel rooms to be built each year to control growth.[72]

The 1990 General Plan reiterated many of the provisions of the 1980 plan. The updated plan stated its objectives as (1) to encourage exceptional and continuing quality in the development of visitor industry facilities; and (2) to control the development of visitor facilities so that it does not infringe upon the traditional social, economic, and environmental values of our community. The 1990 plan included specific language to discourage any additional shoreline resort development and to locate buildings to protect scenic vistas. Language was included for "the concept of a hotel room limit in community plan areas as part of the managed and directed growth plan." It further encouraged the use of local labor to build and run tourism facilities. How that would be accomplished was unspecified.

In a nutshell, Maui County's tourism policies aspire to attain quality (upscale) tourism development, rein in the growth of tourism, and to protect and enhance the well-being of residents. It is difficult to ascertain to what extent the County's plans have made a significant difference in guiding the developing of tourism on Maui. Bank of Hawaii chief economist Paul Brewbaker put it succinctly when he recently pointed out that plans are supposed to be forward looking; by contrast, planning on Maui has been about playing catch-up.[73]

It is quite telling that the most frequently mentioned directional change in the social/cultural impact indicators that Maui residents want to see achieved by the just-completed *Maui County Tourism Strategic Plan, 2006–2015*, is to "reverse the negative trend." While residents are not seeking to halt tourism growth completely—the operative words are "modest increase"—the language of the Strategic Plan suggests that most Maui residents believe that tourism has grown too fast on the Valley Isle! That sentiment has been around since at least the late 1970s.[74] Nonetheless, Maui people still think that they live in a pretty special place and are willing to pay among the highest median housing prices in Hawaii to live there.

It has been suggested by prodevelopment advocates that some of the antitourism development sentiment comes from newcomers, who are accused of being afflicted with "moat mentality"; having found "paradise," they now want to take up the drawbridge over the moat to keep others out.[75] But for many, the desire to go slower genuinely reflects their wish to keep Maui special. Despite the highest ratio of tourists to residents in the Islands, Maui is not yet overrun by people. In 2000, the de facto population (residents plus tourists) on Maui was 215 people per square mile, compared to 1,554 people per square mile on Oahu. Opportunities remain to protect what is best about Maui.

Nice People Don't Always Finish Last

Resort planners Charles Kaiser and Larry Helber note that tourism is first and foremost a human relations business.[76] To enjoy their trips, tourists must be "pleased with what they see and experience in their dealings with local people."[77] Given the importance of the Aloha Spirit in the success of Hawaii tourism, it is curious that the State's annual visitor satisfaction and activity survey does not include questions on the quality of the interaction between tourists and locals. Visitors are queried about their experiences with tourist attractions but not about their experiences in interacting with local people.

There is anecdotal evidence. Every once in a while, a local daily newspaper publishes a letter from a couple about their wonderful vacation experience in Hawaii. The following letter sent in by a couple from Illinois appeared in a recent issue of the *Honolulu Advertiser:* "Mahalo to the kamaʻaina who made our time in Oahu the best. If you: drove our bus or trolley, greeted us each time we returned to our hotel, helped keep our room homey, prepared our food, shared the music and dance with us and nourished our souls, talked with us anywhere and smiled as we passed on the street, then you make a difference in our lives. You are Hawaii, and we will miss you." For this couple, the Aloha Spirit is alive and well.[78]

It would have been nice to receive a letter from a local resident about his/her interaction with that appreciative Illinois couple. Maybe the letter would have been just as complimentary toward them. Kaiser and Helber's prescription for a pleasant visit is one in which a visitor has been well treated by locals. They then provide instructions on how to select and train the right employees who must deal with tourists. But the tourist experience also depends on how tourists regard and treat the local population.[79] If tourists treat their hosts in a disrespectful way, they shouldn't expect excellent treatment in return. The satisfaction derived by tourists from interacting with locals is a two-way affair.

Hawaii Tourism Authority's 2002 *Survey of Resident Sentiments on Tourism* included a few questions about tourism-resident interactions. The study concluded that "residents actually express a strong 'Aloha Spirit' toward visitors as individuals."[80] When asked whether they agreed or disagreed with a number of statements pertaining to their direct interaction with tourists, the majority of the respondents agreed that they usually enjoyed getting to meet and talk with visitors (82 percent), and they agreed that visitors usually treated local people with respect and equality (70 percent).[81] The Hawaii Tourism Authority study did not produce cross-tabulations to allow comparison among the islands. Nonetheless, the central message is clear. Hawaii's residents are able to separate their feelings toward tourism in general from how they view and treat individual tourists. They may not want to have another hotel or resort built in their neighborhood, and they will publicly oppose developers and vigorously lobby the county councils to deny a permit for the development, but they will treat individual tourists they meet with friendliness and hospitality.[82] Hawaii's hospitable people help to make Hawaii a dream destination to millions of people around the world. Leo Durocher, the former and fiery major league baseball manager, published a book in 1975—still available on the Internet—with the title *Nice Guys Finish Last.* The success of Hawaii's brand of tourism provides proof that nice people don't always finish last.

Notes

1. Farrell (1982), p. 139.

2. Scott (2000).

3. McKee and Tisdell (1990), p. 51.

4. The reader is reminded that visitors may visit more than one Neighbor Island during their Hawaii trip.

5. The phrase "visitor accommodation units" includes not only hotel rooms but also apartment hotels, bed and breakfast units, condo hotels, hostels, individual vacation units, time-share units, and others.

6. State of Hawaii DBEDT, *2005 Visitor Plant Inventory* (2006), p. 9.

7. Hitch (1992), p. 196; Allen (2004), chapter 6.

8. Allen (2004), chapter 6.

9. Ibid. It is now the 356-room Kauai Marriott Resort and Beach Club.

10. For a more detailed history of the resort, see Farrell (1982), chapter 4.

11. Kaiser and Helber (1978), p. 61, define a destination as "an area with sufficient attraction to provide primary motivation for tourism visits." Simpich (1971), p. 108 notes that Amfac "put $10 million in the ground at Ka'anapali and watched contractors and hotels, tour drivers and restaurant operators, profit while it, the originator of it all, the one with the greatest risk, stood at the end of the line awaiting a slow return in lease rentals." He opined that if Amfac had owned and operated some hotels and built and sold some condominiums, it would "move the landowner up the line to share in the early profits." Of course, the short-term gains reaped by others would largely be capitalized in the value of the land, which Amfac still owned, and lease rents should reflect the anticipated higher land values stemming from the resort's development.

12. State of Hawaii Department of Planning and Economic Development (1972), p. 123.

13. Ibid.

14. Simpich (1971), p. 110.

15. Dankyi (1996), p. 33.

16. Hitch (1992), pp. 180 and 197.

17. For a detailed history, see Farrell (1982), chapter 4.

18. Ibid., pp. 73–77.

19. Kent (1993), p. 177.

20. See, for example, State of Hawaii DPED, vol. 2 (1972), pp. 53–59.

21. Kent (1993), p. 168.

22. LaCroix (1992), pp. 135–141; Hitch (1992), pp. 292–294.

23. Hitch (1992), pp. 292–294.

24. Kent (1993), p. 169.

25. Ibid., p. 180.

26. See, for example, Fry (1979).

27. Ibid.

28. Wenkam (1975), p. 116.

29. Schneider (1978), p. 15. See also Crampon (1976), chapter 15; Southward (1968), p. A11; and Southward (1969), p. 10. To prevent them from competing against the interisland air carriers, the CAB added a stipulation that the major carriers could not fly passengers solely between Hilo and Honolulu.

30. Ibid.

31. In 2005, Hilo counted 2 million visitor days compared to 8 million visitor days for Kona. State of Hawaii DBEDT, *2005 Annual Visitor Research Report* (2006), p. 10.

32. For a chronological history of Big Island airports, see http://www.state .hi.us/dot/publicaffairs/archive/presskits/ito/history.htm.

33. Hitch (1992), p. 238.

34. Mak (1993).

35. Simpich (1971), p. 102.

36. Fujii, Im, and Mak (1992). Direct flights to Kauai were terminated in September 1985 and replaced with one-stop service via Honolulu. Both Kauai and Hilo now have direct flights to the U.S. mainland again.

37. Mak (1993).

38. Among westbound visitors to Hawaii, the average length of stay on Oahu jumped from 5.77 days to 6.96 days between 1982 and 1983; the increase on Maui County was from 4.26 days to 5.61 days; from 3.62 days to 4.52 days on the Big Island; and from 3.51 days to 4.22 days on Kauai. Hawaii Visitors Bureau (1986), p. 33.

39. Ibid.

40. State of Hawaii DBEDT, *2005 Annual Visitor Research Report* (2006), p. 8. By comparison, the average length of stay in Hawaii (per trip) is around nine days. The Japanese stay the fewest number of days (less than six days), while Canadians stay the longest (thirteen days). These numbers apply only to visitors arriving by air and not by cruise ships.

41. I thank Paul Brewbaker (Bank of Hawaii) for bringing this point to my attention.

42. Purchasers of time-shares can either choose an ownership plan or a use plan; the latter only confers use rights and the purchaser has no ownership interest. In Hawaii, nearly 70 percent of the time-share units statewide are ownership units. Hobson Ferrarini Associates (2002), p. 40.

43. State of Hawaii DBEDT, *2005 Visitor Plant Inventory* (2006), pp. 18–19.

44. Hobson Ferrarini Associates (2002).

45. Knox (1978).

46. Hawaii Tourism Authority, *2002 Survey of Resident Sentiments on Tourism in Hawaii* (2003), pp. 56–57. While these responses are suggestive, it is not entirely clear what they mean.

47. Recall that 1930 was the start of the Great Depression in the United States, which also struck hard at Hawaii's sugar and pineapple industries—then the main economic base in the Islands. Afterwards, improvements in the technology of sugar and pineapple production, combined with the enactment of U.S. sugar legislation that limited production in Hawaii, reduced demand for labor on the plantations.

48. Boylan and Holmes (2003), p. 197.

49. Even more so than Oahu, as Oahu enjoys a broader economic base. First Hawaiian Bank (1984).

50. State of Hawaii DBEDT, *2000 Annual Visitor Research Report* (2001), p. 9.

51. Turner and Ash (1976), p. 163.

52. Coffman (2003), p. 169.

53. Lind (1969), p. 39.

54. See, for example, Apo (2002), pp. B1 and B4, and Apo et al. (2003).

55. Ebel and Mak (1974), chapter 32.

56. State of Hawaii DBEDT, *State of Hawaii Data Book 2005* (2006), Table 1.40.

57. "Kauai World's 2nd-Best Island" (2006), p. C1.

58. *Honolulu Advertiser,* October 2, 2004, p. C1.

59. Hawaii Tourism Authority, *Maui County Tourism Strategic Plan, 2006–2015*, p. 11.

60. Doxey (1976).

61. Ap and Crompton (1993).

62. 2006 data from Hawaii Tourism Authority, *2006 Survey of Resident Sentiments on Tourism in Hawaii*, vol. 2 (2006), p. 3; 1975 data from Public Affairs Advisory Services, Inc. (1976), p. 3.

63. Blackford (2001). See also review of Blackford's book by LaCroix (2001). Dankyi (1996) also provides detailed accounts of group conflict in two high-profile Maui cases: the State's plan to extend the Kahului Airport runway and a proposal to build a golf course at the Hotel Hana Maui. Blackford notes (p. 229) that even when emotions ran high on some high-profile proposals, opponents remained in face-to-face contact and on speaking terms.

64. Blackford (2001), p. 190.

65. Ibid., p. 189.

66. Hawaii Tourism Authority, *Maui County Tourism Strategic Plan, 2006–2015*, p. 16.

67. Farrell (1982), pp. 145–161.

68. Ibid., p. 145.

69. Ibid., p. 147.

70. Mayor Cravalho's political power and his passion for independence from the State government were legendary. I add a personal story here. In 1973, during the first energy crisis, I was on loan from the University of Hawaii to the

Legislature to serve as the chief economist of the House Select Committee on Energy, which had been charged with investigating the oil companies doing business in Hawaii. While at the Legislature, I was also asked to develop a contingency (coupon) gasoline rationing plan for the State. The completed draft plan was presented to the individual counties for comment. I briefed Mayor Cravalho on the draft plan during one of his visits to the Legislative session. After hearing my presentation, he said that Maui had no desire to be part of the plan. He pointed out that on Maui, if someone was using more gasoline than they should, the County would send someone to their house and tell them to behave or be cut off from future gasoline supply. On Maui, he said, they knew what everyone was doing! A coupon rationing system would be too costly to implement on Maui.

71. Farrell (1982), p. 87. But Figure 8-1 shows that during Tavares' administration, tourism growth did not slow down.

72. County of Maui (1980).

73. Personal communication.

74. Farrell (1982), p. 87.

75. Dankyi (1996).

76. Kaiser and Helber (1978), p. 199.

77. Ibid. NFO Plog Research, a large market research firm, conducts an annual survey of American travelers to ascertain which U.S. state provides the most satisfying vacation experiences. The firm notes that the most satisfying vacation destinations must have at least three of the following attributes: beautiful outdoor scenery, warm weather, a variety of activities, and well-maintained lodgings and attractions. Tourist-resident interaction is not one of the four. Mak (2004), p. 205, fn 7. Hawaii topped the Plog's Delightful Dozen List in 2003 (the most recent ranking located on the Internet), as it did for six straight years before that. Florida came in second.

78. June 6, 2007, p. A17.

79. Knox (1978).

80. Hawaii Tourism Authority, *2002 Survey of Resident Sentiments on Tourism in Hawaii* (2003), p. 57.

81. Ibid.

82. Noel Kent, who subscribes to the view that Hawaii's tourism industry profits off the backs of oppressed workers, nonetheless concedes (and is puzzled by) "how friendly and helpful they [the workers] remain in their human relationships on the job" (1993), p. 181.

References

Allen, Robert C. 2004. *Creating Hawaii Tourism.* Honolulu: Bess Press.

Ap, John, and John L. Crompton. 1993. "Residents' Strategies for Responding to Tourism Impacts." *Journal of Travel Research* 32(1): 47–50.

Apo, Peter. 2002. "Can Hawaii Have Tourism without Hawaiians?" *Honolulu Advertiser,* November 3: B1 and B4.

Apo, Peter, Dennis "Bumpy" Kanahele, Cheryln Logan, and Davianna McGregor. 2003. *Socio-Cultural Impacts of Tourism in Hawaii—Impacts on Native Hawaiians.* Prepared for the State of Hawaii Department of Business, Economic Development and Tourism (DBEDT), Planning for Sustainable Tourism Project. Honolulu: DBEDT (August).

Blackford, Mansel. 2001. *Fragile Paradise: The Impact of Tourism on Maui, 1959–2000.* Lawrence, KS: University Press of Kansas.

Boylan, Dan, and T. Michael Holmes. 2003. *John A. Burns: The Man and His Times.* Honolulu: University of Hawaii Press.

Coffman, Tom. 2003. *The Island Edge of America: A Political History of Hawaii.* Honolulu: University of Hawaii Press.

County of Maui. 1977. *General Plan.* Wailuku: Maui County (December 28).

———. 1980. *The General Plan of the County of Maui.* Wailuku: Maui County (June 24).

———. 1990. *1990 General Plan,* at http://www.co.maui.hi.us/departments/ Planning/generalPlan1990.htm.

Crampon, L. J. 1976. *Hawaii's Visitor Industry: Its Growth and Development.* Honolulu: University of Hawaii School of Travel Industry Management.

Dankyi, Stella S. 1996. "Discord in Paradise: Tourism Development and Public Controversy in Maui Hawaii." M.S. thesis in sociology and anthropology, Simon Fraser University, Burnaby, B.C. (September).

Doxey, G. V. 1976. "A Causation Theory of Visitor-Resident Irritation: Methodology and Research Inferences." In *The Impact of Tourism: The Travel Research Association Sixth Annual Conference Proceedings,* 1975 (San Diego: Travel Research Assn.): 195–198.

Ebel, Robert, and James Mak. 1974. *Current Issues in Hawaii's Economy.* Honolulu: Crossroads Press (June).

Farrell, Bryan H. 1982. *Hawaii: The Legend that Sells.* Honolulu: University Press of Hawaii.

First Hawaiian Bank Research Department. 1984. "Hawaii: A Quarter-Century of Change." *Economic Indicators* (January/February).

Fry, Maxwell J. 1979. "Economic Growth and Capital Shortage in Alaska, Hawaii, and Puerto Rico." *Growth and Change* 10(2): 17–21.

Fujii, Edwin, Eric Im, and James Mak. 1992. "Airport Expansion, Direct Flights and Consumer Choice of Travel Destinations: The Case of Hawaii's Neighbor Islands." *Journal of Travel Research* 30(3): 38–43.

Hawaii Tourism Authority. 2006. *2006 Survey of Resident Sentiments on Tourism in Hawaii.* Honolulu: HTA (November). See also the 2002 report.

———. 2006. *Maui County Tourism Strategic Plan, 2006–2015,* at http://www .hawaiitourismauthority.org/.

Hawaii Visitors Bureau. 1986. *Trend Analysis of Hawaii's Visitor Industry, 1976–1985.* Honolulu: HVB (August).

Hitch, Thomas K. 1992. *Islands in Transition: The Past, Present and Future of Hawaii's Economy*. Honolulu: First Hawaiian Bank.

Hobson Ferrarini Associates. 2004. *Overview of the Hawaii Second Home Market and Opportunity Analysis for Ko Olina Resort, Honolulu, Hawaii*. Portland, OR: Hobson Ferrarini Associates (December 9).

Honolulu Advertiser. 2004. October 12: C1.

John M. Knox & Associates. 2004. *Sustainable Tourism in Hawaii: Socio-Cultural and Public Input Component, section 4: Socio-Cultural Impact Study—Native Hawaiians*. Honolulu: John M. Knox & Associates (April).

Kaiser, Charles, Jr., and Larry E. Helber. 1978. *Tourism Planning and Development*. Boston: CBI Publishing.

"Kauai World's 2nd-Best Island." 2006. *Honolulu Advertiser*, July 14: C1.

Kent, Noel J. 1993. *Hawaii: Islands under the Influence*. Honolulu: University of Hawaii Press.

Knox, John. 1978. *Resident-Visitor Interaction: A Review of the Literature and General Policy Alternatives*. Submitted for PEACESAT Conference on the Impact of Tourism Development in the Pacific (April).

LaCroix, Sumner. 1992. "Can Government Make Housing Affordable?" In Randall W. Roth, ed., *The Price of Paradise: Lucky We Live Hawaii?* (Honolulu: Mutual Publishing): 135–140.

———. 2001. "Review of Fragile Paradise: The Impact of Tourism on Maui, 1959–2000." *Journal of Economic History* 61 (December): 1160–1161.

Lind, Andrew W. 1969. *Hawaii: The Last of the Magic Isles*. London: Oxford University Press.

Mak, James. 1993. "Tourism and Hawaii's Economic Development." Paper presented to the Philippines Exchange Mission to Hawaii, Sheraton Waikiki Hotel, Honolulu (September 16).

———. 2004. *Tourism and the Economy: Understanding the Economics of Tourism*. Honolulu: University of Hawaii Press.

McKee, David L., and Clem Tisdell. 1990. *Development Issues in Small Island Economies*. New York: Praeger.

Pacific Affairs Advisory Services. 1976. *What Hawaii's People Think of the Visitor Industry*. Honolulu: DPED (January 2).

Schneider, Bruce A. 1978. "The Evolution of Mainland-Hawaii Air Travel." Unpublished paper. Honolulu (December 15).

Scott, Julie. 2000. "Peripheries, Artificial Peripheries and Centers." In Frances Brown and Derek Hall, eds., *Tourism in Peripheral Areas: Case Studies* (Toronto: Channel View Publications): 58–73.

Simpich, Frederick, Jr. 1971. *Anatomy of Hawaii*. New York: Coward, McCann & Geoghegan.

Southward, Walt. 1968. "Direct Hilo Flights: Impact is Gradual." *Sunday Star-Bulletin and Advertiser*, January 7: A11.

———. 1969. "Jets Boost Hilo's Sagging Economy." *Honolulu Star-Bulletin*, February 18: Special Section 3.

State of Hawaii Department of Business, Economic Development and Tourism (DBEDT). 2006. *2005 Annual Visitor Research Report.* Honolulu: DBEDT.

———. 2006. *State of Hawaii Data Book 2005.* Honolulu: DBEDT. Also see 1976 edition.

———. 2006. *2005 Visitor Plant Inventory.* Honolulu: DBEDT (May).

———. 2006. *2005 Visitor Satisfaction & Activity Report.* Honolulu: DBEDT.

State of Hawaii Department of Planning and Economic Development (DPED). 1972. *Tourism in Hawaii: Hawaii Tourism Impact Plan,* vol. 1. Honolulu: DPED.

———. 1972. *Tourism in Hawaii: Hawaii Tourism Impact Plan,* vol. 2: Regional, West Hawaii. Honolulu: DPED.

Turner, Louis, and John Ash. 1976. *The Golden Hordes.* New York: St. Martin's Press.

Wenkam, Robert. 1975. *The Big Island: Hawaii.* New York: Rand McNally & Company.

Chapter Nine

Lessons from Hawaii's Experience

Statehood and the coming of the jet plane opened up tremendous opportunities for the development of tourism in Hawaii in 1959.[1] Within a short period of time, Hawaii was transformed from a "sleepy exotic resort," barely a speck in the middle of the vast Pacific Ocean, to become "a booming tourist Mecca."[2] This transformation was not the result of some grandiose government plan. Nor was it the vision of one person. It happened because of the resourcefulness of many individuals.[3]

To be sure, Hawaii held a number of early advantages over other places in developing a dream destination. At the conclusion of a study mission to the Caribbean in 1975, Tom Hamilton observed that Hawaii's advantages were: "Language; Beauty; Climate; Beaches; Different but secure; Good infrastructure; Food; Water; Currency. The Aloha Spirit is the vital one."[4] Of course, he was thinking about tourists from the U.S. mainland. Only about one in four (28 percent) of Hawaii's visitors came from foreign countries in that year.[5]

Hawaii's tourist industry in 2005 had become vastly different from what it was in 1959. For one thing, the tourism enterprise had become very much larger. In 2005, there were 7.4 million visitor arrivals, or nearly twenty-nine times the number in 1959. The 2005 tourists spent nearly $12 billion in Hawaii versus $109 million in 1959 (or $708 million in 2005 dollars). There were over ten times as many hotel rooms in Hawaii in 2005, with half of them now on the Neighbor Islands. In 1959, the Neighbor Islands' share was just 19 percent. The percentage of international tourists in 2005 was also much higher (29 percent versus 19 percent) than in 1959, even after Japanese travel to Hawaii had fallen so sharply since 1996. In 1996, foreign visitors made up almost 45 percent of total visitor arrivals in Hawaii. Americans continued to make up most of the tourist traffic in 2005, with 66 percent of all visitor arrivals. U.S. and Japanese visitors comprised 86 percent of all visitors to Hawaii. Tourists outnumbered residents nearly six to one in 2005—but luckily, not all of them were in Hawaii at the same time. On a typical day, about 185,000 of them were in Hawaii, meaning that statistically nearly one out of every eight people in Hawaii was a tourist.[6] Although Oahu had the most tourists, the number of tourists relative to the local population (i.e., the tourist density) was actually much higher on the less populated islands of Maui and Kauai.[7]

By the early 1970s, tourism had assumed a central role in the Hawaiian economy and was a leading producer of state income and jobs. But it also had become an object of controversy. How best to develop tourism became a topic of much debate around the state.

In 1976, the Hawaii State Legislature passed Act 133, a pioneering piece of legislation, which called for a ten-year master plan to guide the growth of tourism in Hawaii. The act required that the plan address the following issues: (1) planned growth of tourism, (2) visitor satisfaction, (3) protection of Hawaii's natural beauty and attractions, (4) Hawaii's heritage, (5) resident requirements, (6) education and training, and (7) criteria for growth. In sum, Act 133 called for a blueprint for sustainable tourism development in Hawaii. Technical studies were commissioned. An action plan was developed two years later, and many of the suggestions were acted upon. Then in 2001, the State Legislature appropriated $1.2 million to fund another massive tourism study. This time it was called the Sustainable Tourism Study. The study was completed in late summer of 2004. In 2005, the Hawaii Tourism Authority released a new ten-year strategic tourism plan for the state. Action plans are still being crafted. County strategic plans for tourism (2006–2015) were completed a year later.

In this final chapter, I highlight the following eight main lessons that can be learned from Hawaii's experience in developing a premier destination since statehood:

1. Tight and pervasive government control is not always necessary to produce a dream destination.
2. Government can exacerbate or be a solution to tourism's ills.
3. Taxing tourism need not harm tourism.
4. Admission fees are an excellent source of revenue to pay for the upkeep of popular natural attractions.
5. Responsibility to raise revenues should go hand in hand with the responsibility to spend.

6. Incentives may not be necessary to induce tourism investment.
7. Money spent on collecting basic tourism data is well spent.
8. In developing tourism, the welfare of residents must be paramount.

Lesson 1

Lesson 1 is that tight and pervasive government control is not always necessary to produce a dream destination. After more than half a century of astonishing growth, the Hawaiian Islands remain one of the world's greatest tourist destinations—one of the "50 places of a lifetime," declared the *National Geographic Traveler* magazine. It all seemed to have happened by chance. The State government did help by contributing money for promotion. It also put in the necessary infrastructure, such as airports and roads, and provided job training at the University of Hawaii, the normal responsibility of any government. It regulated the industry when it felt regulation was necessary to protect the interests of tourists and residents. Other than that, it pretty much stayed on the sidelines.

Hawaii's experience is very much at odds with the popular notion that tourism development must be carefully planned and tightly controlled by government. Hawaii's State government planned but generally did not impose tight control over tourism development. Longtime Hawaii resort planners Charles Kaiser and Larry Helber recalled that there was little or no inhibiting legislation in existence at the time major resort developments were launched in Hawaii during the post–World War II tourism boom. Hawaii's first strategic tourism plan (1980) was not elevated to the level of a statute. Like the other eleven State Functional Plans, the Tourism Functional Plan identified areas of State concern and suggested strategies and budget priorities (chapter 3). Critics noted that it was also unenforceable. Authors of the plan made it very clear that the development of tourism belonged to the private sector; the government's role was to support and regulate the industry in the manner that was believed to best serve the public interest.

There was careful planning and tight control of tourism development in Hawaii, but it was not by the State and local governments. On the Neighbor Islands, large landowners, sometimes working with developers, created master-planned—and upscale—mega-destination resorts that have been kept in attractive condition. Thus, "tight control" of tourism development on the Neighbor Islands has been exercised to a large extent by private resort developers (chapters 3 and 8). This was not true in Waikiki (chapter 7).

Hawaii's model of tourism development is not the only approach capable of producing attractive destinations. When Hawaii's delegates visited Bermuda as part of their study tour of the Caribbean, Bermuda was their overwhelming favorite. Careful planning and tough government controls over just about every aspect of tourism development had made Bermuda a popular destination for tourists (chapter 3). "Bermuda is a delightful place to visit and a shining model of how tight controls, pride in the product and a friendly beautiful environment can make for a 'gem of a resort,'" wrote the editor-in-chief of the *Honolulu Advertiser*.[8] But the delegates were also quick to note that Bermuda's approach to tourism development would have been unworkable in Hawaii. Hawaii's residents no doubt would find the degree of government intervention in Bermuda far too intrusive and oppressive and thus unacceptable. Everything considered, which approach is best is constrained by local political and socioeconomic cultures. The choice of more or less government involvement in tourism development is ultimately determined in the political arena, and the outcome must achieve political equilibrium.

An additional lesson from the development experiences in Hawaii and Bermuda is that tight control of tourism development invariably leads to higher prices, whether control is exercised by private developers or the government. A recent visitor to Bermuda observed that "there is no such thing as a cheap vacation in Bermuda."[9] Hawaii is not a cheap place to visit either. In both Hawaii's Neighbor Islands and Bermuda, high prices were also equated with high quality. However, there is no assurance that stringent government regulations necessarily produce higher quality service. Government-imposed restrictions on supply, for example, may give profits only to incumbent businesses and result in a lower quality tourism product.

Lesson 2

Lesson 2 is that government can exacerbate or be a solution to tourism's ills. Markets don't always produce the best outcomes for society. What's good for tourism is not always also good for everyone else in Hawaii. When individuals pursuing their own interests make others worse off, government intervention can help to remedy the problems. Most of us don't object when governments intervene to reduce congestion and pollution created by tourism because we know that intervention, properly designed and implemented, can make society better off. For example, the implementation of a management plan at Hanauma Bay Nature Preserve, despite a few early glitches, is generally regarded as a success story in government intervention (chapter 6).

Obviously, government intervention cannot make everyone better off. More often than not, some people will be made worse off. At Hanauma Bay, commercial tour operators were worse off after the management plan went into effect because they were denied access to the preserve. But it is necessary that more people gain than lose for society's welfare to be improved. Ideally, a way can be found to compensate the losers, but that is not usually possible.

Taxing hotels and dedicating some of the money by formula to fund destination tourism promotion was another successful intervention by Hawaii's State government. Hawaii's own history and experience with industry funding in other states such as Colorado and California clearly show that not enough revenue can be generated to pay for the desired amount of promotion through industry efforts alone. The incentive is to free ride on someone else's contribution toward generic tourism promotion. In the absence of adequate funding, the whole state loses because tourism is unable to achieve its potential in bringing visitors to Hawaii.

Taxing tourism to pay for destination tourism promotion is not a subsidy to the industry. It is an efficient way to compel the industry (and tourists) to pay for the benefits they receive from tourism promotion. A dedicated tax on tourism to fund tourism promotion is different from using tax revenues from the general treasury to pay for promotion. The latter is a subsidy to tourism that reduces the benefit of tourism development to the community.[10]

Governments also have a legitimate role to play in alleviating poverty, because markets cannot guarantee that the poorest in the community get a fair share of the economic benefits derived from tourism development. Around the world, more is being asked of tourism to take a more direct role in alleviating poverty.[11] Economic growth alone is insufficient to ensure that there would be less poverty. It will require governments to be more aggressive in formulating policies and programs that benefit the poor.[12] In Hawaii, there is special concern for Native Hawaiians, who make up nearly 20 percent of the state's population. Native Hawaiian unemployment, substance abuse, and prison incarceration rates are significantly higher than the corresponding statewide averages, while their educational achievement, health status, and other indicators of social well-being fall significantly

below the statewide averages.[13] In 2005, per capita income for Native Hawaiians was $16,932 compared to the statewide average of $25,326, or 66.9
percent of the state average. By comparison, in 1979, per capita income of
Native Hawaiians was 73.1 percent of the statewide average. The poverty
rate for Native Hawaiians in 2005 was 15 percent compared to the state
average of 9.8 percent.[14] Despite the centrality of the Hawaiian culture—
especially music and dance—in the development of Hawaii's tourism product, resident surveys consistently show that Native Hawaiians as a group
are the least supportive of tourism development. A recent (August 2003)
report prepared for the States' Sustainable Tourism Study and authored by
a Native Hawaiian Advisory Group concluded that "the majority of Native
Hawaiians do not fully and comfortably embrace the prevailing business
model of corporate tourism as generally contributing to the betterment
of conditions of Native Hawaiians."[15] The State government has not done
much to address the fairness issue in its tourism strategic plans. It needs to
find ways to do more.[16]

Sometimes the outcome of government intervention is not what was intended or desired. For example, efforts to regulate commercial tour boating
on the Hanalei River on Kauai stalled because the State and county governments failed to enforce their own regulations and didn't work together to
resolve issues of overlapping jurisdiction (chapter 6). No one was in control.
The community became bitterly divided over the issue and ultimately re-
sorted to costly legal battle. Hanalei River commercial boating is a textbook
example of "government failure" and not "market failure." Enforcing regulations and intergovernmental cooperation where relevant are essential to
making intervention work.

Government intervention can also make the situation worse. When Puerto
Rico's tourist industry was ailing in the mid-1970s, its government stepped
in to buy up failing hotels (chapter 3). Puerto Rico's decision to participate
directly in its tourist industry is not unique. The government of one South
Pacific country directed the country's social security system (provident fund)
to buy equity shares in failing and new hotels to support tourism development. The downside of such a policy is that if the hotels perform poorly,
politicians may find it expedient to continue appropriating taxpayer money
to keep them operating instead of closing them. It becomes a classic case of
throwing good money after bad. By taking ownership in the ailing industry,
government becomes part of the problem and not a solution to the problem. Wisely, Hawaii's State government has thus far avoided making direct

investments in tourism businesses. (By contrast, it has participated as an equity owner in high-tech development.) Even as privatization of tourism enterprises is becoming more common globally, public ownership of tourism businesses is still prevalent in one of the most important tourist destinations in the world: China.

The State's ownership of the Hawaii Convention Center is a more complicated story of government intervention (chapter 5). Convention centers in the United States typically lose money.[17] According to Darling and Beato, that's because in the United States most convention centers are publicly owned and financed, and the local governments that own them don't care if they lose money. (In Asia, most convention centers are privately owned.) Local government officials believe that the additional tourism revenues the centers are expected to bring to the community will more than cover the red ink at the facility. Hence, convention center management typically underprices the use of the facilities, resulting in the red ink. As demand for convention travel is declining but the amount of convention space is rising, the promise of large spillover benefits to the community is proving to be empty for many communities. It is probable that most convention centers in the United States, and perhaps the one in Honolulu as well, will never pay back the cost of building and operating them. At the very least, the promise of convention centers as significant economic catalysts will not be realized. It was predicted that the area around the Hawaii Convention Center would be totally transformed after the center was built. That has not happened. In other cities on the mainland, urban blight can be seen around modern convention centers. This is not to argue against building convention centers. For many communities, building a brand new world-class convention center is a feel-good investment. There is nothing wrong with that, as long as residents are willing to pay for it. It is like remodeling your house when realtors tell you that the investment can never be recouped. It does suggest that a community that is thinking about building an expensive new convention center or expanding an existing one should contemplate the reality that it is not going to be a big economic bonanza to its community. Local government officials should be wary of consultants who predict rosy attendance figures. At the very least, consultants should be required to perform sensitivity analyses on their forecasts. Too often, consultants are allowed to get away by citing themselves as the authoritative source of information; instead, they should be asked to document their assumptions.

Lesson 3

Lesson 3 is that taxing tourism need not harm tourism. Nothing riles tourist industry officials more than the mention of tourist taxes. The industry was so upset by the proliferation of tourist taxes around the world during the 1980s that the World Travel and Tourism Council—an influential tourism interest group comprising the top executives of some of the world's biggest tourist businesses—put up money to establish the World Travel & Tourism Tax Policy Center at Michigan State University in 1993. The mission of the center was to "track and monitor the status of taxes imposed on travelers and travel and tourism companies around the world. . . . Its aim is to provide timely information and analysis of tax policy issues and considerations to government policy makers, industry leaders, and the general public."[18] In other words, its ultimate objective was to put a damper on the global proliferation of tourist taxes. (The center has been disbanded.)

Taxation of tourism was also a heated issue in Hawaii for a long time (chapter 4). In Hawaii, the controversial tourist tax turned out to be the transient accommodation tax, widely known in the rest of the country as the hotel room tax, or the bed tax in some foreign countries. For over a decade, the local industry fought to defeat efforts to impose a room tax. It was argued that a tax would discourage tourists from visiting Hawaii and hurt the industry and, indeed, everyone in Hawaii. Studies indicated that a hotel room tax would not discourage large numbers of people from visiting Hawaii. After Hawaii's modest tax was finally enacted in 1986, more studies confirmed that it did not hurt the industry. If the tax rate was set much higher, it might have. Opponents of the hotel room tax also argued that tourists to Hawaii already were paying their fair share of taxes and should not have to pay more. That claim is debatable.[19]

Hawaii's hotel room tax turned out to be more good than bad for the tourist industry. The industry wanted more money for tourism promotion, and both the industry and the State wanted to build a world-class convention center to diversify sources of visitors and to fill empty hotel rooms during the slack periods. The dedicated hotel room tax made it possible to achieve both. It is unlikely that Hawaii's residents would have approved giving more of their own tax dollars toward tourism promotion or to build a $350 million convention center.

Lesson 4

Lesson 4 is that admission fees are an excellent source of revenue to pay for the upkeep of popular natural attractions. We learned that lesson at Hanauma Bay Nature Preserve. Yet the World Bank notes that in the 1990s, only half of the world's protected areas charged admission fees. Even when they were levied, the fees tended to be quite modest and often well below what tourists were willing to pay.[20] It is also not uncommon for money collected from the admission fees to be siphoned off to the general treasury, leaving the upkeep of the attraction underfunded.

Despite the reluctance of destinations to fully take advantage of admission fees, there are a number of reasons why admission fees should be levied at popular public tourist attractions.[21] First, they can help to reduce crowding. (It may not be very effective in reducing crowding, however, if the tourist attraction is extremely popular—such as a "must visit" attraction.) Second—and most importantly—it can generate revenues to pay for upkeep. And third—and the most controversial—revenues collected beyond the amounts needed to pay for the attraction's upkeep could be used to pay for other needed public services. For example, in Uganda a gorilla viewing fee subsidized all of the country's national parks in the 1990s.[22] Excess revenues can also be used to pay for more mundane things such as schools, salaries of civil servants, and other public services that mostly benefit residents.[23]

At the Hanauma Bay Nature Preserve, the institution of an admission fee did not dramatically reduce attendance, and thus nonprice rationing was also needed to reduce crowding at the preserve. But the $3 to $5 admission fees levied on tourists (residents exempted) generated a lot of money for much-needed improvements. There was some grousing about how all the money was spent, but there was no dispute that more money was badly needed to pay for upkeep and improvements at the preserve.

Another important lesson learned at the Hanauma Bay Nature Preserve is that a modest admission fee is legally not an infringement on anyone's fundamental right to enjoy the preserve. It is also legally permissible and nondiscriminatory to exempt local residents from paying the admission fee. These features should open the way for greater use of admission fees in the management of natural recreational resources in the United States.

Lesson 5

Lesson 5 is that responsibility to raise revenues should go hand in hand with the responsibility to spend. In the literature of government finance, it is referred to as the "accountability principle." In practice, it is too often a forgotten principle. Hawaii's State government guards its taxing powers jealously (see chapter 4). It uses just about every tax that's available, but it denies the county governments the same options. Yet the responsibility for providing services to tourists and the tourist industry falls more heavily on the county governments.[24] When the power to tax is centralized and the responsibility to spend is decentralized, as they are in Hawaii, a serious mismatch between tax and spending responsibilities may arise.

Hawaii's situation is not unique. Many countries have strong central governments but weak local governments, especially among developing countries, and fiscal mismatches of the kind described here are quite common. Unless local governments are granted taxing powers corresponding to their service responsibilities or some intergovernmental transfer system is designed to allocate revenues from the central to the local governments, the development of tourism could be negatively affected. In Hawaii, the counties often do not have the money to pay for large expenditure projects such as upgrading Waikiki or widening the Nimitz Highway between the Honolulu International Airport and Waikiki, and they must seek grants from the State Legislature. Hawaii's example makes a strong case for fiscal decentralization.

Lesson 6

Lesson 6 is that incentives may not be necessary to induce tourism investment. To give or not to give tax incentives to stimulate investment remains a controversial question. Most economists do not like them.[25] Politicians regard them as the weapon of choice in the war among the states to attract outside investments.

Historically, Hawaii has not played the fiscal incentive game to induce or attract out-of-state investment in tourism in any significant way. This all changed in the late 1990s, when the State created a number of incentives to attract high-technology investment and to induce hotel remodeling and new construction (see chapter 4). Compared to some of the truly generous tax incentives seen in other tourist destinations, Hawaii's hotel tax credits were relatively modest. The purpose of the hotel tax credits was to induce hoteliers to remodel their aging properties, especially where it was needed the most—Waikiki.

Did the hotel tax credits work? Evidence suggests that they did increase hotel investment, although not everyone agrees. The doubters argue that the spike in spending on hotel investment following the enactment of the tax credits only moved up inevitable investment from the future. It was like borrowing money from Peter to pay Paul. Eventually Peter had to be repaid. The increase in current investment means there will be a decrease in future investment.

Even assuming that the tax credits did spur hotel investment, how big a difference is hard to tell because other factors favorable to hotel investment—in particular, falling interest rates—were also at work. When efforts to increase the generosity of the tax credits died at the Legislature, it did not cause hoteliers to scrap plans to make hundreds of millions of dollars of private improvements in Waikiki. It appeared that the hotel tax credits were not a crucial determinant of hotel investment. Other factors were more important.

Lesson 7

Lesson 7 is that money spent on collecting basic tourism data is well spent. Ken White and Mary Beth Walker noted that tourism data are some of the worst economic data in the world.[26] By contrast, Hawaii has had a long history of producing pretty reliable basic data on tourism (see chapter 5). It has been money well spent.

A quality basic data program is essential for marketing and planning. For example, Hawaii Tourism Authority's latest strategic plan shifts the State's traditional emphasis in marketing from attracting the maximum number of visitors to attracting fewer but upscale visitors. How would one know who are the upscale visitors and whether or not the goal has been achieved without reliable data? And how would one know if visitors are satisfied with their vacation experiences unless they were asked? Hawaii's tourism strategic plans could not have been written without the voluminous and high-quality data Hawaii has produced for decades.

A good basic data generation program is costly, and no individual business, especially a small one, has the inclination or the resources to have one. And most tourism businesses are small businesses. Research departments also are not profit centers. At the first sign of financial distress, research is often one of the first departments to be downsized. Indeed, the state's two largest commercial banks, Bank of Hawaii and the First Hawaiian Bank, shut down their respected research departments during the economic malaise of the 1990s.

Because basic tourism data can help so many users—and once collected, the distribution costs are miniscule—it makes sense to have the data collected by a single research department and then distributed at little or no cost to anyone who wants them. Until 1998, the Hawaii Visitors Bureau (HVB) was the designated producer of basic tourism data for the State. The transfer of the research program from the HVB was inevitable with the establishment of the Hawaii Tourism Authority. The State's Department of Business, Economic Development and Tourism (DBEDT) inherited the former HVB research program and has improved on it. But more importantly, DBEDT's prolific output of tourism data is now available via the Internet to anyone who wants it, free of charge. Under the HVB, members of the bureau received "free" copies of its *Annual Research Report* and the *Visitor Expenditure Report;* nonmembers had to either pay several hundred dollars for the thin reports or go to the public library to find them.

Lesson 8

Lesson 8 is that in developing tourism, the welfare of residents must be paramount. The famous hospitality of Hawaii's people—often referred to as the Aloha Spirit—is one of the most important factors in the success of Hawaiian tourism (see chapter 8). Some would argue that it is Hawaii's *most important asset*. However, not everyone could agree on *what* it is.[27] The State Legislature even waded in and passed a statute (HRS 5-7.5) to define it.[28]

Obviously, maintaining the good will of residents toward tourism (and tourists) is essential to the continued success of Hawaii's tourist industry. A sure way to kill off tourism would be if the locals became hostile toward tourists. Hostility could surface if residents felt that their well-being was being sacrificed for the benefit of tourists. Thus, Hawaii's continuous monitoring of resident attitudes toward tourism takes on special significance.

Hawaii has been conducting surveys of resident attitudes toward tourism since the early 1970s. Surveys using pretty much the same questions were completed in 1988, 1999, 2001, 2002, 2005, and 2006. Until the 2005 survey, most of the respondents believed that their interests were not being sacrificed for the benefit of the tourists (see chapter 2). But the size of the majority has been shrinking, and in 2005 for the first time, over half (55 percent) of the respondents agreed with the statement that their "island is being run for tourists"; that percentage took a sharp jump to 62 percent in 2006. Unfortunately, the surveys have not explored the reasons for the shift in resident attitudes, and thus one can only speculate on the causes. A reading of the local daily newspapers provides a few potential sources of rising irritation among residents. For instance, residents in eastern Honolulu have become more vocal about the number of traffic-snarling distance races (human and bicycle) that attract largely tourists. Many residents of Waikiki complain about the frequency of parades—averaging over one per week—that prompt the closure of Kalakaua Avenue, the main street in Waikiki.[29] Residents complain about the proliferation of commercial activities in neighborhood recreation areas by tourist businesses. A number of Kailua (Oahu) residents are also unhappy about the inability or unwillingness of the City government to contain the spread of illegal bed-and-breakfast establishments in their community.[30] Some surmise that this change in local attitude merely reflects the general unhappiness with the current living conditions in the state of Hawaii—the failing public school system, terrible roads, frequent sewage spills, worsening traffic congestion, escalating cost of housing—even as more money is being spent on tourism promotion.[31]

On the other side of the ledger, there are some things that Hawaii does where the residents' welfare remains paramount. The State's long history of commitment to direct citizen participation in the development of tourism policies and plans is one example. The open—and highly unusual (for governments)—practice of offering kamaaina rates (i.e., local resident discounts) at public establishments is another example.[32] But arguably, none is more important than the protection of everyone's access to Hawaii's shoreline and beaches.

In some tourist destinations, beachfront hotels are permitted to own the beach, and they can (and do) deny beach access to anyone other than hotel guests. By contrast, from the late 1960s, the Hawaii Supreme Court ruled in several seminal cases that private land in Hawaii ended at the vegetation line. The rulings established the shoreline above the upper annual reaches of the wash of the wave rather than the lower "mean high water" line.[33] The series of decisions essentially reserved more of the shoreline for public use. The Supreme Court's definition was subsequently adopted in Chapter 205A of the Hawaii Revised Statutes. By law, the public now has a right to "lateral access" along any shoreline property in the state of Hawaii.[34] In other words, all the shoreline and beaches in Hawaii belong to the people, and reasonable public access must be provided. While there are still occasional resident complaints about resorts (and beachfront private homes) not providing adequate public access to the beach, it is reassuring that people—and not only hotel guests—are seen enjoying their right to picnic on the beach and swim in the ocean in front of some of the poshest hotels in the state.

Concluding Observations

To be politically correct, everything we do today seemingly has to be "sustainable." Most people still do not know what the buzzword means. So much attention is currently being devoted to the development of tourism in a sustainable way that one cynic complained it is taking the fun out of tourism.[35] There are some who believe that truly sustainable tourism is unachievable for the foreseeable future.[36]

The concept of sustainable tourism is thought to have started with the 1987 *Brundtland Report* by the World Commission on Environment and Development.[37] The report highlighted the three pillars of sustainable development: (1) economic growth, (2) environmental protection, and (3) social equity. J. R. Brent Ritchie and Geoffrey I. Crouch offer four complementary pillars—economic, social, cultural, and political—and suggest that sustainability is not achieved if any one of the four is unsustainable.[38] This is a tough order!

The gist of sustainability is that we need to look after the well-being of the current generation and at the same time not jeopardize opportunities for future generations. Sustaining tourism is not only about the "greening" of the tourist industry.[39] The World Bank puts it simply as "enhancing human well-being through time."[40]

The World Tourism Organization (UNWTO) began promoting the idea of sustainable tourism at the Rio Earth Summit in 1992. In 1995, the World Conference on Sustainable Tourism adopted the charter for sustainable tourism and declared sustainable tourism as "any form of development, provision of amenities, or tourist activity that emphasizes respect for and long-term preservation of natural, cultural, and social resources and makes a positive and equitable contribution to the economic development and fulfillment of people living, working, or staying in these areas."[41]

To develop tourism in a sustainable way, the UNWTO suggests the following be attained:[42]

1. The natural, historical, cultural, and other resources for tourism are conserved for continuous use in the future, while still bringing benefits to the present society.
2. Tourism development is planned and managed so that it does not generate serious environmental or sociocultural problems in the tourism area.
3. The overall environmental quality of tourism areas is maintained and improved where needed.
4. A high level of tourist satisfaction is maintained so that tourist destinations will retain their marketability and popularity.
5. The benefits of tourism are widely spread throughout society.

In their recent article, Pauline Sheldon, John Knox, and Kem Lowry report on Hawaii's latest effort to develop sustainable tourism, kicked off by a $1.2-million Sustainable Tourism Study (see chapter 3). It remains too early to tell whether the study or the Hawaii Tourism Authority's ten-year Strategic Tourism Plan will make a real difference. They note that a late 1980s proposal for a tourism management impact system was scuttled in the 1990s when tourism was ailing and the State's resources were directed to marketing. It could happen again if the current tourism boom becomes a tourism bust. Nonetheless, they conclude by professing optimism that Hawaii "will emerge as a pioneer in the real-life application of sustainability concepts to the complex realities of a mature mass-tourism destination."[43] A new Hawaii 2050 Sustainability Plan is also underway to replace the now obsolete State Plan first passed in 1980. As pointed out by Ritchie and Crouch, planning does not guarantee success, but it can enhance the chances of success.[44]

Sustainable tourism is about looking ahead. *Developing a Dream Destination* looks back to see how Hawaii has managed to cope with rapid tourism growth in the forty-six years (1959–2005) since statehood. Chapter 3 notes that concepts of sustainable tourism were widely discussed in Hawaii long before the 1992 Rio Earth Summit and were embodied in Act 133 passed by the Legislature and signed into law in 1976. The act was a pioneering piece of legislation long before the phrase "sustainable tourism development" was even invented. How much of a difference Act 133 and the subsequent State tourism plans made in shaping the development of tourism in Hawaii during the past half century is hard to say. So much of how tourism developed in Hawaii was determined not by the public sector but by the private sector. The process that led to Act 133 did sensitize Hawaii's people to the opportunities and impacts of mass tourism development on the community more than thirty years before the latest Sustainability Tourism Study and HTA's new 2005–2015 Tourism Strategic Plan.

In nearly fifty years of rapid tourism development, Hawaii remains a magical dream destination for millions of people around the world. This occurred without heavy-handed government control. Maybe Hawaii's enduring allure stems from the fact that it is still one of the most secluded places on earth. As Ritchie and Crouch correctly observe, "What makes a tourism destination truly competitive is its ability to increase tourism expenditure, to increasingly attract visitors while providing them with satisfying, memorable experiences, and to do so in a profitable way, while enhancing the well-being of destination residents and preserving the natural capital of the destination for future generations."[45] Everything considered, Hawaii has done pretty well in the manner that tourism has developed since statehood.[46] For the future, *Developing a Dream Destination* suggests that there needs to be (1) improvement in the coordination between the State and county governments in managing tourism development; (2) more attention given to determine who gains and loses from the development of tourism in Hawaii; and (3) a determination of what needs to be done to enhance social equity.

Notes

1. Until 1990, tourism in Hawaii grew at a much faster pace than international travel. Mak (2004), p. 196.

2. Allen (2004), p. x.

3. To learn more about these early "icons" of Hawaii tourism, see Allen (2004).

4. Hamilton (June 24, 1975).

5. State of Hawaii DBEDT (2005).

6. This includes an estimate of the number of local residents who were away from the state on any given day.

7. Indeed, more than three times as high.

8. Chaplin (June 23, 1975).

9. Limone (May 21, 2007).

10. Mak (2005), pp. 441–443; also Mak (2004), chapter 12.

11. See, for example, Jamieson (2003).

12. See Jamieson (2003) for specific suggestions.

13. Office of Hawaiian Affairs (June 2002); also the 2006 edition.

14. Naya (2007).

15. Apo et al. (August 2003).

16. In carrying out its new ten-year strategic plan, the Hawaii Tourism Authority (HTA) spent nearly $2 million on Hawaiian cultural programs in 2006. HTA also hired a Hawaiian cultural coordinator. According to the president and CEO of HTA, the main purpose of these initiatives was to promote Hawaii's uniqueness as a destination. In other words, its primary aim was to use Hawaiian culture to differentiate the State's tourism product and not explicitly to give Native Hawaiians a bigger share of the tourism profit. Indirectly it could, if any subsequent increase in demand for authentic Hawaiian cultural assets in tourism increases opportunities for Native Hawaiians. Arakawa (July 29, 2006), pp. C1 and C3. Recent efforts by a group of Native Hawaiian artists to protect their (authentic) creations against fakes by developing a cultural trademark could benefit them if such a trademark could be designed and enforced. Leidemann (July 30, 2006), pp. A31 and A35.

17. Darling and Beato (April 2004).

18. Cited in Mak (2004), pp. 145–146.

19. Mak (2006).

20. International Monetary Fund, United Nations Environment Programme, and the World Bank (2002), pp. 25–26.

21. Provided the fees can be collected at reasonable costs. It is difficult to imagine that admission fees can be collected easily at Waikiki Beach.

22. Mastny (2002), p. 114.

23. At that point, the user charge becomes a tax.

24. U.S. Advisory Commission on Intergovernmental Relations (December 1989), pp. 142–143 and 190.

25. Mak (2004), chapter 11; Bird (1992), pp. 1145–1158; Zee et al. (2002), pp. 1497–1516.

26. White and Walter (1982), pp. 35–57.

27. See, for example, Lind (July 27, 1975), pp. G1 and G6.

28. http://www.hawaiischoolreports.com/culture/aloha_spirit.htm.

29. The Honolulu City Council has been grappling with the issue of how to limit the number of parades and other events in Waikiki. Bill 84 was first introduced in November 2004, and finally in August 2006 the council capped the number of street closures in Waikiki due to parades and other events to thirty-nine per year. The number of events that required street closures in 2005 was fifty-eight. Shikina (August 17, 2006), p. B2.

30. Leidemann (April 23, 2007).

31. Arakawa and Nakaso (April 11, 2006), pp. A1 and A5.

32. Curiously, the Chinese government has abolished resident discounts for admission fees to the Forbidden City (Beijing) and other tourist attractions. Price discrimination is not necessarily about being generous or being fair. Under the right conditions, for-profit businesses also engage in price discrimination because it is profitable to do so. See Mak (2004), pp. 13–14.

33. See Lee (1993), pp. 160–161 for summaries of these landmark cases. The State and federal courts have clashed over the definition of the public boundary line.

34. State of Hawaii Department of Land and Natural Resources (December 2005).

35. Butcher (1997), pp. 27–38.

36. Goodall and Stabler (1997), p. 298.

37. World Commission on Environment and Development (1987). Ritchie and Crouch suggest that the concept of sustainable development can be traced as far back as 1973. Ritchie and Crouch (2003), p. 33. See also Mak (2004), chapter 14, and Swarbrooke (1999).

38. Ritchie and Crouch (2003), p. 30.

39. Mak (2004), chapter 14.

40. World Bank (2003), p. 13.

41. A summary and chronology of the actions taken by international organizations and conventions to promote sustainable tourism can be found in Perez–Salom (2001), pp. 801–803; Gossling et al. (2002) point out that tourism development can be sustainable at the local level but not at the global level. For example, air travel for long-distance tourism accounts for more than 90 percent of a journey's contribution to climate change. Gossling et al. argue that long-distance air travel, from an ecological perspective, should be discouraged.

42. World Tourism (2002).

43. Ibid.

44. Ritchie and Crouch (2003), p. 30.

45. Ibid., p. 2.

46. Of course, not everyone agrees. See, for example, Kent (1993).

References

Allen, Robert C. 2004. *Creating Hawaii Tourism: A Memoir.* Honolulu: Bess Press.
Apo, Peter, Dennis "Bumpy" Kanahele, Cheryln Logan, and Davianna McGregor. 2003. *Socio-Cultural Impacts of Tourism in Hawaii: Impacts on Native Hawaiians.* Prepared for the State of Hawaii Department of Business, Economic Development and Tourism (DBEDT) Planning for Sustainable Tourism Project. Honolulu: DBEDT (August).
Arakawa, Lynda. 2006. "HTA Honors Cultural Leaders." *Honolulu Advertiser,* July 29: C1 and C3.

Arakawa, Lynda, and Dan Nakaso. 2006. "Islanders Growing Weary of Tourism?" *Honolulu Advertiser,* April 11: A1 and A5.

Bird, Richard. 1992. "Taxing Tourism in Developing Countries." *World Development* 20(8): 1145–1158.

Butcher, J. 1997. "Sustainable Development or Development." In M. J. Stabler, ed., *Tourism and Sustainability: Principles to Practice* (New York: CAB International): 27–38.

Chaplin, George. 1975. "Bermuda: Planned Growth Keeps It a 'Gem.'" *Honolulu Advertiser,* June 23.

Darling, Arthur H., and Paulina Beato. 2004. *Should Public Budgets Finance Convention Centers?* Economic and Social Studies Series RE1–04–005. Washington, D.C.: Inter-American Development Bank (April).

Goodall, Brian, and Mike J. Stabler. 1997. "Principles Influencing the Determination of Environmental Standards for Sustainable Tourism." In M. J. Stabler, ed., *Tourism and Sustainability: Principles to Practice* (New York: CAB International): 279–304.

Hamilton, Thomas. 1975. "Trip Procedure Encouraged Insight." *Honolulu Advertiser,* June 24.

International Monetary Fund, United Nations Environment Programme, and the World Bank. 2002. *Financing for Sustainable Development.* Washington, D.C.: World Bank.

Jamieson, Walter. 2003. *Poverty Alleviation through Sustainable Tourism Development.* New York: United Nations Economic and Social Commission for Asia and the Pacific.

Kent, Noel. 1993. *Hawaii: Islands under the Influence.* Honolulu: University of Hawaii Press.

Lee, Anne Feder. 1993. *The Hawaii State Constitution: A Reference Guide.* Westport, CT: Greenwood Press.

Leidemann, Mike. 2006. "Hawaiian Artists Call for Cultural Trademark." *Honolulu Advertiser,* July 30: A31 and A35.

———. 2007. "City Considers Tougher Tactics for Illegal Rentals." *Honolulu Advertiser,* April 23: A1–A2.

Limone, Jerry. 2007. "Pink Beach Has the Ingredients to Keep Guests Coming Back." *Travel Weekly Daily Bulletin,* May 21: 34.

Lind, Andrew W. 1975. "Aloha Spirit: Is It Just a Tourist Attraction?" *Honolulu Advertiser,* July 27: G1 and G6.

Mak, James. 2004. *Tourism and the Economy: Understanding the Economics of Tourism.* Honolulu: University of Hawaii Press.

———. 2005. "Tourist Taxes." In Joseph J. Cordes, Robert D. Ebel, and Jane G. Gravelle, eds., *The Encyclopedia of Taxation and Tax Policy* (Washington, D.C.: Urban Institute Press): 441–444.

———. 2006. "Taxation of Travel and Tourism." In L. Dwyer and P. Forsyth, eds., *International Handbook on the Economics of Tourism* (London: Edward Elgar Publishing): 251–265.

Mastny, Lisa. 2002. "Redirecting International Tourism." In *State of the World 2002*, A Worldwatch Institute Report on Progress Toward a Sustainable Society (New York: W. W. Norton & Company): 101–126 and 225–234.

Naya, Seiji. 2007. "Income Distribution and Poverty Alleviation for the Native Hawaiian Community." Presented at the Second Annual Business Conference, Organized by the Office of Hawaiian Affairs. Hawaii Convention Center, Honolulu (May 22–23).

Office of the Auditor. 2005. *Hawaii 2050 Sustainability Task Force Report.* Honolulu: State of Hawaii Office of the Auditor (December 24).

Office of Hawaiian Affairs (OHA). 2002. *Native Hawaiian Data Book.* Honolulu: OHA (June); also the 2006 edition.

Perez-Salom, Jose-Roberto. 2001. "Sustainable Tourism: Emerging Global and Regional Regulation." *Georgetown International Environmental Law Review* 13(4): 801–803.

Ritchie, J. R. Brent, and Geoffrey I. Crouch. 2003. *The Competitive Destination: A Sustainable Tourism Perspective.* Cambridge, MA: CABI Publishing.

Sheldon, Pauline J., John M. Knox, and Kem Lowry. 2005. "Sustainability in a Mature Mass-Tourism Destination: The Case of Hawaii." *Tourism International Review* 9(11): 47–59.

Shikina, Robert. 2006. "Council Limits Street Closures in Waikiki." *Honolulu Advertiser,* August 17: B2.

State of Hawaii Department of Business, Economic Development and Tourism. 2005. *2004 Annual Visitor Research Report.* Honolulu: DBEDT. Also 2005 edition.

State of Hawaii Department of Land and Natural Resources. 2005. *Requesting a Review and Analysis of the Issues Surrounding the Shoreline Certification Process for the Purpose of Establishing Shoreline Setbacks.* Report to the 23rd Legislature, Regular Session of 2006, December 2005.

Swarbrooke, J. 1999. *Sustainable Tourism Management.* Wallingford, UK: CAB International.

U.S. Advisory Commission on Intergovernmental Relations. 1989. "Intergovernmental Fiscal Relations in Hawaii." In *Tax Review Commission: Working Papers and Consultant Studies,* vol. 2 (Honolulu: State of Hawaii Department of Taxation): 139–314.

White, Kenneth J., and Marry B. Walter. 1982. "Trouble in the Travel Account." *Annals of Tourism Research* 9: 35–57.

World Bank. 2003. *Sustainable Development in a Dynamic World.* World Development Report. New York: Oxford University Press.

World Commission on Environment and Development. 1987. *Our Common Future.* New York: Oxford University Press.

World Tourism Organization (UNWTO). 2002. *Tourism and Poverty Alleviation.* Madrid: UNWTO.

Zee, Howell, Janet Stotsky, and Eduardo Ley. 2002. "Tax Incentives for Business Investment: A Primer for Policymakers in Developing Countries." *World Development* 30(9): 1497–1516.

Index

About the Author

James Mak is professor of Economics at the University of Hawai'i. He is the author of *Tourism and the Economy: Understanding the Economics of Tourism* (University of Hawai'i Press, 2004) and *Japan: Why It Works, Why It Doesn't: Economics in Everyday Life* (with S. Sunder, Y. Abe, and K. Igawa, eds.) (University of Hawai'i Press, 1998). He serves on the editorial board of the *Journal of Travel Research*.

Production Notes | DEVELOPING A DREAM DESTINATION
Cover and interior designed by April Leidig-Higgins in WarnockPro,
   with display type in Bodega Sans, Marydale, and Seria Sans
Composition by Copperline Book Services, Inc.
Printing and binding by Versa Press
Printed on 60# Accent Opaque, 435 ppi